FACE THE FUTURE

DAVID OWEN was born in 1938 in Plymouth, and educated at Bradfield College, at Sidney Sussex College, Cambridge, and at St Thomas's Hospital, where from 1964 to 1966 he was Neurological and Psychiatric Registrar and from 1966 to 1968 Research Fellow in the Medical Unit.

After his election to parliament in 1966 as Labour Member for the Sutton Division of Plymouth he became Parliamentary Private Secretary to the Minister of Defence, Administration. From 1968 to 1970 he was Parliamentary Under Secretary of State for Defence (Royal Navy). When Labour went into opposition in 1970 he became Opposition front bench spokesman on defence until his resignation in 1972 on the question of Britain's membership of the European Community. Since the general election of 1974, following constituency boundary changes, he has represented the Devonport Division of Plymouth.

As Minister of State with responsibility for Health (1974–6) Dr Owen guided through parliament for Children Act, and in 1976 he became Minister of State at the Foreign and Commonwealth Office, where he was responsible for European Community affairs. In 1977 he was appointed Foreign Secretary, at 38 the youngest since Anthony Eden. He was Opposition Spokesman on Energy from 1979 to 1980.

In 1981 he co-founded, with Shirley Williams, Roy Jenkins, and William Rodgers, the Council for Social Democracy and he is now part of the joint leadership of the Social Democratic Party.

The editor of *A Unified Health Service* and contributor to *Social Services for All*, he is also the author of *The Politics of Defence* and *Human Rights*.

David Owen's wife Deborah is a literary agent. They have three children.

FACE THE FUTURE

DAVID OWEN

Oxford Toronto Melbourne
OXFORD UNIVERSITY PRESS
1981

Oxford University Press, Walton Street, Oxford OX2 6DP
London Glasgow New York Toronto
Delhi Bombay Calcutta Madras Karachi
Kuala Lumpur Singapore Hong Kong Tokyo
Nairobi Dar es Salaam Cape Town
Melbourne Auckland

and associate companies in
Beirut Berlin Ibadan Mexico City

© David Owen 1981
First published 1981 by Jonathan Cape Ltd
First published in abridged form with revisions and new Preface 1981 as an
Oxford University Press paperback

British Library Cataloguing in Publication Data
Owen, David, 1938–
Face the future. – (Oxford paperbacks)
1. Socialism in Great Britain
I. Title
355.5'0941   HY244
ISBN 0-19-285117-9

Printed in Great Britain by
Richard Clay (The Chaucer Press) Ltd
Bungay, Suffolk

For Tristan, Gareth and Lucy,
whose future it is.

CONTENTS

ACKNOWLEDGEMENTS

My first debt is to my wife and three children for all their support, particularly in cheerfully accepting that our time together has been constantly eroded while the book was being written. Many friends and experts have been extremely generous with their time and advice and I wish to thank them all. No one has taken a greater burden of the work than Margaret Smart and I am deeply grateful to her and to David Stephen and to my research assistant, Alan Robinson. All at Jonathan Cape willingly accepted a heavy workload and none more so than Jill Sutcliffe and Xandra Hardie.

In this paperback edition I have had to shorten the book for it was inordinately long with 526 pages. I have concentrated the cuts on the original chapters, mainly descriptive, concerned with Industrial and Energy Policy, State Intervention and Co-operatives, and in a revised chapter on Economic Policy I have omitted the detail of monetary policy. The section on Northern Ireland has been deleted from the chapter on the Constitution. Much of the discussion of NHS structure has gone from the chapter on Community Care and of law and order from the chapter on Freedom with Security; of those chapters only those parts relating to local government have been retained and added to the local government chapter. Two chapters, The Internationalist Tradition and The Community of the Twelve, have been dropped in their entirety. There have been minor changes throughout referring to the tasks ahead for Social Democrats and I have removed inner Labour Party arguments. There is also a Preface covering the founding of the Social Democratic Party. Many critics commented on the absence of a final chapter drawing together the strands of the argument running through the book, not least Paul Barker writing in the *Sunday Times*. It is to him that I owe the title of the last chapter, The Enabling State. The whole book has been reset and I am grateful to Will Sulkin of the Oxford University Press for his support and encouragement.

D. O.

PREFACE

The launching of the Social Democratic Party on 26 March 1981 represents an historic opportunity for the electorate to challenge the Labour and Conservative Parties' monopoly of Government estab-lished ever since the Liberals lost power in 1924. Yet no one should underestimate the electoral difficulty of the task that lies ahead. The 'first past the post' system entrenches in particular the class and geographical basis of the Labour Party's support. The Social Demo-cratic Party is drawing its support from across the classes, and must do this if it is to fulfil its objective of breaking the class antagonisms that the two old Parties have fostered. Yet this means it will be difficult to win seats in the old industrial areas. Successive elections have shown that the Liberals have been unable to win over the traditional supporters of the Labour Party, running second in only two of Labour's 268 Parliamentary seats. Social Democrats, to form the next government, must capture the Labour vote in these constituencies at the next election or the Labour Party could well be the largest Party in Parliament, despite the Social Democrats and Liberals winning a substantial number of Conservative held seats. It is vital that the electoral facts of life in the particular constituencies are not forgotten in the heady atmosphere of national opinion poll ratings based on an overall percentage lead. The Social Democrats have to convince Labour Party voters at a time when the Party is in Opposition, not in Government, and where there is no performance yardstick of Government to feed the disillusionment that surfaced in 1970 and 1979. Since it must not be done on the basis of a class appeal it can only be done by demonstrating that Social Democrats can best represent the interests of traditional Labour voters by reviving the whole country's fortunes.

The founding of the Social Democratic Party is not a febrile reaction to a temporary change of direction in the Labour Party after the defeat in 1979. It has a much deeper and more profound genesis. That is why the Limehouse Declaration of 25 January 1981 which created the Council for Social Democracy stated: 'We do not believe in the politics of an inert centre merely representing the lowest common denominator between two extremes. We want more not less radical change in our society, but with a greater stability of direction.' This is not a plea for centrism, a soft and flabby compromise. It is an appeal for radicalism, for fundamental changes in attitude and in direction; it carries with it a readiness to eradicate poverty and to challenge privilege.

It is extremely easy to fall into the trap of believing that over the last two decades the only criticism of the policies and direction of all Governments has come from the Labour Left or the Conservative Right. The disillusion in July 1966, felt by those of us who had entered into Parliament in the election only a few months before, triggered fundamental criticisms. We had campaigned in the confident years of the early 1960s and believed that Labour only had to win – the Conservatives to leave office – for all to be different. Suddenly we found our Government, our Party, introducing the same deflationary economic measures which most of us had bitterly attacked under the stop-go cycle of Conservative governments' economic management. Left-Right labels within the Labour Party have always hidden a much deeper divide between Radicals and Corporatists. It was this division which began to fuel criticism amongst some new MPs by 1967. The Labour Government was unrealistically making the value of the pound a symbol of political virility, deflating the economy and holding on to an exchange rate which was wildly out of line. The Government was hanging on to a defence role East of Suez, unduly influenced by Establishment attitudes and refusing to make the fundamental reappraisal of our defence effort that we all thought was necessary. The Government was also extraordinarily timid in responding to the Rhodesian UDI in 1965 and we began to sense, even then, the start of the equivocation over race. Not surprisingly, some of us began to ponder the future. If I had to trace the first of the decisions that sowed the seeds for the emergence of the Social Democratic Party it would be to the deflation of the economy and of expectations in July 1966.

Three Labour MPs, David Marquand, John Mackintosh, and I, in September 1967 before the Labour Party Conference spelt out a clear warning in a special supplement to *Socialist Commentary* called 'Change Gear'.[1] Almost all of its predictions have been fulfilled. We wrote in 1967, 'unemployment is rising, investment is sluggish, and the rate of growth will be much lower than we hoped to achieve. The pound has been strengthened – but at a high and bitter price in terms of resources unused, production foregone, and men out of work. The price in terms of disappointed hopes has been higher still.' We could almost have been writing in September 1981 about the present Conservative Government, though unemployment in September 1967 stood at 450,000; in 1981 at over two-and-a-half million. We went on to say, 'there are unmistakable signs of disillusionment among many of Labour's most steadfast supporters'. We wrote and warned of indications that the Party had 'lost some of its original drive and sense of purpose'. Above all, we said, 'there are signs that the Labour Movement as a whole no longer has a clear strategic vision of what it wants to achieve in the next three years, and how its aims can be related to its fundamental principles. For a Party of the Left, this is a situation of appalling danger.'

We recognized that many reforming Governments in the past had undergone a temporary period of doubt and uncertainty, two or three years after coming to power: that this had happened to the Liberals after 1906, to the American Democrats after 1932, and to the Labour Party itself after 1945. All three, however, recovered the initiative, and went on to make revolutionary changes in their respective societies. Yet they did so not by continuing along their old paths, at their old speeds, but by decisively changing direction or changing gear. Looking back, I do not believe that the Labour Party ever responded to the challenge we then posed. 'Change Gear' advocated a more adventurous, radical path. We stated then: 'The most vital of all political attributes is confidence in one's purpose, and in one's ability to achieve it. In parties of the Right, such confidence often comes from the elitist assumption of a traditional governing class. In a party of the Left, it can only come from conviction and commitment: from the certainty that one knows what one fights for, and loves what one knows. It is this certainty', we wrote, 'that is now being undermined, and it can be corroded and destroyed with fatal ease if temporary disillusion is allowed to escalate through despair to defeatism.' I believe that this is exactly what happened to the Labour Party over the following years.

A different criticism has been mounted on the record of Conservative governments by previous supporters who have now become Social Democrats but their conclusion as to what is now needed is much the same.

The real importance, in retrospect, of 'Change Gear' was its championing of a more active democracy. We wrote: 'Socialism is not only about the things the Government does for people, it is also about the things people do for themselves. Since its foundation, the Labour Movement has struggled, not only for greater equality and an end to poverty, but for human emancipation, for the right of ordinary men and women to decide their destiny for themselves and to become the subjects of history instead of its objects.' We asked why we should bother with a subject which some would feel was at best an academic irrelevance and at worst a positive obstacle to a Government anxious to use the power of the State with greater efficiency. We challenged the attitude behind such cynicism, saying that it carried serious political danger for a party of the Left to ignore the issue of democracy. We warned that modern societies are bound to be bureaucratic. Individual citizens inevitably find themselves again and again at the apparent mercy of vast and impersonal organizations whose purposes they do not understand, with nominal heads they have never heard of and in whose decisions they have no voice. We saw then, in 1967, growing signs of the sense of individual powerlessness creating dangerous social tensions, and warned that it was not an accident that the age of the giant firm (and since then this phenomenon has greatly increased), the giant trade union, and the giant State machine, should also be the age of revived minority nationalism and irresponsible fringe movements. Meanwhile, we warned, the power of the State was increasing steadily and would increase further, as it has done under both Conservative and Labour Governments.

Another aspect of the British character, all too easily forgotten, is that no people on earth so detest the nosey-parker, and active Government will tend to cross the traditional demarcation lines between the Government's sphere and the private citizen's. Since a Government of the Left must be an active, radical government it is therefore in constant danger of allowing itself to be identified as the Party of arbitrary and over-centralized Government. It was because of this that we sensed the need in 1967 for Parliamentary reform, devolution, regionalism and a greater emphasis on the politics of quality, not just quantity. We saw, for example, devolution for Scotland as a serious issue which had to be grappled with, within the framework of overall constitutional reform; and, coming from the far South-West region, I felt it was vital that we dismantled much of the centralized decision-making of Whitehall, and argued for a radical transformation of the administrative structure of the regions, so as to foster greater participation in decision-making. In the years that followed, all Labour's attempts at constitutional reform failed, and the sense of failure that this produced over Scottish devolution in particular compounded the overall failure to successfully manage the economy. Labour tended to foster a belief that economic growth would create equality, without a fight: justice without tears. It was a self-deception in 1967 and it is a self-deception now. The enemies –

poverty on the one side and privilege on the other – remain. To resist the forces of privilege, prejudice, inertia, and corporatism, requires political courage. The record shows clearly that since 1964 both Labour Governments and the Labour Party have been incapable of overthrowing these forces. Why? Far too often, because Labour has actively embraced all these forces within itself. It has become in practice a very conservative and even at times a reactionary political force locked in to a bureaucracy of inertia. The prediction of a Fabian Tract written as long ago as 1886 was in 1981 fulfilled. It said, 'there is a mass of socialist feeling, not yet conscious of itself as socialism, but when the unconscious socialists of England discover their position, they will also probably fall into two parties – a collective party supporting a strong central administration, and a counter-balancing anarchist party defending individual initiative.'[2] The division between centralists and decentralists goes very deep, and has far more significance than the labels of Left and Right.

It is this division, even though it was predicted so long ago, which divides the present-day Labour Party from the Social Democrats. It is why the present-day Labour Party can now no longer claim to be the only vehicle for socialism in this country; why the present deeply centralist Conservative Party offers so little for the 1980s; why 'my Party, right or wrong' is now the only slogan holding the Conservative and Labour Parties together. Both Parties are locked into dogmatic, doctrinaire, divisive policies, which many of their supporters deplore. Yet their leaders appeal to a blind loyalty – Party first, country second. Adversary politics thrive on polarization, polemic, and fear. The two-Party system survives by depicting the other Parties as having no sensible policies. They deny any common ground between the Parties, or any hope of agreement. Above all they fear electoral reform, for it challenges their respective monopoly. It was totally predictable that Mrs Thatcher, when speaking to young Conservatives in Eastbourne in 1981 and rattled by the powerful challenge of Social Democracy, not then even launched into a Social Democratic Party, depicted us as the 'Limehouse Left' and as slow-motion socialists. It is equally predictable that the Labour Party tries to depict us as the 'Limehouse Right' and as genteel conservatives. What the two Parties and their leaders cannot understand is that the Limehouse Declaration marked a liberation for millions of voters in this country, progressively disenfranchized in the past.

Such voters find it a refreshing change for Social Democrats and Liberals to acknowledge that they have many common policy aspirations and to begin to explore ways of working with, rather than against, each other; to attempt to widen the areas of agreement rather than heighten the areas of disagreement. The Labour Party has in many constituencies grown mindlessly intolerant. It now advocates many policies which do not reflect the broad-based generosity of spirit that inspired the founding fathers of the Labour Movement, which do not reflect the wish to eradicate class hatreds and divisions, but instead, all too often, perpetuate them. Many of the policies which have been advanced by the Labour Party are policies that fellow-socialists, existing and recent members of the Labour Party, believe to be profoundly damaging to the best interests of the country. A political party has ultimately to be judged by what it will do, not by the breadth of its traditions nor the width of the opinions expressed within its ranks. The last straw for many previous Labour supporters was the decision to allow the Trade Union block vote to influence the choice of a potential or actual Prime Minister. It was the absolute antithesis of a democratic reform and meant the end of any chance of changing the Labour Party from within. The last straw for many previous Conservative supporters was their government's total insensitivity to unemployment. Of course, it was theoretically possible for any of us to have stayed members of our political parties while our parties advocated, and possibly even implemented, policies with which we profoundly disagreed. But to have done so would have been to perpetrate a deceit on the electorate and on the British people.

Social Democrats do not believe it is in the national interest to abandon our membership of the European Community. We are well aware that that is an unpopular view. But opposition to appease-ment was unpopular throughout the 1930s. Politicians have to be prepared at times to swim against the tide of opinion and to swing opinion around. The European Community is not just a foreign policy issue in this country, nor one purely of Parliamentary sovereignty. It is a fundamental political and economic issue, which affects the livelihood of every single family in this country. It affects people's employment prospects, their prosperity, our trading future as a country, and provides a massive export market for our goods. If one sincerely believes, as I do, that Britain's withdrawal from the European Community in 1984 would substantially increase unem-ployment, weaken our economy and reduce the chances of new investment and the possibility of attracting the new technologies, then how can one accept the policy to withdraw, the policy to which the Labour Party committed itself in the 1980 Conference? Further, if

one believes that to unilaterally amend the European Communities
Act – even if the election were to be won on the basis of that issue –
would itself raise a major question mark over whether this country
could, or is likely to, remain a member of the European Community,
and that, similarly, this would profoundly damage foreign investment in Britain, damage employment prospects and create uncertainty and political instability among the other nine Member States,
then how can one conscientiously go to the electorate with such a
commitment? It can hardly be suggested that we should have made
our reservations clear to our own constituencies, obtain their en-
dorsement, but then vote against the proposition if and when we
ever had another Labour Government.

The Social Democrats' commitment to achieving genuine measures of arms control and multilateral disarmament is total but if
unilateral nuclear disarmament means anything a Labour Prime
Minister and Cabinet in 1984, if elected, would have to make a
decision on Day One: should the Polaris patrols be stopped and the
submarines be brought home to port, their weapons systems
dismantled and all nuclear weapons in this country scrapped? An
affirmative decision is one which the Labour Party expects and
which the Conference resolutions overwhelmingly endorsed. Now,
if one believes, as I do, and the majority of the Labour Shadow
Cabinet used to believe, that such action would be profoundly
damaging to NATO, and to the security and stability of the West,
then how on earth can one possibly fight for and support such an
election commitment?

These however are only some of the policy issues. Similar queries
can be applied to nationalization without compensation, to proposals for ever-increasing State nationalization, to the refusal of the
Labour Party to face up to the choosing of priorities for public
expenditure. The most cowardly course would have been for people
like myself to have waited until the actual Manifesto was published
and then to have endorsed the inevitable 'fudge and mudge' that
has become the hallmark of Labour leadership, and perhaps half
hope for an electoral defeat. For the critics of the Conservative
Government the most cowardly course would have been to hang on
hoping too for catharsis from defeat.

The decision that the people of this country can now make is
whether the Social Democrat Party can provide the framework
for a new, radical, political drive to revitalize our country. It was
President Roosevelt who, at a time of fear and recession, in the
1930s, offered a new start to the American people. We who believe

in the immense potential of Social Democracy will bring the same message to the British people, that they have nothing to fear but fear itself. They can break the system. They can elect a Social Democratic Government. Frances Cairncross wrote in the *Guardian* early in 1981 that the great gap in politics in Britain is that there is no party which believes simultaneously in promoting social equality and encouraging the free market to work. 'If you believe in redistribution,' she says, 'you are on the Left, and must also believe in nationalisation and in interventionist industrial policy and incomes policy. If you admire the market and think the price mechanism is usually more efficient than a Civil Servant's decree, then you are on the Right, and must also believe in public schools, company cars and cutting social security.' That is a good shorthand précis of the dilemma that many electors face. The task for Social Democrats is to bridge that gap and to show that the new political Party can resolve that dilemma.

The identity of the Social Democratic Party as it establishes itself will be an amalgam of some of the best policy elements of the major parties, a feature facilitated by the fact that its membership will include people hitherto in the Labour, Conservative, and Liberal Parties. But the distinctive ingredient must be a readiness to rethink old issues, to change attitudes and to challenge the record of the past, and this will more readily be achieved because many who have joined the new Party have never hitherto been members of any political party. In essence the Social Democrats will draw on the traditional Labour Party commitment to social justice and social conscience. It will champion a high quality National Health Service available to all and free at the point of demand, believing in the serenity that comes from knowing that ill health will not mean bills from doctors or hospitals or heavy insurance premiums for those with a poor health record. It will endeavour to ensure that the public educational system gives not just a good education, allowing the talents of all to develop and flourish, but also responds to the industrial and technical needs of the country. It must openly recognize that the disadvantaged, handicapped, and elderly are a rightful charge on the talented, fit, and young and that a society is healthier if there is a readiness among those richer and stronger to shoulder the burdens of those poorer and weaker. Social Democrats will draw on the traditional Conservative commitment to the merit of private enterprise and a market economy. They will not shrink from acknowledging that in the main people work harder if they can ensure as a result a better standard of living for themselves and their family and, equally, that the degree of burden-sharing that society can ask of its individual citizens has to allow for the incentive to work and so for financial rewards which stimulate people to innovate, experiment, and build for the future. There will be an open acceptance of the need for profits, to allow for wealth creation in a person's lifetime, to encourage investment and risk-taking and a realization that our country's prosperity depends on our ability to sell in the markets of the world at a price, design and delivery time that is competitive. Social Democrats, in genuinely championing the mixed economy, must ensure that the mix will become a partnership between the public and the private sectors, devoid of the obsessive dogma of privatization or nationalization and the oscillation of policy that has meant uncertainty and discontinuity for many of our basic industries. It is a sad commentary on post-war Britain that this combination of policies has never been unequivocally on offer to the British electorate.

Some will identify the Party with the post-war Socialism of Clement Attlee, others may identify the Party with the 'one nation' tradition of Conservatism, others with the radical Liberalism of David Lloyd George. Certainly the Party must have roots in the past and draw on the traditions of the past. A Social Democrat has a distinctive identity, Left of Centre, drawing on definable roots and tradition of Conservatism, others with the radical Liberalism of Daviid Lloyd George. Certainly the Party must have roots in the past and draw on the traditions of the past. A Social Democrat has a need for steady and considered moves towards a more decentralized form of government in Britain. It unequivocally espouses the introduction of a fairer electoral system through proportional representation, a form of devolution for Scotland and Wales that recognizes their separate and distinctive needs as nations within the United Kingdom, and a pattern of decentralization for England that will recognize the needs of its regions and the case for a greater measure of autonomy for truly local government.

The Social Democratic Party was founded in the realization that it would not be easy to win power at the next election, that to do so it would be necessary to maximize support, and that an electoral arrangement with the Liberals, who share many of our objectives, should be attempted from the outset. In those seats where the psephological evidence points to a Liberal having a better chance than a Social Democrat of winning, it would be folly for Social Democrats to field a candidate simply for the satisfaction of putting candidates forward in every constituency. For that reason the Social Democratic Party has been established on an Area basis, grouping constituencies to allow for some constituencies to be fought by Liberal candidates and yet permitting Social Democrats to work within the Area Party and not feel disenfranchized by perhaps not having their own candidate in their constituency. There is little point in disguising the fact that it will be difficult to achieve such an electoral arrangement, for it will mean that the Liberals will have to agree to stand down in seats which they have fought in the past. In some parts of the country where a Social Democrat would have a better chance of success there may well be no agreement. The best means of achieving a centrally and locally negotiated arrangement to cover most of the constituencies is for members of both Parties to grasp the significance and magnitude of the opportunity that such an arrangement presents. What is at issue is the future well-being of our country. An electoral arrangement clearly must be an agreement in principle, not just a carve up of seats. It must at the minimum assure both Parties that, while their separate identities will be fully preserved, by the time of the election major elements in the programme of both, and of the new government, will have been agreed beforehand between them. In no area is it more important to agree the detail of legislation than the proposed constitutional reforms, on which there is in principle far more common ground between Social Democrats and Liberals than either has with the Labour or Conservative Parties. It is important too for Social Democrats and Liberals to grasp that an electoral arrangement for the next election, if successful, will not mean that either Party will be swallowed by the other, because proportional representation will be in operation before the following election. Their separate identities will not just be maintained but the very existence of four distinct Parties offers a far better prospect to both Social Democrats and Liberals that they will participate in government; the separate identity of each is likely to narrow the appeal of the Labour and Conservative Parties. On the other hand a single merged centre party would more easily be squeezed by either or both the Labour and Conservative Parties, allowing them to widen their electoral base and broaden their appeal. The principal factor which must motivate the whole attempt to forge an electoral arrangement is that the British nation has been ill-served by its political parties over the last quarter of a century. Social, political, and racial tensions grow and a country which was once envied by the world appears unable to shake itself free, to revive its self-confidence, to unleash its energies, and restore its fortunes. Adversary politics continue to fan the embers of class divisions. Our standard of living as a nation and as individuals is falling behind that of our neighbours in Europe. The present economic decline is deep-seated and shows every sign of continuing against a mood of despair and disillusionment. Except for a few short periods of reasonably successful economic management between 1957–9, 1968–70 and 1976–8, the record overall is one of failure. Government is not the sole or even the major factor in ensuring economic prosperity and social stability but the nation has suffered deeply from not having had a sustained period of good government.

The task of Social Democrats is nothing less than to revive the fortunes of our country, to allow the resourcefulness, the boldness, to re-emerge, to halt the drift and to face the future with resolution.

PART ONE

SOCIAL
DEMOCRACY

1

SOCIAL DEMOCRATIC VALUES

The centralist–decentralist argument and the complex issues it raises have little relevance to the rather facile press-labelling of Left and Right which has always dominated public comment about British politics. It is the question of decentralization which now forms a real divide in British politics. The last decade has seen a growing public debate on the merits of small-scale institutions, a reaction to the centralization of government, and criticism of the growth in the size of industrial companies, hospitals and schools. The challenge for Social Democrats is to develop a philosophy that will be welcomed by those voters who identify with the social values of the Left but who do not want to see further nationalization or a growth in bureaucracy and who believe in the mixed economy. There is a yearning for a fresh and valid political alternative, a widespread realization that the continuation or extension of past trends and policies is no way forward for the future.

What is needed is a political philosophy outside the restrictive confines of much of the present polarized political debate, which asserts the radical democratic libertarian tradition of decentralized socialism, which revives the concept of fellowship and community within a participatory democratic society, and which sees change not as a threat but as a challenge. Change carries with it the assumption of choice and choice implies values, judgement and balance. 'Liberty–Equality–Fraternity' the old radical cry still emphasizes an eternal truth: that none of the three can properly be fulfilled without being combined in some measure with the other two. For more than a century political thought has been dominated by the interaction and balance between liberty and equality, but surprisingly little attention has been given to the other element of this historic triad, fraternity, representing the sense of fellowship,

cooperation, neighbourliness, community and citizenship. This neglect of fraternity, particularly by socialist thinkers, has meant that
the espousal of equality has lacked a unifying force to bridge the
gaps and contradictions between equality and liberty. Even more
importantly, the foundations for the values and attitudes which
must underpin a democratic society are lacking a strong and secure
base. Even the most fervent proponents of liberty feel it necessary to
qualify the description of a state of liberty or freedom as being 'that
condition of man in which coercion of some by others is reduced as
much as is possible in society'.[1] Without fraternity neither liberty
nor equality will flourish.

Socialist thinking has concentrated too much on the mechanics of
equality and has paid insufficient attention to the attitudes which
underpin the pursuit of equality, particularly how to foster altruism,
which is the human drive behind the aspiration to eradicate inequalities and to strive for a more egalitarian society. 'No money
values can be attached to the presence or absence of a spirit of
altruism in a society. Altruism is giving to a stranger . . . it may
touch every aspect of life and affect the whole fabric of value. Its role
in satisfying the biological need to help – particularly in modern
societies – is another unmeasurable element.'[2]

For all socialists, whether they use the label social democrat,
democratic socialist, or whatever exact position they may occupy in
the political spectrum of the Left, there is common ground in one
particular set of beliefs, the need to redress poverty and to reduce
inequality. At the heart of socialism lies the combination of an
abhorrence of the misery which poverty brings and positive belief in
the virtues of a just and equal society in which equality of means,
treatment and respect lay the fraternal foundation for any community.

Equality is a noble ideal. We know it will not be achieved, but that
of itself does not invalidate an aspiration – any more than the fact
that wages and salaries will reflect different responsibilities and
opportunities means that it is wrong to strive for a system which
endeavours to make financial rewards fairer. Right wing propaganda which portrays the socialist desire for a greater measure of
equality as nothing more than pure envy of the rich, a blind
vindictiveness and hatred of the successful[3] is simply the weakest
defence of vested interest and privilege. A more powerful argument
from the Right is that the real choice is between more equality with
low living standards for all and on the other hand greater, or at least
some, inequality but with higher standards for all. This is at least a

practical argument and though it exaggerates the effect of inequality as a motivating force for economic growth it at least does not criticize the attempt to reduce poverty, to alleviate the problems of families haunted by a lack of basic necessities and the desire to free people from the shackles of low income and of low status.

It is the insensitivity to those in society, a high percentage of people, who are unable to compete and achieve, which is the unattractive face of the Right and the counterpart of those on the Left who allow envy to predominate. When the Prime Minister, Mrs Thatcher, asks, 'What is it that impels the powerful and vocal lobby in Britain to press for greater equality – for total equality even, when there is little evidence to show that ordinary people want it? Undoubtedly one important pressure is the *simpliste* desire to help the underprivileged. But more often the reasons boil down to an undistinguished combination of envy and what might be termed "bourgeois guilt",'[4] she reveals the fundamental insensitivity which to date at least has narrowed her capacity to lead the whole nation. The desire to help is not just *simpliste*, it is deep, genuine and basic. Envy of course exists and can demean the movement for greater equality, but it is a minority motive. 'Bourgeois guilt' exists too, and when coupled with a wish to deny one's own upbringing or to ape the social background of others, is deeply unattractive, but guilt is not a motive to be so lightly disparaged if it can engender concern and a wish that others shall enjoy the same benefits.

Arguments against economic redistribution are made by the Right's social theorists, who are convinced that equality is undesirable on the grounds that it is unobtainable, and that therefore the search for it is futile. Reference is sometimes made by the more extreme participants in the debate to genetics, environment and intelligence, and undigested and erroneous deductions are drawn from the works of Professors Jensen, Bernstein and Eysenck. The arguments continue despite the evidence that social class is not determined by IQ that educational success depends less on IQ than on family background and that biological inequality does not necessarily dictate that society should be hierarchical and rigidly stratified.[5] The Right have also argued that any society will always have so-called functional stratification, in which important decision-makers will either have more status or more material rewards than the mass of the people, and that this kind of inequality will inevitably remain in any complex industrialized society, whether free-market or state-controlled. This theory assumes that individuals will always be motivated predominantly by a desire to maximize their own or their families' financial rewards or status and that it is impossible to create a climate where rewards based on job satisfaction or an ethos of public service tend to predominate.

There is a Right-wing theory that though social and financial inequalities clearly are very great and difficult to justify, it is doubtful whether they can be removed except at unacceptable cost. This argument is stronger, for a democratic system allows the privileged to organise in defence of their position and tends to accept as the price for democracy a measure of individual freedom which does run counter to what may statistically or theoretically be in the best interests of the whole of society. Democratic politicians are rightly unwilling to put at risk or to dismantle Western liberties and democracy in order to remove inequality. Gradual persuasion in a democracy is the only sure way of bringing about greater equality without degenerating into the kind of undemocratic and restrictive society that is spawned by authoritarian state control. This will necessitate a more value-orientated discussion of politics, and while some politicians, particularly those who profess no religious belief, may be wary of such an approach, that reluctance must be challenged. For it is this very reluctance which has prevented discussion of issues like fraternity and altruism, and encourages politicians to espouse equality while confining their theories to the mechanics of distribution.

That socialism is about much more than just equality was a theme William Morris well understood when he wrote that socialism was 'a condition of society in which there should be neither rich nor poor, neither master nor master's man, neither idle nor overworked, neither brain sick workers nor heart sick workers; in a word, in which all men would be living in equality of condition, and would manage their affairs unwastefully and with full consciousness, that harm to one would mean harm to all.'[6] The use of the terms 'brain sick' and 'heart sick workers' is an evocative reminder that there is much more to the process of living than the redistribution of material wealth, and a clear pointer to the relevance of industrial democracy in attaining job satisfaction and encouraging job enrichment. The emphasis on managing our affairs unwastefully involves the use of words which evoke part of the current ecological debate, which is rightly a dominant concern for many and an issue in which politicians should be particularly engaged. The quality of our social environment is as important as the quantity of social provision. The concept of harm to one meaning harm to all goes deeper and wider than more familiar phrases.

If socialism depicts equality only in terms of distribution, then, when inequalities persist or when socialists and socialist governments not only perpetuate but defend certain inequalities of income in terms of differential payment for different tasks, a deep sense of failure is engendered, leading to disillusionment, and this will be used as a justification for abandoning liberty in order to be sure of achieving equality. The record of state controlled societies in overcoming inequality is not such as to make any thinking democrat change his or her predisposition for liberty.

Unfair distribution of talents does not preclude equality of respect, for this can be applied equally to men or women, to the habitual drunkard, to a judge or a doctor, to the mentally handicapped, or to a sporting personality, regardless of social status or professional earning capacity. Equality of respect covers equality under the democratically passed laws essential for the maintenance of liberty. Again and again one is driven back to the democratic imperative as the means for resolving the conflicts and contradictions of life. 'If we wish to remain human, there is only one way, the way into the open society. We must go into the unknown, the uncertain and insecure, using what reason we may have to plan for both security and freedom.'[7]

Yet such an outlook runs counter to what is, together with democracy, one of the constant themes of Western political thinking in recent centuries, the quest for certainty. This quest is not unique to political thought, but runs strongly through much religious, scientific and economic thinking. Some of the frustration and even despair of modern thought and writing stems from the inability of those who search to find simple answers or solutions to ever more complex problems. Many socialists in particular search endlessly for an all-embracing unity of political purpose and thought. Sensing the value of collective action they turn in varying degrees to totalitarian bureaucratic or democratic collectivism. The attraction of the totalitarian analysis stems from the security and faith its all-embracing structure engenders among its adherents.

Certainty is easier to achieve if one can totally abandon or lower the priority given to democracy. It is impossible to give the highest priority to democracy and still find a great measure of certainty. Democracy carries with it an acceptance of the infinite spectrum of views, aspirations and demands of human beings that cannot be perfectly structured or systemized. Democratic politics carries with it the necessity to put the sum of human happiness before philosophy, dogma or doctrine. Even to categorize human behaviour is fraught with danger. No one falls perfectly within any category. Yet that risk has already been faced by two writers who have had a powerful effect on contemporary thought, Isaiah Berlin and G. D. H. Cole. Isaiah Berlin's 'The Hedgehog and the Fox'[8] defines two personalities using the saying of the Greek poet, Archilochus, 'The fox knows many things, but the hedgehog knows one big thing'. The personality of hedgehog relates 'everything to a single central vision, one system less or more coherent or articulate, in terms of which they understand, think and feel – a single, universal organizing principle.' The foxes 'pursue many ends, often unrelated and even contradictory, connected, if at all, only in some *de facto* way, for some psychological or physiological cause.' The foxes are the decentralizers who 'lead lives, perform acts, and entertain ideas that are centrifugal rather than centripetal'. Behind this admittedly over-simplified classification lies one of the great divides of thought and writing. Isaiah Berlin used the classification to identify intellectual and artistic personalities, but it can also be applied to political personalities. The greatest dangers to democracy come from those politicians whose certainty means that they espouse dogma and doctrine when facing the complex decision-making of our modern society.

G. D. H. Cole was deeply conscious of the need to develop a form of socialism that would be appropriate to British values and institutions. But he also sought to combine the insights of Marx and Proudhon in a manner that would stress fellowship and community rather as William Morris had done, avoiding collectivism or anarchic libertarianism. Cole recognized that the Marxist ideas of the class war and the dictatorship of the proletariat were both unattractive to the electorate, and likely, if ever carried out, to sweep away many of the liberties that Britain had gradually built up. He rejected those forms of socialism that neglected liberty and fraternity in the overriding quest for equality and he saw democratic participation as the key to maintaining communities and achieving social change that was attuned to the needs of working people.

A political classification to which G. D. H. Cole often referred was originally used by Beatrice Webb: the 'A's' and the 'B's' – the 'anarchists' and the 'bureaucrats'. The 'B's' have long been in the ascendancy in the Labour movement in Britain and the welfare state and the post-war nationalization programme were the crowning achievements of 'B' thought.[9] Few in the Labour movement have championed the anarchists' dislike of the state and centralization. The label 'anarchist' is clearly inappropriate for Cole since his thought was more deeply influenced by a socialist theory of power rather than by Proudhon's mutualism, and he was firm in his advocacy of social justice and in his support for welfare policies. The Labour Party has always lacked a theory to explain how the distribution of power was to be altered in order to achieve socialism and how power was to be distributed in a socialist society. These questions have been neglected since it was too easily assumed that the achievement of a much greater degree of state ownership would of itself spread to all citizens the power previously held by private business. In practice, however, the redistribution of power in favour of Whitehall, the executive, the civil service and a huge administrative apparatus has not automatically achieved the socialist objective of common ownership. It has in practice impeded the creation of a participatory democracy by removing the power to take initiatives from the community and encouraging 'corporatism' and rule by committee.

That nationalization was an insufficient basis for changing society was always accepted by G. D. H. Cole. He identified the task ahead as stimulating democratic activism and wrote, 'this is precisely what the 'B's' are temporarily unfitted to do by themselves: only the 'A's', held in check by the 'B's' can do it in any effective way'.[10] Throughout his life and in numerous writings Cole advocated 'A' socialism though firmly within a democratic society. Extending democracy and championing the expression of a vigorous plurality of viewpoint undoubtedly make decision taking more time consuming but the decisions become more sustainable once they have been taken. Pluralism offers the prospect of a more interesting, relevant and stimulating democracy, where difficult problems will evoke different solutions and where decisions more fully reflect the wishes of particular communities.

The pluralism which Isaiah Berlin advocates is not a soft consensus but has been characterized by Aileen Kelly as being 'much more tough-minded and intellectually bold; it rejects the view that all conflicts of values can be finally resolved by synthesis and that all desirable goals may be reconciled. It recognizes that human nature is such that it generates values which, though equally sacred, equally ultimate, exclude one another, without there being any possibility of establishing an objective hierarchical relation between them. Moral conduct therefore may involve making agonizing choices, without the help of universal criteria, between incompatible but equally desirable values. This permanent possibility of moral uncertainty is . . . the price that must be paid for recognition of the true nature of one's freedom: the individual's right to self-direction, as opposed to direction by state or church or party, is plainly of supreme importance if one holds that the diversity of human goals and aspirations cannot be evaluated by any universal criteria, or subordinated to some transcendent purpose.'[11]

Such a philosophical attitude, if linked to a political approach which is unequivocally democratic and socialist, radical and bold, could appeal to those who identify with the past values of the British Labour Party but who now see its political counterpart in the social democracy successfully practised by many other socialist governments in Western Europe. It is an approach within the socialist debate which is not uniquely or even predominantly British. French socialism, which was born out of revolution and has never been as resolutely reformist as British socialism, is currently involved in a similar debate. At the 1977 Congress of the Socialist Party at Nantes Michel Rocard challenged the centralist orthodoxy and spoke of the two political cultures within the French Left; the one which has dominated for a long time was 'jacobin, centralizing, étatist, nationalist and protectionist'. The second culture was 'decentralizing, regionalist, refuses arbitrary dominations, the domination of employers as well as that of the state. The culture fears regulations and administration. It prefers instead basic collectivities and experiment.[12] President Mitterand appoints a Minister for Decentralization.

This approach is neither syndicalist nor anarchistic but is concerned with freedom, is sceptical about more power to the state, and believes that workers should have rights in the workplace. The Labour Party has in the past rejected many of these themes as being idealistic or wildly impracticable but they are relevant after the obvious failure of state ownership, continued alienation, and the failure to achieve industrial democracy. That a strong and centralized state has contributed greatly to the welfare of the British population in the last fifty years is not in doubt; it was perhaps naive of nineteenth century anarchists to believe that a strong state was not needed to start the erosion of the dominance of private ownership and the move towards common ownership. The state has, however, now not so much outlived its usefulness but has become itself an impediment to further change towards the development of a participatory democracy, wider ownership, co-operation and community. The state has a continuing role; modern society cannot do away with the state, and those who regard any attempt to reform and redefine its role as being completely insufficient to safeguard freedom, are detached from reality.

Democracy in Britain cannot just be limited to the political life of the country and be confined to the cyclical elections for the Westminster parliament, the European parliament and the local authority. A true democracy will mean a progressive shift of power from Westminster out to the regions, to the county and town halls, to communities, neighbourhood, patients, tenants and parents. Such a diffusion of power will be resisted by the machine politicians, some trade union leaders, industrial managers, and the bureaucrats, all of whose current power base, status and authority will be challenged. To introduce radical reforms it will be necessary to harness the frustration and to retain the support of a public, which, while affected by a myriad of decisions, as yet feel little enthusiasm for participation even in those areas which do interest them, since they do not believe that their participation will have any influence on decision-making. There is now abundant evidence that the relevance and importance of industrial ownership in transforming attitudes within industry has been exaggerated: the two polarized viewpoints that economic prosperity and social progress come from either private ownership or state ownership alone are facile. The emphasis needs to be placed instead on co-operative ownership and industrial democracy, and on distinguishing the different problems facing public and private ownership and developing where appropriate different policies for pricing, profits, wage-bargaining and investment in those sectors. The major argument is that parliamentary democracy by itself is not enough and needs to be buttressed and enriched by an extension of democracy from the community upwards. The trade unions will need to adapt to more varied patterns of ownership in which their members share in the management, and unions will need to make a greater distinction in how they organize to represent the interest of workers within the public and private sectors. The unions must also be prepared to accept a greater measure of democracy and balloting and to encourage their members to develop different forms of industrial democracy within various patterns of ownership.

In advocating devolution we should reject the inward restrictive emotions of nationalism: whether English, Welsh, Scottish, Irish or British, we should enjoy the simple pleasure of genuine patriotism and at the same time the cultural delight and diversity of retaining the distinctive characteristics of the nation state. In espousing internationalism there needs to be a deep-seated commitment to negotiations for a new world economic order and a new world security order. The challenge for Social Democrats is to rediscover traditional values, to reorder many current priorities, to redefine future goals. This calls for a radical reorientation towards a more decentralized society where the immense task ahead is 'that of passing beyond the welfare state, in which people get given things, to the kind of society in which they find satisfaction in doing things for themselves and for one another'.[13]

There is a very genuine and probably growing opinion that Britain should adopt a low growth strategy, create a low energy society, resist the employment and social implications of the new technology, sustain old industries, refuse robots, keep the conventional office, return to the land and dismantle the industrial society. It is easy to scoff at these ideas, but they have appeal because of the despair felt at the consequences of present policies. For people to be persuaded to reject such a strategy, as not just backward looking but a counsel of despair that will itself bring more misery than happiness, they must be able to relate to a future where there is the prospect of a society which they control and where they do not feel the slaves of that society, a future which holds the prospect of individuals coming together freely to master the system under which they all will live. The key to such a new direction lies in persuasion, not in imposition, and the challenge is to design a political system which allows for persuasion. No one single measure can begin to solve the complex issues which face us all but a shift of attitudes in favour of a more involved democracy where persuasion and consent predominate, and away from authoritarianism, bureaucracy and corporatism, is desirable world-wide. Even higher economic growth against the likely world industrial trends looks harder to achieve and its competitive drive has itself substituted values which have contributed to the destruction of community feeling and to widespread alienation and dissatisfaction.

As Britain is forced to grapple with the world's problems so it will be necessary to adapt society, as well as our own material aspirations, to lower growth. The assumption, prevalent in the 1950s and 1960s, that high growth would automatically transform the problems of poverty, squalor, inequality and injustice has clearly been proven wrong. There is now a greater wish to explore the underlying values within our society: to question, though not to reject, materialism; to ponder, though not to embrace, the morality of sharing fairly the fruits of the earth. Yet all experience indicates that it will be more difficult to correct fundamental inequalities in a situation of low economic growth. A low energy strategy which takes as its central assumption the desirability of low growth can logically argue for a moratorium on the development of nuclear power. Yet aiming for higher economic growth means that, while one can reduce energy consumption more rigorously than in the past, and while much of the new technology is itself less energy-demanding, there will still be a need to provide more energy as a precondition of economic growth.

The dilemma is well illustrated by the Western democracies' most vigorous current public debate which is about the future role of nuclear power. The leaders of communist and developing countries have been able to espouse nuclear power without any debate. Yet, so far, all Western democratic leaders have found it necessary to argue for the continuation of a nuclear power generation programme, in the face of legitimate public anxieties about nuclear waste disposal and a less justified, though nevertheless widely felt, public fear associated with the more remote risks of a serious incident involving a nuclear power station.

Britain is better supplied than most countries with coal, gas and oil, and energy self sufficiency looks feasible, at least for twenty years, which allows us to proceed with more caution over nuclear power. Diversifying our energy sources and progressively developing alternative decentralized sources of energy is a prudent policy on economic, social and environmental grounds. Yet there will continue to be a need for national energy policies and an energy grid for electricity and natural gas; and few who want higher economic growth feel able to square likely forward energy demand with a moratorium on further nuclear power electricity generation.

It is similarly impossible to aim for higher economic growth and to shut out the new technology, to turn one's back on the micro-chip, abandon the office revolution or hold off the robot factory with one manned shift out of three. Such developments have profound social implications for our traditional way of life, but we are responding to the challenge with little imagination and in the belief that the old political structures and attitudes can cope with the new challenges. In Britain more than in most countries we have suffered for some time from a lack of national self-confidence. The British resistance to change is very pervasive and is well documented as existing long before the Great Depression – itself part of the legacy of our being the first country into the industrial revolution. The pessimism that came with the Great Depression was fostered by the savage unemployment and its memory lived on. It became institutionalized within the trade union movement, within management and within Whitehall. Helped by the Second World War, the memory fed the development of corporatism. The growth of central-ism and its manifestation in corporatism are described later in some detail, but here it is only necessary to assert that it is this institutional trend, the committee consensus, which has contributed to the peculiar reluctance in Britain to welcome and adapt to change. Our European neighbours and most comparable industrial competitors have shown – in France in the last two decades, through most of this century in Germany – a greater readiness to make the industrial changes which have contributed to their far more impressive eco-nomic performance.

Yet even over the last decade, with all its disappointments, there has been in Britain a steady rise in the standard of living. Although European comparisons show it to be relatively lower than in other countries, it has nevertheless contributed to a clear improvement in the overall standard of life. In 1970 virtually no manual workers had four weeks' paid holiday. In 1980 over 35 per cent did. Real personal disposable income in fixed prices rose from £1,000 in 1970 to £1,400 in 1980. These are but two statistics indicative of the general improvement.

The industrialized developed world, or the North as it is referred to in the context of the North-South dialogue, has little real understanding of the depth of poverty existing in the Third World, the underdeveloped South. The television screen brings home to many people's sitting rooms the ravages of famine, floods and earthquakes, but the poverty, illiteracy, malnutrition and illness which haunt vast tracts of the world are difficult to comprehend. The Report of the Independent Commission on International Develop-ment Issues under the Chairmanship of Willy Brandt is the most readable and authoritative account of the problems that is easily available.[14] The World Bank estimates that 800 million people can be classified as destitute. Some 40 per cent of the people in the South are not able to secure the basic necessities of life. Four large countries – India, Pakistan, Bangladesh and Indonesia – account for around two-thirds of the world's poor. The bare statistics can easily have a deadening effect. Between 20 to 25 million children below the age of five die every year in developing countries and a third of these deaths are from diarrhoea due to drinking polluted water.

To provide safe drinking water is an achievable goal and the UN in 1977 aimed to do this by 1990. Yet three years later it was clear that the target would not be reached without a doubling of rates of investment in the urban areas and a fourfold increase in rural areas. The 1980s have been declared a 'Decade for Drinking Water and

Sanitation'. The cost of simple standpipes or wells is estimated at $10 per person for water in rural areas; for sanitation the cost is $5 per person in rural areas. Some sceptics decry international action and believe that fixing ambitious world targets is the wrong approach; yet the World Health Organization's successful smallpox eradication programme in the 1970s vindicates such an approach and demonstrates what can be done by a united and determined world.

The Brandt Report necessarily aims at rich governments, whether in the industrialized West or OPEC. It therefore takes as a major theme the divide between North and South and aims to convince powerful Western interest groups that substantial cash transfers to the South, reflation of the world economy by increasing demand, and the rejection of protectionism, are mutual or common interests. It is arguing, however, for economic expansion at a time when the dominant view in Britain and in much of the West is against monetary inflation. Instead the world is experiencing monetary restraint which it is hoped will cut down inflation and not harm medium to longer term production. It is very hard to see how, until there is greater consensus of view amongst governments about the basic tenets of economic policy and how they run their own national economies, there can be a concerted international response to the world's economic problems. It is, therefore, important that in stressing – rightly – enlightened self-interest politicians do not play down or neglect the arguments of common humanity.

This particularly applies to the eradication of hunger where the arguments of self-interest are not easily discernible and yet where the moral case for action is widely accepted. The need for this duality of purpose, self-interest and common humanity, is important not just to convince the Western industrialized world, but also the OPEC countries. In a world where *Realpolitik* dominates, and is likely to continue to dominate, the most rapid movement in tackling the problems of the South will come if OPEC, which is in a pivotal position, decides to force the Western countries to respond. Because of their oil and gas reserves, they are uniquely placed to use their power and leverage. Hitherto their key decision makers have had little self-interest in changing the world economic order; but as OPEC changes its political leaders, as the tension between the older and younger leaders grows, their links with Third World countries strengthen. As a grouping of predominantly Muslim nations, they draw on their moral traditions. The balance of power is very slowly but inexorably changing.

The West has believed for far too long that it has a monopoly of civilized and moral values. The quickest, most dramatic and probably the most radical way of tackling the economic imbalance in the world would be for the OPEC countries to negotiate with the North not only on their own behalf but also on behalf of the South. If they agreed to keep up oil production levels and to recycle their forward surpluses only on condition that the North also expanded their economies and opened up their trading patterns, this would be a powerful force for change, since it could be backed by the realistic threat of cutting back on oil production. As OPEC becomes progressively more radical, so it will be less influenced by the monetarist theories which tend to be favoured by many of their highly traditional banking sources of financial advice. They are listening more to the grievances of the Third World even if they retain their traditional royal family leaderships. If they ignore the South and OPEC puts its interests exclusively in with those of the North, the prospects for any real negotiations taking place over a new economic order in the next decade are very slight.

At the start of the 1980s all the key trends point in the wrong direction. It is amazing how few leading political figures seem aware of the perilous state of many Third World countries' finances. The chance of a major country defaulting on debt repayments is now very high unless there are more generous write-offs, better debt recycling and greater commodity price stability. Deflation in the West has limited the ability of many of the Western countries to purchase goods from the Third World yet we continue to lend to them at previous levels; the risk of a default is also compounded by the continuing rise in oil prices, adding to the Third World countries' costs. A major default would precipitate a financial crisis, since some large financial institutions in the United States in particular are by now severely over-exposed. The repercussions would be very serious and it can be in no one's interest for this chain of events to be triggered. Nor should private banks be allowed to continue to lend at high risk and therefore at high interest to countries which then use all their much needed aid to finance these debts. Aid itself is dropping all the time, as politicians seize on the fashionable questioning of the purposes of aid to reduce their aid budgets. OECD countries in 1961 gave 0.54 per cent of GNP in aid, their highest ever level. This had dropped to 0.31 per cent by 1977, and with the subsequent fall in the rate of growth in the US and the UK, the OECD percentage must be dropping still further. The 1979 Conservative government totally reversed the previous Labour government's forward expenditure priorities which allowed for a 6 per cent per year real terms' increase in the aid budget. Britain has been singled out for criticism by the President of the World Bank for planning to cut aid to 0.38 per cent of GNP by 1985 from the 0.49 per cent average for 1977–9. A more short-sighted policy would be hard to contrive.

The Brandt Report stresses the case for untied aid, automatic disbursement and programme lending and suggests financing it by taxes on foreign trade, energy consumption and arms sales. These are all praiseworthy recommendations, but they stand little chance of being adopted other than under pressure from OPEC by a West which already feels itself economically beleaguered, and only too eager to excuse itself by pointing to the abysmal record on aid of the Soviet Union and other COMECON countries. The reluctance of some Western leaders to discuss the Brandt programme for survival should be a signal to the Third World to give a higher priority to trying to persuade OPEC to negotiate on their behalf with the West in the various world negotiating forums. If the West see this as a possible development, they might move to open discussions with OPEC as a pre-emptive action. There is no justification for inaction, for a resigned acceptance of continued world economic recession; a mixture of inactivity and pessimism will result in continued decline.

Here in Britain politicians need to heed André Malraux's aphorism as we enter the 1980s that a mixture of pessimism and activism breeds fascism. The new Conservative government elected in 1979 showed an untypical activism in the sense that it started as a radical government with initially considerable optimism. Then pessimism took over as the government acted to reduce employment, reduce services and cut the money supply. If the public mood matches this resigned fatalism, pessimism could easily become a way of life, fed by headlines that highlight only what goes wrong. Britain could become so fearful of unemployment, nuclear war and nuclear melt-down, so alarmed about the finite nature of resources, whether of energy or food, so concerned about the breakdown of values and of traditional family life, and so fatalistic about progressive de-industrialization, that it is unable to see a different perspective.

The start of the 1980s with very high unemployment may not appear the best time to advocate a new perspective, but there are well-founded grounds for believing that over the next two decades we will grope towards a new economic and security order, a world that does ease poverty and hunger, does control the arms race, develops new safe sources of energy, new sources of protein, adopts new patterns of child care with a new family structure, works less and has more flexible hours and patterns of work involving far more leisure. The highly centralized society of the Western industrialized democracies will either give way to a more decentralized, disaggregated way of life or it will become more authoritarian and centralized. The question is whether politicians in the Western democracies chart the course of a more decentralized democratic society or resist. Do we develop our democracy so that we become the masters of our destiny, or do we become more state controlled, more subservient to the system? There is already plentiful evidence that individuals within society are straining to be given more choice and to take more responsibility for their lives. The most important task for Social Democrats is to allow that feeling to surface and to extend democracy. At present only twenty to thirty of the member states of the United Nations can be classified as genuine democracies; governments everywhere centralize and bureaucratize and, in doing so, stifle the roots of democracy. The new politics must challenge the increasing centralization of society which is fast becoming the hallmark of government in East and West, North and South, and insist on a greater measure of decentralization as the natural partner of genuine democracy.

2

THE DECENTRALIST
TRADITION

For Social Democrats intent on reviving the decentralist strand of thinking and in advocating specific policies for the 1980s it is worth first reexamining the historical debate. The socialist societies of the 1880s and 1890s, with their mixed membership of socialists and anarchists, focused most of their attention on the issue of *decentralized worker-control* versus *nationalization*. William Morris, although not an anarchist, criticized both the Fabian definition of socialism and the means by which the Fabians expected socialism to be realized. Morris wrote that the Fabians' 'municipal socialism' might seem to work but, 'it may do nothing of the kind: the highly centralized municipal administration of the Roman Empire did not in the least alter the economic basis of chattel slavery.' The mistake of the Webbs, Morris argued, was 'to over-estimate the importance of the mechanism of a society apart from the end to which it may be used.'[1] The decade which included the First World War saw the Fabian view prevail. The belief in centralization and nationalization was given a further boost by the Russian Revolution and the world economic situation. Margaret Cole wrote that 'it was the Russian Revolution itself which soon spelt the end of Guild Socialism as an organized movement. Immediately the Russian factory workers did in fact take over control of factories, and the resultant chaos was so disastrous that the Bolsheviks quickly put a stop to it and introduced centralized discipline.'[2]

The outcome of that debate profoundly influenced the political thought of the Labour movement and in particular the policies of the Labour Party. The flavour of debate is best captured through the contrasting words of two of the key participants, not so much for their particular policies or suggested structures but for what they reveal about their underlying attitudes to people. Looking back on that debate in 1934, G. D. H. Cole wrote that, 'the familiar brands of collectivist socialism were somehow things one wanted for other people rather than oneself, in order to eradicate the deprivations and injustices of capitalism, whereas the Guild doctrine offered me a kind of socialism that I could want as well as think right' . . . 'as having personalities to be expressed as well as stomachs to be filled.'[3].

It is salutary to contrast this with the paternalistic attitude of Sidney Webb, in a lecture entitled 'A Stratified Democracy'. 'The great mass of the people,' he said, 'will always be found apathetic, dense, unreceptive to any unfamiliar ideas, and your eager active spirit with the unfamiliar idea . . . frets and fumes at being held in check by this apathetic mass. But after all, the apathetic mass are individually God's creatures, and entitled to have a vote, and it is no use kicking against their apathy and denseness. You have got to work your governmental machine in some way that will enable you to get on notwithstanding their denseness'[4]

At the February 1918 Labour Party Conference the Fabian collectivist tradition emerged as the dominant influence in formulating the wording of the Labour Party constitution. Clause 3 of the constitution stated '. . . to secure for the producers by hand and by brain the full fruits of their industry and the most equitable distribution thereof that may be possible, upon the basis of the common ownership of the means of production, and the best obtainable system of popular administration and control of each industry or service.' The latter part was a bow to the Guild Socialists but the direction was henceforth towards nationalization. In 1929 Clause 4, para 4 of the constitution, which was to become so contentious after the electoral defeat of 1959, emerged. 'Means of production' was altered to 'means of production, distribution, and exchange', and 'producers' was amended to 'workers'. It is interesting that the early debate between the centralists and decentralists was so dominated by the discussion over workers' control and did not widen out to cover other areas in the centralist – decentralist debate. The reason was probably that the Labour Party in Parliament and in the boroughs was still building up its support. It had not yet held power and there was a tendency therefore to concentrate on the main industrial issue on which decisions had to be taken and which from day to day divided both the Party and the Trade Union movement.

It was significant that the Webbs, while being strong advocates of the consumer co-operative movement, were suspicious of industrial co-operatives. The Webbs did not object to the profits of retail co-ops being distributed to the population at large but they were very sceptical of the ability of workers to manage factories and preferred that industry should be nationalized and professional managers be employed. For Morris, influenced by his romantic notion of a return to the dignity and craftsmanship of the medieval guilds, this was an inadequate vision. In criticizing Graham Wallas, one of the Fabian essayists, he wrote that, 'Socialism is emphatically not merely "a system of property-holding" but a complete theory of human life, founded indeed on a distinct system of religion, ethics and conduct, which . . . will not indeed enable us to get rid of the tragedy of life . . . but will enable us to meet it without fear and without shame.'[5] There was no dissent about the need for democracy: the argument was about the form democracy should take. Common ownership was seen to be of fundamental importance; the issue was whether ownership should be by the state on behalf of everyone, or by workers within the organization. The Webbs and their fellow Fabians stressed the virtues of collective action in every sphere, not only in the ownership of industry but also in social activities. As Anthony Crosland put it in *The Future of Socialism*, they thought that 'any extension of collective [action] at the expense of individual activity constitutes an advance towards socialism, including the registration by the state of playing-card makers, hawkers, dogs, cabs, places of worship and dancing rooms.'[6] Yet while mocking these collectivist Fabian attitudes Crosland also questioned the reality of the all embracing participatory society, when he wrote, 'if what is meant by participation is an active and continuous process of participating in decision-making, then all experience shows that only a small minority of the population will wish to participate . . . the fact is that the majority will continue to prefer to lead a full family life and cultivate their gardens. And a very good thing too. For a continuous political activism by the great bulk of the population would not only run counter to most people's desires for privacy and a leisured family life, but it would also (as G. D. H. Cole used often to say) pose a real threat to the stability of our democracy. Indeed it would mark the breakdown of normal social cohesion.'[7] That criticism evokes Oscar Wilde's supposed comment that socialism would take too many evenings. Yet participation and political activity cannot be so lightly dismissed. John Stuart Mill was right when he argued that liberty is morally better than slavery, that even if slaves like being slaves it is still right to free them, because only free men are fully human.

It is of course true that the movement towards greater participation will always operate within the bounds of human nature; for some growing vegetables on the allotment will always be of more concern than air pollution. But plan to cut a motorway through an allotment area and suddenly activism will be unleashed. The momentum towards participation has its roots in the very educational advances for which socialists and others have striven. In no area is this drive for participation more difficult for established authority to comprehend than in the industrial place of work. Yet no other activity occupies so much time in an individual's life and should more naturally be at least subject to that person's influence.

The movement in favour of workers' control grew out of syndicalism, the revolutionary trade union movement which arose after 1880 in France and in the United States. Its leading advocates were the American Marxist, Daniel DeLeon and the Frenchman, Georges Sorel. In Britain syndicalist doctrines were spread most effectively by the trade union leader, Tom Mann. In South Wales the syndicalists formed the Unofficial Reform Committee of the South Wales Miners Federation, and in 1912 the Committee published a pamphlet entitled *The Miners' Next Step* in which they rejected nationalization and instead favoured a process by which each industry would be run by the workers with the various industries of the country being controlled by a Central Production Board. This they asserted 'would mean real democracy in real life, making for real manhood and womanhood. Any other form of democracy is a delusion and a snare.'[8] The National Union of Mineworkers (NUM) to this day is resistant to any form of worker representation on the National Coal Board, preferring the Tripartite mechanism for representation, with the Unions, National Coal Board and Government discussing the wider issues affecting the industry, and with all retaining independence for negotiations on wages and conditions. The NUM, itself a deeply federalist union with considerable autonomy given to the union leaders in different parts of the country, has maintained its legendary unity largely by the widespread use of the pit-head ballot.

The influence of the syndicalists was minimal in Britain because their revolutionary doctrine and advocacy of direct action through the general strike had little appeal. Most union leaders who were interested preferred the theory of Guild Socialism elaborated initially by two journalists, A. R. Orage and S. G. Hobson on the Left-wing weekly *New Age*. The Guild Socialists differed from the syndicalists in that they did not believe that the state should be abolished or that revolutionary means should be adopted. They argued that the best basis for representation was by function rather than by territory since modern legislators could not reflect all the diverse interests and opinions of their constituents. They felt that a democratic system based on the workplace or industry would more fully reflect the interests of the workers and would help to prevent the dilution of democracy which occurs when representatives are overstretched or remote. The Guild Socialists believed that the means of production should be collectivized but be controlled by guilds rather than by the state. Guildsmen would elect their own legislatures and executives and these would select representatives to serve on a council of all the important guilds. This council would co-ordinate the plans of the guilds and settle disputes between them but would not act as a replacement for parliament.

The disparity of thinking can be seen by analysing the two viewpoints presented to the Sankey Commission on the coal industry in 1919. Sidney Webb supported the formation of joint committees of workers and managers to offer advice and criticism to the owners, whereas G. D. H. Cole called for the establishment at once of the greatest amount of industrial democracy – meaning direct control by the workers and their unions – that was practicable, and for the most rapid subsequent extension of that control that was practicable. Beatrice Webb saw the self-governing workshop as 'that "charmer" within the order of thought, but "gay deceiver" within the order of things.'[9] This slightly deprecating and condescending judgement still represents the tenor of much establishment thinking within the Labour movement even today. Workers' control is seen as a romantic idea, harmless provided it does not get too strong, a potential but remote threat to the authority of the trade union movement: but basically irrelevant to the real issues of managing the economy. Industrial co-operatives are something to which lip service may be paid, or which can be disparaged with a knowing smile and an evocative reference to the well-publicized failures of KME in Kirby, or the *Scottish Daily News*, and a question about the Meriden Motor-Cycle Co-operative. These attitudes fail to absorb the impact of the quantum shift in the educational level of the industrial labour force. The wish to have more say and greater involvement in the decisions which dictate a peron's daily pattern of work is not just a feature of education but also of greater leisure and security. Even seventy years ago, however, some powerful trade unions like the National Union of Railwaymen were sympathetic to workers' control. The issue split the Independent Labour Party but with the Miners Federation, the Post Office Workers and others there was an influential minority within the Labour movement sympathetic to the concept of workers' control.

Guild Socialism was essentially a movement of middle class intellectuals and as such it was limited in its appeal. Trade union leaders were reluctant to adopt the very radical solution that the Guild Socialists favoured and without union support the Guild Socialists could not hope to confront the hostility of private owners. The advocacy of workers' control was also coming at a time when many workers and all women still did not have the vote and the proposed downgrading of parliament and the civil service was far too radical for many people sympathetic to the broad idea. There was also considerable doubt by those who favoured central control that the degree of economic planning which they favoured could be achieved by the national guilds. As a result, after the collapse of the building guilds, Guild Socialism has left only a theoretical legacy. But these early debates did ensure that the Webbs moved off their initial position of total opposition to worker participation in industrial control and their 'Constitution for the Socialist Commonwealth' did allow for participation within a system of organized groups. It was a shift of emphasis, an acceptance of worker directors – like those in 1977 on the Post Office Board and in 1967 for the regional Boards of British Steel – and it was illustrated by their seeing as a 'real social gain that the General Secretary of the Swiss Railwaymen's Trade Union should sit as one of the five members of the supreme governing body of the Swiss railway administration'.[10]

The concept of the public corporations evolved from the writings and speeches of Herbert Morrison. It is too easy, however, to see Morrison himself as the archetypal centralist. He was in fact the most committed supporter of local government who has ever held senior Cabinet office in the Labour Party. In the 1945–51 Labour government it was frequently Herbert Morrison who challenged the accretion of powers to the state particularly if they were taken from local government, as they were over the NHS. Morrison, ever the practical politician, wanted to establish in the 1930s a detailed management structure for nationalized industry which would allow for a clear-cut decision making procedure, and this was far more important to him than a theory of democratic control. The concept of nominated members of public corporations was, however, strongly challenged by the advocates of greater worker representation and the Labour programme of 1934 said, 'the employees in a socialized industry have a right which should be acknowledged by law, to an effective share in the control and direction of the industry'.[11] But the 1945 Labour government was not committed to the concept. Stafford Cripps could say in 1946, 'there is not yet a very large number of workers in Britain capable of taking over large enterprises . . . until there has been more experience by the workers of the managerial side of industry. I think it would be almost impossible to have worker controlled industry in Britain, even if it were on the whole "desirable".'[12] This comment reflected a confusion which remains to this day between the concept of workers acting as managers, and the more realistic objective of managers acting for workers or with them, rather than for capital.

The government of which Stafford Cripps was such a prominent member was deeply rooted in the Fabian collectivist centralist tradition – like all its successors. The dominance of this tradition contributed to the fact that by the 1979 election the Tory philosophical Right was the radical challenger to the status quo in relation to the debate about public sector industry and public services generally. The Right had picked up the public's concern about government bureaucracy and cleverly created a political climate in Britain which identified the target for these concerns as being the Labour Party. The Labour government and the Party appeared intellectually exhausted: standing pat on the status quo. It was the Right which stood against nationalization, bureaucracy, state interventionism, for a materialistic personal freedom and the privatization of industry which, against an intellectual vacuum and lack-lustre espousal of trade union dominated industrial democracy from the Left, meant that the Right had a more than passing appeal – around 40 per cent of trade unionists voted Conservative, among them many workers in state industries. At no time since the end of the 1920s had the Labour movement seriously engaged in the intellectual debate about the role of the individual in relation to the state, the company and the community. With few new ideas to invigorate its supporters and with which to chart a course for the 1980s, the Labour government was bound to appear defensive, and even though there was a Manifesto commitment to industrial democracy, it never came alive as an issue, in part because the key democratic issues had not been resolved.

In contrast nationalization in the 1945 Manifesto was not a vote loser and it had considerable public support. It was natural then to retain much of the machinery evolved in wartime, to continue to plan the economy, so as to ease the transition to a peacetime system of production and to ensure that full employment was maintained. There was a strong practical case, which had been argued over the past few decades, for the 1945 government to take the large public utilities into state ownership. Yet many socialists even then saw nationalization as much more than a practical industrial policy. It represented a means of achieving greater socialism in the long run by easing the conditions of manual workers through better paid and more secure jobs and by allowing the economy to be planned. Tawney wrote that nationalization 'will benefit the mine-worker by removing the downward pressure of capitalism on his standard of life, by making room for considerations of social well-being which are at present subordinated to the pursuit of dividends, and by securing him an effective voice in the policy and organization of the industry.'[13] Some of these advantages have been achieved, but mainly through the pressure of collective bargaining and the role of the state as a good employer, not through the involvement of those who work in the industry. In the 1960s, when the coal industry was deliberately run down by both Conservative and Labour governments, not many miners were convinced that nationalization had brought great benefits to their industry. In comparison to the attitudes of the coal owners in the 1930s there had been great changes, but these had also taken place over the same period in most of British industry, both private and public. In 1972 it took the first miners' strike since 1926 for miners' wages to start to improve their relative position. The fourfold increase in oil prices saw the coal industry, in 1974, at last experiencing the steady investment and government support that it had lacked for the first twenty-five years of nationalization. The record of nationalized industries is not as bad as its critics pretend but neither has it lived up to the hopes of its early advocates. Not one State Industry can point to a really pioneering role in relation to workers' control.

Sadly no Labour government can point to any significant measure of decentralization. Only Richard Crossman showed in government a genuine radical wish to change the structure of government. In 1966, when he was Minister of Housing and Local Government, he established a Royal Commission with terms of reference designed to produce positive reform. As Lord President of the Council he also attempted to reform both the House of Commons and the House of Lords. The Labour Party in Opposition in the 1950s never challenged the centripetal tendency of post-war Britain. In government in the 1960s Labour advocated large-scale industry and large government departments, and argued for economies of scale and the extension of the public sector.

The establishment of the Royal Commission on the Constitution under Lord Kilbrandon in 1969 could and should have been a constitutional landmark, a turning point in our history. Instead it was a cynical reaction to the electoral success of the Scottish Nationalist Party, taken not as a convinced devolutionist response to a genuine issue but as a way to defuse a new and threatening political force. The subsequent ten-year debate which ended in the referendum and parliamentary debacle of 1979 was no more than an accurate reflection of a deep division of opinion, both in the Labour Party and in the country, that had been glossed over under the threat of a continuous SNP challenge to the Labour Party in Scotland. The Royal Commission on Local Government's Report[14] came too late in the lifetime of the 1964–70 government to be implemented, as did the proposals to end the tripartite structure of the National Health Service. It was left to another centralist government, the Tory one of 1970–4, to bureaucratize and nearly destroy the structure of local government and the National Health Service. Social historians will probably judge these as the two most disastrous administrative reforms this century. The 1979 Conservative government is demonstrating an even stronger centralist sentiment in its control of local government.

Even the establishment of the Committee on Local Government Finance in 1974[15] reflected a short-term political reaction to protests over rate increases. It never had as its prime motivation a wish to examine seriously the case for greater financial autonomy for local authorities. The virtual rejection of its recommendations in the Layfield Report, while the ink was still wet, was a triumph for centralism amongst both politicians and civil servants. The decision to appoint the Enquiry into Industrial Democracy was also flawed by the acceptance of demands for terms of reference which circumscribed the enquiry so as to emphasize the centralist, legislative, trade union dominated, option for industrial democracy. As a result the Bullock Report[16] gave some consideration to the other more radical options, but reflected in its membership and in its approach, the centralist approach.

The task for Social Democrats is to try to develop and build a fresh decentralized philosophy, and put forward a detailed programme of legislative and administrative reforms to diffuse power in Britain. To carry electoral support such a programme will need to have an inner coherence, and honestly face the genuinely conflicting arguments and attitudes that are posed within the centralist – decentralist dilemma. How great is the risk of widening inequalities by decentralizing, and how effective is centralization in achieving equality; what is the role of inspectorates; how efficient are smaller units? Most postwar British governments have at times said that they are in favour of administrative and political decentralization but they have failed to pursue these beliefs when it has been realized that the result would be a reduction in their existing powers. What is needed is nothing less than a radical reappraisal of British society. It will not be resolved by referring those political issues to a civil service bureaucracy or establishing another round of Royal Commissions or Committees of Enquiry. It needs a fresh political philosophy and commitment. It needs to be a society where quality is weighed with quantity, where diversity is the friend of order not its enemy.

This is not a prescription for consensus, middle of the road politics. There are hard choices to be made, large bureaucracies to be dismantled, vested interests to be challenged, whether represented by the First Division of the Civil Service Association or the National Union of Public Employees, whether that of the Institute of Directors or the Transport and General Workers Union, the British Medical Association or the National Union of Teachers. What is required is a break with the past not a revolution; not replacing an extremism of the Right by an extremism of the Left but an evolution of attitudes, which is the only democratically acceptable method of making change and ensuring that the changes last beyond the lifetime of one government. A society seeking greater decentralization faces a more radical challenge than a society dominated by the centralist belief in state control and nationalization. A decentralized society widens the goals which its citizens seek to realize and it takes on more of the existing centres of power than does a strategy that has the relatively narrow goal of transferring power from the private to the public sector.

Enhancing democracy is a long-term policy. John Stuart Mill argued that men would learn by being free, that freedom produces morally better people because it forces them to develop their potentialities. Only change of attitude will produce lasting social change. By deliberately increasing the opportunities for the individual to become involved, a decentralized society can focus the attention of a wider section of the population on its economic weaknesses, social failings and persistent inequalities. The task is to explain more about the nature of society or to enable voters to find out for themselves rather than merely to trade in single slogans such as 'nationalization' or 'private enterprise'. Political values ought to underpin the appeal of any political party to the electorate. Social Democrats will need to elaborate theirs if they are to change the political climate. The values of the Right have made headway recently and these were shown in 1979 to be as important in terms of voter appeal as detailed policies or manifestos.

The most stimulating writer on socialism in the 1950s was Anthony Crosland, though his analysis was surprisingly centralist in concept. This was masked to some extent by Crosland's own personality and his ability lightly to deride every facet of any organization and to extol individualism in a way which made his form of socialism beguilingly sensitive, warm and attractive. Who could fail to respond to a plea for liberty and gaiety in private life? 'We need not only higher exports and old-age pensions, but more open-air cafés, brighter and gayer streets at night, later closing hours for public houses, more local repertory theatres, better and more hospitable hoteliers and restaurateurs, brighter and cleaner eating-houses, more riverside cafés, more pleasure-gardens on the Battersea model, more murals and pictures in public places, better designs for furniture and pottery and women's clothes, statues in the centre of new housing-estates, better-designed street-lamps and telephone kiosks, and so on *ad infinitum*. The enemy in all this will often be in unexpected guise; it is not only dark Satanic things and people that now bar the road to the new Jerusalem, but also, if not mainly, hygienic, respectable, virtuous things and people, lacking only in grace and gaiety.'[17]

Crosland asserted in 1950 that 'Britain has in all essentials, ceased to be a capitalist country'[18] and later in 1974 that 'I see no reason to alter the revisionist thesis that government can generally impose its will (provided it has one) on the private corporation'.[19] The revisionist case was that fundamental changes were needed in the structure of society but that these changes could be imposed. They tended to under-estimate the importance of changing attitudes seeing change in terms of legislative or administrative reform. Being dominated by the need to obtain economic growth, the Crosland analysis spent little time on capitalism or aspects of alienation.

Crosland was firmly in the tradition of those, such as Tawney, who emphasized the ability of the government to bring socialism about by economic reforms. Despite his appeal for 'grace and gaiety' he tended to believe that a combination of politicians and administrators would be able to cure social problems with only minimal involvement by the bulk of the population. Little attention was given to how to achieve a fundamental change in attitudes in the values of community by eroding the values of capitalism, and by the involvement of individuals in decision-making at their place of work. Marxists who argue that economic changes precede changes in values and that the economic basis of capitalism must be removed before any change in values can be expected also ignore the importance of attitudinal change. Both under-estimate the ability of old value systems to adapt to institutional changes in such a way that despite radical-sounding legislation little real change results. That changes in values and structures need to proceed together in order to achieve significant changes in the actual working of institutions is one of the major lessons that should be derived from the revisionist experience through the 1960s and 1970s. The revisionists formed a coalition with the corporatists without realizing the extent to which that very corporatism had embraced capitalist values and had become a stultifying brake on introducing any radical change. Crosland was not unaware of this when writing in 1962 that: 'A dogged resistance to change now blankets every segment of our national life. A middle-aged conservatism, parochial and complacent, has settled over the country; and it is hard to find a single sphere in which Britain is pre-eminently in the forefront . . . Our Parliament and Civil Service, brilliantly adapted to the needs of a bygone age, and which we still seek to export unmodified to ex-colonial territories, are in fact in need of drastic modernization.'[20] Successive Labour governments saw change as primarily arising out of structural organizational and administrative reform. So 1964–80 saw the establishment of endless Committees of Enquiry, Royal Commissions and Inter-departmental Working Parties. Their findings were implemented by politicians only if they did not pose a challenge to the role of the centralized state. Few socialists saw that corporatism was as much the enemy of socialism as capitalism, perhaps more so because it proved a less obvious challenge – more adaptive and just as corrosive. Yet it is with corporatism that the Labour Party has unwittingly become ever more closely identified. The decentralist socialist case which at the start of the century was diffuse and utopian, was in retrospect bound to be defeated by the organizational and practical arguments for centralized socialism, particularly when that form of a socialism had never even been tried. Half a century later, after the experience of centralized government through the two post-war periods it is possible to identify its off-spring, corporatism. For the Social Democrats' decentralist analysis to carry conviction the nature of corporatism must be exposed and its further extension rejected.

3

THE GROWTH OF
CORPORATISM

There is clearly a legitimate and responsible role for the state and in
certain areas such as defence, international relations and world
trade, its tasks are obvious. The state has also developed a role in
domestic policy which has been sufficiently successful to make it
difficult to argue in principle against the welfare state; the question is
whether the trend towards increasing the role of the state can be
checked or reversed so as to shift towards a more decentralized
society.

The argument that Britain has begun to move inexorably towards
a corporate state is not new, and in recent years that critique has
been vigorously mounted from the New Left as well as from the
Hayek Right. The year 1979 saw the return of a Conservative
government which, for the first time, meant a government that was
openly critical of the corporate state. The challenge for Social
Democrats is not to allow this political critique to be mounted only
from the viewpoint of the Right, but to ensure that the Social
Democratic Party is seen to be reassessing the strength of the
corporate state with conviction and coherence. The dominant tradition within the Labour Party is deeply centralist, and large sections
of the Party are so firmly embedded in the structure of the state that
they see an attack on the corporate state as an attack on them. The
signs are that the Labour Party has become so defensive that it will
automatically oppose all of the Conservative Party attitudes to the
corporate state, to the extent of becoming the defender of the
bureaucracy and resisting any cutback in the tasks and functions of
the state.

Driven to accept the inevitability of the continued private ownership of much of industry yet disliking the concept of market
forces, many socialists seek to control private industry through the
apparatus of the state. Such socialists do not accept the Marxist[1]
analysis that corporatism is a capitalist strategy for subordinating
labour when for a variety of reasons the normal capitalist device of

market forces is not operating. They see corporatism as a way of enhancing the position of labour through agreement, forming a tripartite negotiating forum between trade union organizations, the state and employer organizations. Hitherto many Conservatives have found that the mix between private and public ownership is inevitable and have tried to instil artificial disciplines of market forces into the public sector through the apparatus of the state. Between the Conservative and Labour position corporatism develops as a system where the traditional distinction between capitalism and socialism is eroded. Instead of the majority view prevailing as is the essence of democracy, committee decision-making produces a consensus which erodes decisive democratically elected and responsible decision making. This form of Conservative status quo corporatism is in marked contrast to the attempt at a redistributive corporatism in Scandinavia or the bland mixture of the kind that has evolved in Britain under Labour governments.

The growth of the interventionist state began in Britain with the social welfare reforms of the 1906–14 Liberal governments. This was a radical change, the first example of the state actively promoting social goals for a large sector of the population. By 1914 expenditure on the social services had doubled and the First World War saw an acceleration of this trend and a qualitative change in the role of the state under the challenge of total war. Trade union and business co-operation was essential for victory and so the state adapted its structure and role to ensure their co-operation.

The historian, A. J. P. Taylor, has described the impact of the war in the following terms: 'until August 1914 a sensible, law-abiding Englishman could pass through life and hardly notice the existence of the state, beyond the post office and the policeman . . . All this was changed by the impact of the Great War. The mass of people became, for the first time, active citizens. Their lives were shaped by orders from above; they were required to serve the state instead of pursuing exclusively their own affairs.'[2]

In the First World War the British government encouraged the growth of labour and employers' organizations to secure public consent for mobilization, while the organizations welcomed the increase in power. The British government was forced to bargain for the support of the public as it was vital to produce the munitions and obtain the manpower to achieve victory. The state apparatus was partly dismantled after the First World War but several newly created Ministries survived, such as the Ministry of Labour and the Ministry of Transport and 'by 1922 it had become clear that a number of unions and employers' leaders had accepted the need for formal political collaboration with the state. TUC and employers' organizations crossed a threshold which had not even existed before the war, and behaved thereafter in some degree as estates of the realm, to the detriment of more ancient, obsolete estates, the municipalities, the churches, the "colleges" of professional men, and the panoply of voluntary bodies, so important in the political system of the nineteenth century.'[3] The significance of the 1926 General Strike was that it killed workers' control and the syndicalist tradition and though it did not break trade union power it did turn trade union power in a corporatist direction to work henceforth with employers and government. It publicly demonstrated that TUC and employers interests had to be recognized for the country to be governable. The General Strike also brought to prominence trade union leaders such as Ernest Bevin who, despite their records as strike leaders, recognized that there was a place for conciliation rather than conflict in winning better returns for their membership. In 1929 the TUC, the National Conference of Employers' Organizations and the CBI had their first joint meeting without government present and with a wide remit covering the national economy, unemployment and industrial legislation. It was the start of a long road towards institutional co-operation.

In the United States and in Europe during the depression more interventionist governments adopted many of what we now identify as corporatist remedies. As with Mussolini's Italy, Hitler's Germany could not strictly be termed corporatist since a false consensus was imposed by very effective propaganda, backed by the threat and use of force rather than by consultation and representation. The Italians attempted to reduce the independence of non-state institutions and to create a rigidly hierarchical society, and the same pattern was discernible, too, in Nazi Germany. In the United States, President Roosevelt and 'the New Deal' created a series of institutions to pay out government finance and to influence and plan sectors of the economy. The US trade unions also became more corporatist but given their weak structure there was little danger of these measures developing into full-blown corporatism. Even so Roosevelt was endless attacked by big business for whom state intervention lacked any legitimacy. This resistance was fortified by the deeply federal structure of US government with the individual states jealous of any federal government encroachment on their powers.

An intellectual justification for government intervention was provided, in all developed countries, by the economic analysis heralded in Keynes's *General Theory*. Keynes showed that capitalist economies were not self-regulating and in particular that they did not automatically create full employment. Demand-management by the state was legitimized and, with the development of new economic tools by the Keynesians, governments were now able at least to pose as being able to control macro-economic variables such as the level of investment, the rate of inflation and the amount of unemployment. Henceforth, governments could no longer claim that a poor economic performance was due to factors wholly outside their control and in the first flush of enthusiasm governments began to intervene in the economy, claiming that they were creating the economic conditions which would justify their re-election.

Ernest Bevin as Minister of Labour in 1940 acquired powers under the Emergency Powers (Defence) Act that had never been held by central government before. The wages of agricultural workers and railwaymen were raised, and so was excess profit tax. With craftsmen enlisting in the armed services attempts were made to negotiate dilution agreements to use semi-skilled workers. Wages Tribunals were established under the Conditions of Employment and National Arbitration Order No. 1305. Prices were held, real wages increased slightly and the net effect was redistribution of wealth. The foundation was laid for repeated experiments in forms of incomes policy allied, to a lesser or greater extent, to prices and dividend restraint.

The Second World War again accelerated the growth of corporatism. In five years the institutional framework of a semi-planned economy was built up to such an extent that A. J. P. Taylor could write: 'this produced a revolution in British economic life, until in the end direction and control turned Great Britain into a country more fully socialist than anything achieved by the conscious planners of Soviet Russia.'[4] The government intervened in all aspects of industry in order to increase the production of armaments. The financial powers of the banks were curtailed, welfare policies were brought forward to secure the acquiescence of workers and foreign trade was regulated. 'The common struggle against an external enemy provoked in both Labour and Conservative Parties acceptance of the ideas of a mixed economy, a modified imperial role, a welfare state and the perpetuation of institutional consensus.'[5] Many war-time controls were later removed but the process of representation and consultation was now formalized.

The 1945 Labour government, in its centralizing measures, was broadly governing within a trend established even before the outbreak of the Second World War. Since then governments have demanded centralized restraint, often with public support, at times of economic crisis, to cope with a collapse in the balance of payments or inflation. Then, as support has been eroded, interest groups have flourished and the restraint has been replaced by a compensatory spiral. The economic crises have followed one another with depressing regularity. Hard choices have been frequently ducked and no fundamental solution has been found, and the pattern of institutional compromise, built up during wartime, has been legitimized and retained in peacetime.

Britain after the Second World War was not compelled to create new institutions to rebuild the economy as were Japan and Germany. Instead old institutions were adapted, particularly parliament, the civil service and local government. The country as a whole shrank from truly radical reform and important permanent institutions such as the universities and schools continued much as before. Even the 1944 Education Act, important though it was, did little to challenge the class structure within Britain.[6] Comprehensive education, bitterly fought over for two decades, has only now gained wider acceptance and is producing good results, and our technical and engineering education is still given far too low a priority.

Britain, the first country to enter the Industrial Revolution, was also the first to confront many of the problems of an industrial society: the alienation of the worker at the place of work, the demoralization of the assembly line worker, the loss of satisfaction that came with the decline of craftsmanship and the growth of the semi-skilled. With strong and numerous trade unions it has become apparent that many groups of workers, particularly in the public sector, have the potential to cause industrial and social disruption; and the aims of one group often depend on the support of other like-minded groups for success. Division of labour is now so complex that as workers, consumers and citizens we have all come to depend on the actions of other people. The pensioner depends on the single large civil service computer for his or her weekly pension, the housewife on the water engineers, the surgeon on the electricians. A society which recognizes that a degree of co-ordination is necessary in order to make life tolerable soon develops the framework for co-ordinating institutions, committees, representation procedures and, to support it all, proliferating administration. The state not surprisingly soon develops a role as integrator, regulator and arbiter, and this happens even in countries where belief in the free market economy has produced a far less interventionist state than in Britain. Yet just as the complexity of life makes it easy for the state to adopt this central role the centralization makes society strangely vulnerable.

The peculiar nature of British corporatism owes much to the strange way in which the mixed economy has come to mean a mix not just between public and private ownership but a mixing of objectives and management attitudes within each sector. A public corporation under Labour governments adopts the accounting techniques of private enterprise, its profits are expressed and its productivity measured in line with the practice of private enterprise despite the fact that this may then pose a challenge to the very purpose of having the corporation publicly controlled in the first place. The fact that the railways are a public service becomes secondary or that the National Coal Board has a strategic energy function is ignored in pursuit of profit in its annual accounts. The quantification of service in terms of consumer satisfaction or strategic return is forgotten. A similar criticism can be made of the private sector which, while publicly criticizing state intervention, has quietly exploited state intervention and the corporate attitudes of Ministers and civil servants for its own advantage. 'State intervention in economic life in fact largely means intervention for the purpose of helping capitalist enterprise. In no field has the notion of the 'welfare state' had a more precise and apposite meaning than here: there are no more persistent and successful applicants for public assistance than the proud giants of the private enterprise system.'[7] It is a perfectly fair criticism that successive British governments have been prepared to pay out public money to firms that not only refuse to follow government guidelines but frequently do not respect regional policy or even minimal criteria of trade union recognition and good employer practice.

Advocates of the mixed economy must be prepared to question the extent to which it is desirable to mix the objectives of the public and private sectors – the extent to which inducing a sense of social responsibility in the private sector is compatible with the economic dynamic that should come from the private entrepreneur. While it is true that Anthony Crosland argued that 'a mixed economy is essential to social democracy', his revisionism has been criticised for, 'in the increasingly controlled bureaucratized and centrally directed economy now prevailing and always favoured by Crosland . . . a firm will hang on to its profits, export more than is economically justified, butter up its trade unions, never dismiss redundant workers, charge only "fair" prices, site new plants where the government wants it to, operate expensive welfare programmes, make gifts to education, patronize the arts, and participate in local community affairs: "Its goals are a 'fair' rather than a maximum profit, reasonably rapid growth, and the warm glow which comes from a sense of public duty" – and a title doubtless for the chairman to boot . . . Crosland thus sees managers as floating rudderless in a sort of vacuum, blown hither and thither by alternate gusts of public duty and non-economic self-interest, responsible to nobody in particular and to everyone in general.'[8] It is a serious criticism that socialists who advocate a mixed economy must face up to; that they risk emasculating the private sector, by constraining its driving force, so limiting its scope for initiative that its strengths and economic contribution are fatally sapped. The charge has substance. It would be better to give the private sector more freedom from central governmental detailed control and legislate instead for local democratic rights for its own employees, freeing it to operate commercially as a force within the economy with the differences between the private and public sector being openly recognized, not incorporated or amalgamated.

A very wide range of institutions is possible and viable within the framework of western industrialized countries. 'The dozen developed capitalist economies are more alike in the goals they pursue than the specific policy techniques and institutions used to achieve them. Each country has its own style in managing the economy, determined largely by its political institutions and social history. The French have contrived a technique of economic planning which requires intimate collaboration between civil servants and private business firms of a sort which English and American tradition abhors. Italy has had success with mixed enterprises owned jointly by government and private stockholders. Swedish co-operatives play stronger economic roles than those in other countries . . .'[9]

In the 1980s Labour Party policy shows every sign of still giving an unquestioned central and dominant role to the state but, while state intervention has been advocated in every area of political activity, there has never been agreement about the role of the state in relation to the trade unions. Trade unionists and the trade union leaders may call for more State intervention in industry, but the majority of trade union leaders have never accepted that the state should interfere with free collective bargaining and most are opposed to any statutory interference in industrial relations. It is an odd position to be advocating state intervention into other people's activities but resenting any state intervention in one's own trade union activities.

A breakdown in the relationship between Labour governments and the trade unions has been at the root of the last two election defeats. There was genuine anger at the attempted legislation by the Labour government in 1968 into the conduct of trade unionism. In 1978 and 1979 there was bitterness over the attempt to impose a fourth year of incomes policy. A root cause of these two breakdowns in relations has been that while Labour governments have continued to foster centralized socialism the trade union movement itself has been progressively moving towards a more decentralized structure. The Royal Commission on the Trade Unions chaired by Lord Justice Donovan, in its major report published in 1968[10] recognized that there had been a shift in the bargaining strength of unions from the offical structures to the shopfloor. Since the nineteenth century some unions have had representatives at the workplace to collect subscriptions and report to union bodies. Gradually those stewards came to act as representatives when day to day issues arose especially in the munitions factories and in the overall war effort in 1914–18. By 1917 their power was at its zenith, official TUC leadership was unable to endorse strike action and besides taking direct unconstitutional action, the stewards began to campaign for peace and opposed conscription. They were supported by ILP leaders such as Ramsay MacDonald and Philip Snowden. During the Depression of the 1920s and 1930s their role was limited by the danger of victimization, but since the onset of post-war full employment there has been a tremendous rise in their number and influence. Today there are about 300,000 shop stewards,[11] about a third of these in the engineering industry, which represents 30 per cent of all industrial output. In the 1960s their numbers increased rapidly because of increasing government intervention in collective bargaining and the frustration felt on the shopfloor at the support often given by national union leaderships to this degree of state intervention.

It also became the policy of some unions, notably the Transport and General Workers Unions, which is the largest single union with a current membership of two million, deliberately to give positive support to the downward shift in bargaining levels.[12] To some extent the T&GWU wanted to avoid government-imposed controls and to deal with opportunities at individual factories to exploit productivity deals and any other loopholes or agreed flexibilities made necessary by successive national incomes policies: but there was also a conviction that shopfloor bargaining was a better and more democratic way of settling wage levels than central bargaining.

It is amazing, that the Labour movement continues to ignore this dichotomy between the Labour Party and the Trade Union Congress. The centralist tendency of the Labour Party carries the seeds of conflict with a decentralized trade union movement and the fundamental lesson for the Social Democrats is that this issue must be faced. It is little use wistfully recalling the past with its strong trade union leaders, the era of Arthur Deakin, or of 'Caron's law' in the AUEW. The trade unions are very unlikely to reverse the decentralist trend or to agree to vest much authority in the TUC itself. If this is the case, there is an obvious contradiction in any political party, still pursuing a centralist incomes policy with its norms, flat rate increases and detailed procedures. Logically there is a need to define a new decentralized form of incomes policy which matches the realities of the negotiating structure specifically in the private sector.

It is also very apparent that the Co-operative Movement feels that the centralist tradition within the Labour Party has ensured that that Party is less receptive to their underlying philosophical concepts. In particular, the inability to see the potential of state incentives for an expansion of industrial co-operatives as an alternative to state ownership has been a source of immense dissatisfaction. The 10 million consumer co-operators, in addition to the more committed 12,000 members of the Co-operative Party, are a substantial potentially sympathetic electoral target for the Social Democratic Party. They probably represent a more naturally receptive audience in terms of underlying attitudes than those many trade unionists who are not co-operators.

A growing number of people identify with the theme of decentralization and there are strong electoral, as well as philosophical, arguments for stressing the decentralist beliefs of the Social Democratic Party. The expanding ecological movement has strong decentralist elements within its arguments, as have the campaigns of the various minority groups which gain from the depth of feeling within a locality on a particular issue rather than relying on overall national support. The Labour Party by refusing to reassess its centralist tradition and its continued support for the trend towards greater corporatism invites the electorate as a whole, dissatisfied with many of the practical consequences of the workings of the centralized state, to vote against it, even though they may be attracted to the justice and humanity of its social policy. Many people appear already to feel that remote bureaucracies are as hostile to their needs as private vested interests used to be.

It is necessary to distinguish these criticisms. Some represent a passing mood or are symptomatic of a general frustration directed against our overall national economic decline. Others are serious criticisms of the existing structure of government. However, it is too easy to lapse into generalized condemnation of the state and to avoid facing the disadvantages of some decentralized structures. The case in favour of the network and scale of existing British state institutions is that they attempt to meet specific demands made over the years by the electorate. It can be argued with some justice that they have been established as a direct response to democratic pressures, and are a mechanism for trying to implement democratic government. Democracy, corporatists will argue, is enhanced by involving non-elected but representative persons, as well as the elected, in the decision-making process. Power and influence is thereby dispersed, so the state is able to establish more support for the implementation of its policies. The growth of corporatism in Britain may have helped our success in meeting the challenge of the last fifty years without the social unrest experienced by other countries. It is true that, broadly speaking, the welfare state and in particular the National Health Service and some of the nationalized industries, have been approved by the electorate and successive governments. Even the much criticized 'quasi-autonomous non-governmental organizations', Quangos, have proved their usefulness and are easier to decry than to abolish.

Though these arguments present a case for the retention of corporatist elements in more or less their present form they are mostly far too complacent. Corporatism is rarely as democratic as its proponents argue. Superficially it appears to be democratic that interest groups should be represented at all levels of government and that powerful institutions such as the TUC and CBI are able to make their views known. As an extension of democracy it is unobjectionable; but it is not acceptable that it should replace democracy or that so much of the dialogue should be held in private. In consulting interest groups it is necessary to take into account how representative they are and to what extent their spokesmen are democratically elected and accountable. It is also necessary to guard against giving the formal interest groups exclusive access. It is difficult to ensure plurality when opinions are dispersed and hard to assemble. Powerful groups are often given weight, and sometimes a veto, to the detriment of less organized groups and the public good. Employers often find it easier to obtain a hearing than employees. Individual firms or local authorities are either large enough for their case to be heard or they can join forces and make representations to government as a coherent group far more easily than wage or salary earners. Small business has remained unorganized and uninfluential compared with big business: it lacks both the finance and the personal contacts to be able to lobby government as effectively. The homeless and other vulnerable minorities are completely unorganized and are represented only because of the efforts of small protest groups and the campaigning charities. The contrast in strength where, for example, a ratepayer's association or a suburban action group speaks out against having a community project such as a hostel for alcoholics located in its area, is obvious. Producers' organizations organize more easily than groups of consumers and have the necessary finance to research issues and present a case well.

The advocates of interest group democracy make an unspoken assumption that the groups themselves are internally democratic, but often this is not so. Some trade unions have an active democratic structure electing their officials and holding ballots of the membership on policy; others have very little internal democracy. Many interest groups have undemocratic constitutions and a structure which makes no provision for the whole membership to be involved or consulted so that active members have an influence and express views which are not representative of their real support. Where the active members hold minority views the distorted power of their representation can be serious. This is not to criticize activism, since it reflects desirable political commitment, but merely illustrates that the corporate form of representation falls short of the democratic claims so often made for it. If, as is fairly certain, many of our political activities must take place through interest groups then far more effort should be put into helping the groups to be more fully accountable to their members and for members to take a more active interest in what is being done in their name. Publicity is an important check on the unrepresentative exercise of influence. The balloting of members is another way of checking the validity of the representation and is an extension of democracy. Financial support from the state for ballots should be made available on request to all organizations that have a democratic structure, not just to trade unions. Funding should come from an independent commission answerable to parliament not to government, and therefore not capable of being associated with controversial governmental legislation. This form of specific state aid is not open to the objection to general funding, that it will help ossify existing political structures and make them less responsive to their membership and to changes in public support.

Western countries are founded on a belief in parliamentary democracy but periodic general elections offer insufficient opportunity to involve an educated and sophisticated public which is aware of the problems of a complex, mixed-economy industrialized society. New legislation passed by parliament each year has grown rapidly since the First World War.[13] It has changed too in character, from being rather general to dealing with specific and detailed questions and we are no longer governed solely by laws passed by the Westminster parliament. Our membership of the European Community carries with it a mass of Community regulations and directives. The framing of legislation has shifted from the House of Commons to discussions between the civil service and interest groups in London and Brussels. Politicians and politics have always been subject to satire and caricature as an antidote to their power and influence but the trivialization of debate, stemming from a sterile adversary relationship and the growth of opposition for its own sake, contrast strikingly with the increasing complexity of the issues to be decided. The extent to which in practice the political parties work together for the national interest is frequently hidden from the public by an unacknowledged conspiracy between politicians, who prefer to retain the myth of adversaries in parliament and who mask the corporatism within Whitehall.

Involvement of the state has also been stimulated by large multinational organizations. Now British industry is dominated by a small number of companies controlled by a small number of men whose allegiance may well be to the main Board situated in another country. The concentrated power of industry through mergers and takeovers is demonstrated by the fact that in 1950 the top 100 companies in Britain produced about 20 per cent of our national output. By 1973 they produced 46 per cent and by 1980 this figure had risen to over 60 per cent.[14] This same trend can be observed among financial institutions: the number of clearing banks fell through amalgamation from eleven in 1960 to five in 1980. In education and health many local small schools and hospitals have been closed. In 1960 there were 29,289 schools: this had fallen to 28,352 in 1977. In 1959 there were 3,027 hospitals: by 1978 this had fallen to 2,592. White-collar workers have been unionized, specialized lobby groups have sprung up and abbreviations such as NUT, BMA, RSPCA and NEDC have passed into such common usage that newspapers or newsreaders use them without spelling out their full title. The state sector in Britain has been progressively enlarged until, of the Western democracies, only Austria has a proportionately larger state industrial sector. The British public service is now the largest in the European Community, as a percentage of population, with one public servant for every ten citizens. The nearest Community country in this respect is Germany, with one civil servant for sixteen citizens. These figures are for public servants and do not include the nationalized industries and public corporations.

Obviously, corporatism is reinforced and deeply influenced by the attitudes of those who work within the civil service, but great care should be taken in defining the relationship of the civil service to society generally. In administering the complex of state services and state industries, Ministries and civil servants have a statutory duty placed on them to consult parliament and interested groups, but for the most part, the civil service consults interest groups in private. Its relationship with parliament is a public one but parliament often lacks the authority and the expertise to probe effectively. Discussing the role of interest groups concerned with education under a Labour and a Conservative Secretary of State for Education, Professor Kogan has written: 'neither Crosland nor Boyle would have thought to move very far without consulting Sir William Alexander, Secretary to the Association of Education Committees, Sir Ronald Gould, Secretary to the National Union of Teachers, and their counterparts in the other local authority and teachers' organizations . . . Such officials as William Alexander constitute a powerful, perhaps the most powerful, entity within the educational service for a longer period than any Minister or Permanent Secretary.'[15]

This requirement to consult interest groups has given rise to another manifestation of corporatism, the network of advisory bodies, consumer groups, regulatory agencies and semi-independent organizations such as the University Grants Committee, all of which enter into a client relationship with the state. By January 1980 there were 489 bodies in this group, accounting for expenditure of £5,800 millions in 1978–9 and employing 217,000 staff. Advisory bodies numbered 1,561 and cost their sponsor bodies, which were usually government departments, £13 million. There are different tribunal systems each containing many individual tribunals as well as some constituted on an ad hoc basis, such as the 2,000 National Insurance Local Tribunals set up each year. The question is whether tribunals are effective in controlling routine administration as it affects the citizen in a way parliament can never hope to be. An approximate count revealed that there were 67 'tribunal systems' with administrative costs in 1978–9 of £30 million. These figures do not, however, include the nationalized industries or the National Health Service. In 1978–9 the Health Service had 900,000 employees and cost £7,000 million. The nationalized industries employed 1,000,000 and had a turnover of nearly £24,000 million. A further unwelcome aspect of corporatism is the number of top jobs at the disposal of Ministers and civil servants. The Department of Health and Social Security, for instance, had 3,100 appointments at its discretion in 1980 while the Department of Employment had 650.[16]

There is a corporatist tendency to stress the need for secrecy to safeguard citizens' rights generally, but to be shockingly insensitive to a particular or individual case. If we are to develop a more responsive form of political activity all our institutions will need to become more accountable and their size will need to be reduced, for the larger an institution the less democratic and the more bureaucratically top-heavy it is likely to be. Clearly institutions must range from the small school to the giant coal industry, but we need a new, more vigilant approach to guard against the tendency for the upper levels of any institution gradually to accumulate power at the expense of lower levels. Each of the three major concentrations of power within the state, the civil service, the trade unions and large-scale industry, whether in private or state hands, will need to adopt a more open atitude to information if power is to be effectively controlled. It is not the paranoid spectre of a civil servant actively misleading or obstructing Ministers which is worrying, but rather that ever-growing civil service power and influence has not been countered by a matching growth in democratic checks and controls. Opening up civil service advice by introducing more short-term outside advisers, allowing decision-making to be subjected to greater public and parliamentary scrutiny and insisting on a more highly developed system of answerability is all feasible. So is a radical Freedom of Information Act and so are reforms of administrative law to protect individual citizen rights.

Decentralization is not without disadvantages nor will it be easy to achieve. For example, the decentralization of the trade unions to meet the demands of shopfloor workers who were dissatisfied with the policies of a remote union leadership, has diminished the authority of the trade union leader and, along with his authority, that of the TUC. No longer can the TUC guarantee the support of individual trade unions, let alone a majority of trade unionists in negotiations over government policy, particularly over incomes policies. This means that any TUC–government or –CBI dialogue must be more realistic in its aims and objectives. The dialogue, though useful, must reflect the limitations imposed by the structure of its constituent participants. The CBI is also unable to deliver the management of many of its individual companies. The importance of industrial democracy is that it realizes that changes in attitudes do not come simply through changes in ownership but only through real worker participation at the factory floor. The First World War and subsequent history has shown that trade union power is something which the state cannot ignore; to that extent the corporatist trend was irresistible, but the way that the state has sought to come to grips with trade union power through a dialogue between the TUC and CBI is no longer enough. The dialogue must increasingly now take place between management and trade unionists at the factory floor. This is why industrial democracy is so essential for it provides the framework for such dialogue and it reflects the realities of decentralized industrial bargaining.

Decentralizing power in any society means that co-ordination of that society becomes more difficult, since no group easily sees the need to safeguard legitimate national interests. Part of the attraction of the new society which has evolved in Britain is its loss of deference and authoritarianism so the state now finds it harder to coerce groups or force them to work together. A decentralized society needs therefore to develop a counterbalancing sense of interdependence where, instead of an identification with the state first and then to the community, one starts with the community and then relates that responsibility to the nation. Hitherto the state has feared the creation of a mass of non-accountable, self-interested factions and has consciously condemned the sectional interests that community identification has produced. The task now, having clung far too long to a dominant role for the state, is to build up through democratic involvement a sense of community in order to rediscover a responsibility from the individual to the state.

There has been an underlying confusion about the nature of democracy that has justified the corporatist trend of the past. The virtue of democracy is that though its processes involve delay and have a definable cost it is a decisive mechanism. The issue for decision is put to the vote and the majority view then prevails. Corporatism with its emphasis on consensus, consultation and committee decision-making carries both the delay in decision-making and the costs of democracy but lacks its decisiveness. Corporatism is a recipe for choosing the lowest common denominator, for the stifling of initiative and innovation. By its very nature it plays safe, it follows the cautious, timid and indecisive path. It is a recipe for drift and decay and it is no accident that it is the corporatist trend which has coincided with Britain's decline. Britain cannot be revived unless corporatism is rejected and democracy allowed to flourish in its place.

4

THE SOCIAL
DEMOCRATIC
TRADITION

Social democracy is part of the development of European socialism.
Not only are most European socialists called Social Democrats, but
particularly in the late 1950s and early 1960s they began to develop a
distinctive character within the Socialist International.

The British Labour Party, which has always avoided being labelled
a social democratic party, convened the first post-war meeting of
socialists in London in March 1945. It was a time of great optimism
for socialism in Europe. Julius Braunthal, the historian of the
International, and a former Secretary General, wrote: 'It seemed as
though a conference to discuss the re-establishment of the International could hardly have met under more hopeful auguries. For the
first time in history, the working class had entered the scene as a
decisive factor in world policy . . . while the fundamental split in
the International Labour movement had not yet been overcome, in
most of Europe, as in France, Italy and Czechoslovakia and all other
Eastern European countries, socialist parties were co-operating with
communist parties in joint action alliances or coalition governments.
An international, based on the power and influence of the European
socialist parties, was for the first time in a position to become a true
power capable of direct influence over world policy.'[1]

It was not long after the May 1946 Conference at Clacton,
however, before fundamental differences began to appear between
those Eastern European socialists, by no means all of them, who
supported their countries' increasingly close relationship with the
Soviet Union, and the socialist parties of Western Europe. It was not
therefore possible for a united International to be re-founded:
instead, the parties decided to set up a small secretariat in London –
The Socialist Information and Liaison Office (SILO) – to exchange
information and organize periodic discussions, meetings and conferences on the international situation. This was staffed by the British

Labour Party. Another international socialist conference – this time in Bournemouth in 1946 – failed to make progress towards re-uniting Eastern and Western European socialist parties. Many Socialists – including British Labour Party members – still tended to believe the wartime propaganda line that all Germans were Nazis, and the conference could not bring itself to make a decision to admit the German socialists.

The decision to admit the Germans, taken at the next international socialist conference, at Zurich in June 1947, marked the beginning of the important role the SPD was to play in European socialism. The other watershed in post-war European socialist politics was marked by Stalin's decision, in September 1947, to revive the Communist International as the 'Cominform', with a clear intention to oppose and be hostile towards the democratic socialist parties of Western Europe. The decision, implemented at a secret meeting in Poland, established the Cominform as an instrument of Stalin's foreign policy: the meeting was attended by the Soviet and East European governing communist parties, but only two Western European communist parties – those of France and Italy – were invited. As Braunthal comments: 'to those communist parties who had not been invited it came as much as a surprise as it did to the rest of the world'.[2] This was certainly not the old Communist International. The politics of European socialism were now inextricably caught up in the geopolitics of the Soviet Union. That same year the United States launched the Marshall Plan to rebuild Europe, strongly influenced by Ernest Bevin, the British Foreign Secretary. The basic outlines of the Cold War were already drawn. The Marshall Plan as such was never conceived as anti-communist; indeed, communist states were eligible to take part in it, and the Soviet Foreign Minister, Molotov, attended a conference in Paris in June to discuss the implementation of the Plan; but Stalin concluded that it was all part of a United States' policy against the Soviet Union, withdrew Molotov from Paris, and embarked on his cold war phase, harnessing communist parties to that basic purpose.

The Cominform was to be the instrument of Stalin's policy, and from that moment onwards, the Soviet Union presented the problem as one of the two opposing 'camps'; the democratic, peace-loving Soviet Union and its friends, on the one hand, facing, on the other, the imperialist United States, bent on the economic and political 'enslavement' of the world, beginning with Western Europe. Soviet propaganda portrayed the socialist parties of Western Europe as 'masks' behind which the evil forces of imperialism did their dirty work. Communist parties like those of France and Italy which had, during and immediately after the war, co-operated with the socialists in the tasks of resistance and reconstruction, now found themselves having to denounce their former colleagues as traitors, and, in carrying out the orders of the Cominform, organizing largely political strikes. The socialists, in their turn, became alarmed at what they saw as increasing Soviet interest in exerting influence, or even control or domination, in Western Europe, disguised as national movements seeking improvements in working-class living and working conditions. In Britain the Communist Party began active opposition to the Labour government during 1947.

Simultaneously, Stalin began to move against the socialists who were in coalition with communists in the Eastern European governments. Two hundred socialist leaders in Poland were arrested in 1947, and the following year 82,000 of the Polish Socialist Party's members were purged. In 1948, following a series of manoeuvres and ruses – involving the publication of a false statement that the social democrats had agreed to an amalgamation with the Communist Party – the Social Democratic Party of Hungary was swallowed up into the Communist Party. In Czechoslovakia in February 1948, after disputes in government between the communist ministers and those from other parties, the communists seized power and formed their own government, the socialists were 'fused' with the communists, and elections were held with only communists and social democrats taking part: 214 communists out of 300 deputies were elected; a few weeks later, by mid-1948, the social democrats had been absorbed into the Communist Party and Czechoslovakia, too, had passed through the complete process of Stalinization. For socialists the Prague coup marked a watershed; few disagreed that Stalin's desire for expansionism and control now represented a grave danger for the whole of Western Europe. Ernest Bevin, robust trade unionist first and Labour politician second, never had any doubts. On 4 April 1949, twelve countries signed the NATO pact; it received the full backing of European socialists, including many on the Left of the British Labour Party. In 1948 European socialists had to concern themselves with what differentiated themselves from the European Communist Parties. They faced, in the words of a 1948 International Socialist Conference resolution, 'the problem of defending democracy'. And in June 1948 the Socialist International defined what it meant by political democracy: 'The parties represented at this conference are opposed to the one-party state and all systems of government based upon it. They are of the opinion that a system of political democracy must combine in itself a recognition of the pre-eminence of the individual which is to be guaranteed by the following freedoms: Freedom of thought, opinion and speech; security in law and protection against interference by other individuals; . . . equality before the law and protection against political tampering with the machinery of justice; unimpeded freedom and guarantees of rights in elections; the right to an opposition; the political and lawful equality of all citizens, irrespective of class, race or sex.'[3]

The Socialist International as such was not formally reconstituted until the Frankfurt Congress of June 1951. 'The Frankfurt Declaration' – the 'Declaration of Aims and Tasks of Democratic Socialism' – stands with the Communist Manifesto of 1848 and the Inaugural Address of the First International of 1864 as fundamental documents in the history of the International.[4] The Declaration was drawn up after weeks of work by member parties and represented, in a way the earlier declaration had not, a clear distillation of the views of the socialist movement as a whole. The Declaration said, 'socialism aims to liberate the peoples from dependence on a minority which owns or controls the means of production. It aims to put economic power in the hands of the people as a whole and to create a community in which free men work together as equals.' At the same time, however, the Declaration insisted on the importance of freedom: 'without freedom there can be no socialism. Socialism can be achieved only through democracy. Democracy can be fully realized only through socialism.' The Declaration also made the point that, despite Marxist doctrine, the advent of socialism was not 'inevitable': 'it demands a personal contribution from all its followers'. But such a contribution did not have to be along narrowly or dogmatically defined lines. The Preamble makes the point, in Article 11: whether socialists build their faith on Marxist or other methods of analysing society, whether they are inspired by religious or humanitarian principles, they all strive for the same goal – a system of social justice, better living, freedom and world peace. These were the beliefs and doctrines which shaped all the European socialist parties whether they were referred to as social democrats, democratic socialists, Labour, or by any other name, in the period following the Second World War.

In a number of countries European socialists held power for long periods. When it lost the 1976 election, the Social Democratic Party in Sweden had been in government for forty-four years. Although there was some unease among some Swedish voters about what they consider to be the semi-'corporate state' established by the social democrats, there can be no doubt about the achievements of that Party. Sweden developed a far greater degree of perceived fairness among wage-earners, and measures such as comprehensive occupational retraining schemes, and the planned provision of housing helped to reduce differentials among manual workers and to lessen resistance to technological innovation. The highly central-ized system of Swedish wage-bargaining, successful for many years, encountered serious problems only in the winter pay-round of 1979–80. Yet interestingly Swedish socialism has never been domi-nated by the debate about the nationalization of private industry as British socialism has. When the Swedish socialists lost power 95 per cent of all industry was still in private hands. Facing recession it has been its non-socialist government successor which has had to take large sections of industry into public ownership.

The Swedish Social Democratic Party has taken an active role in the Socialist International. Under successive social democratic gov-ernments Sweden increased her aid to the Third World. In 1977–8 Sweden fulfilled her target of devoting 1 per cent of her GNP to development assistance, and was one of only three countries which reached the 0.7 per cent target set by the International Development Strategy in 1975. Sweden has refused to join either NATO or the Warsaw Pact, and has been closely involved in international work on disarmament and in supporting UN peace-keeping efforts; but at the same time Swedish social democrats believe in maintaining strong defences and over many years they have spent more per head on arms than any other West European country.

Another highly successful Socialist Party is that of Austria. It has consistently gained over half of the country's votes and its active membership includes nearly a tenth of the total population. Origi-nally strongly anti-clerical, and with a basic programme drawn up in 1926 when a Right-wing coup was a serious possibility, the Austrian socialists met in Vienna in 1958 and adopted unanimously a major reformulation of principles under the New Programme. They then made it clear that theirs was not only the party of the 'working class' narrowly defined, but the party of 'all working people'. On nation-alization they said it should be considered when it was in the 'national interest'.

Part of the secret of the Austrian Socialist Party's success has been the popular and charismatic figure of Chancellor Kreisky. Active in the Socialist International, and a strong advocate of better relations between Europe and the Third World, Kreisky has been particularly effective in encouraging dialogue between Israel and the Arab World. Yasser Arafat, leader of the Palestine Liberation Organization, took part in discussions with socialist leaders at a party leaders' conference of the Socialist International held in Vienna, under Kreisky's auspices, in February 1980.

If the Swedish or Austrian parties had, by the 1960s, become virtually the 'natural parties of government' of their respective countries, the same cannot be said of the British Labour Party or the German SPD. The SPD is the oldest and best-known social democratic party in Europe, and its role in the development of democratic socialism has been extremely important. But in the immediate aftermath of the Second World War it had failed to develop as a dynamic party and, under the leadership of Kurt Schumacher, a survivor from Weimar days, had begun to decay. 'The SPD had begun to display the bureaucratization and ageing that had been so marked in Weimar,' one British scholar noted.[5] When Schumacher died in 1952, 'the organization and programmatic symbols of the party were still intact, but they were decaying from within. Membership had fallen steeply since 1948 and the parliamentary party was becoming the most influential organ of party decision.'[6] After its second electoral defeat, in 1953, efforts to change the party accelerated. These efforts took place against the background of a strong upsurge in Christian Democrat party support and organization, and where the German Democratic Republic, and its claims to be socialist, were constantly before the German public as a permanent and damaging source of confusion between Marxist-Leninist bureaucratic socialism and the democratic socialism of the International.

In 1956 the Communist Party was banned in the Federal Republic. This was the background to the special party conference called by the SPD at Bad Godesberg in 1959, at which a completely new 'Basic Programme' for the party was adopted. There the old aim of nationalization of the economy was abandoned. 'Free competition and free initiative for the employer' were to become 'important elements in Social Democratic economic policy': while 'the private ownership of the means of production has a claim to be protected and promoted, so long as it does not hinder the setting up of a just social order.' This was fully in line with the Frankfurt Declaration, which stated that one of the aims of democratic socialism was 'effective democratic control of the economy'. The co-operative ownership of the means of production was, however, recognized as a 'legitimate form of public control'. Economic and social change, it was argued, had not been taken into account, and a major re-statement of party principles was therefore necessary. Marx was effectively dropped. Thus the SPD became what some observers have termed a 'Volkspartei', in other words a party aiming to bring together as many voters as possible rather than to be the expression of one class. The attainment of government became the main objective of the party. Its emphasis was laid not on 'agitation or extra-parliamentary activity, but rather governing, research and expertise and a pragmatic – some would say technocratic – approach to the problems of the day'.[7] By 1966 the SPD had entered govern-ment as part of the 'Grand Coalition' and after the federal election of 1969 Willy Brandt became Chancellor, at the head of an SPD/liberal (FDP) coalition. The new programme seemed to have brought about an SPD break-through to parts of the electorate which the party had never previously reached – the Catholic working-class, rural voters in general and the female vote. But the Young Socialists rebelled against the new programme, causing difficulties in the party for Brandt, who also faced calls for a tough line against the Young Socialists, right up to the time he resigned as Chancellor in May 1974. But since then the new programme has, by and large, been accepted and supported by the membership and October 1980 saw another electoral victory for Chancellor Schmidt with the continua-tion of the SPD-FDP coalition – though it was the FDP who gained the most electoral support.

Very similar processes have gone on in the Dutch Labour Party. In 1946 the Labour Party had replaced the old Social Democratic Workers Party (SDAP) – partly in order to deal with the religious problem in Dutch politics, by broadening its appeal – but it, too, felt the need – also in 1959 – to embark on a redefinition of its basic objectives. Here too it was the acceptance of the mixed economy and the abandonment of a formal revolutionary social position which provided the real significance of the change. The Dutch Labour Party (PvdA) then became a pragmatic party of government, not afraid of entering government in coalition with others. But divisions in the party came to a head in 1970, when some people left and formed the new 'Democratic Socialists '70' Party. In 1973–7 under proportional representation it was possible for the parties of the Left and Centre to combine in a coalition under a Socialist Prime Minister pursuing policies which were often more radical than those pursued by the British Labour government. This is particularly so in relation to the Third World where the Dutch socialist position is the most radical and enlightened of any other European socialist party.

Most of the major European socialist parties have, formally as well as in practice, accepted the mixed economy. Only in Britain, since the failure of Hugh Gaitskell's formal attempt, following the election defeat of 1959, to get the Labour Party to amend Clause 4 (see Chapter 2, the Decentralist Tradition), has there been real tension between the constitutional commitment in Clause 4 to common ownership of the means of production, distribution and exchange, and Labour's behaviour to the private sector when in office. How important is this tension? Why did Hugh Gaitskell feel it necessary to embark on this struggle at all when so many of his friends advised him against doing so? The whole controversy was deeply emotional and, as his biographer has written, shrouded with biblical terminology with warnings against tampering with Tablets of Stone, touching the Ark of the Covenant and bothering about the 39 Articles, so much so that Gaitskell said he 'wished he led a political party and not a religious movement'.[8] In the aftermath of the defeat over changing Clause 4 in the Constitution even Gaitskell admitted that if he had foreseen the kind of opposition he would never have raised the issue. He did so because he knew, and many others knew too, that the reputation of wanting to nationalize everything was damaging the party with the electorate. In the 1960s it was possible to believe that nationalization was dead as an issue, buried by the emphasis on technology and the search for economic growth and that the statement adopted by the 1960 Labour Conference had succeeded in shifting the emphasis away from 100 per cent nationalization and in emphasizing other aims. However, as so often in Labour history emotive issues keep reappearing. The 'idolators' on the Left, as the defenders of Clause 4 were called, recognized that this was an issue on which they could rally the party activists and particularly in the wake of the electoral defeats in 1970 and again in 1979 this issue was used as a lever in the inner power struggle as much as to attack the whole concept of the mixed economy. If it could be said that the issue was only a problem in Opposition it could no doubt be shrugged off but there is now considerable evidence that it is a running problem for Labour governments in office. The stark fact has to be faced that a considerable body of influential people in terms of policy formation in the British Labour Party are not content to adopt a pragmatic case by case attitude to state ownership. It is an exaggeration to claim that the controversy over state ownership has been a dominant factor in Britain's economic decline but it has been a contributing factor. The refusal of the Labour Party to face the need for a fundamental reassessment of attitudes, such as took place for the SPD at Bad Godesberg the same year as the Clause 4 controversy, has meant the Labour Party cannot claim and does not wish to claim, that it is a Social Democratic Party. It prides itself on being instead a Democratic Socialist party. In fact in post-war European socialism the two terms have been until recently widely regarded as interchangeable. The Campaign for Democratic Socialism, which played an important part at the grass roots in overturning the 1960 Labour Conference decision for unilateralism, 'was originally conceived by some of the younger Labour candidates who had written to support Gaitskell over Clause Four'.[9] Yet slowly as European socialists became the governing party and demonstrated that their rejection of Marxism and their less ideological approach to the mixed economy was successful in Sweden, Austria, Germany and Holland, a Social Democrat became a description not just of a socialist but of a socialist who worked constructively within the framework of a mixed economy, not against the framework of the mixed economy, as is the more prevalent attitude in Britain within the Labour Party.

Within the British Labour Party it is acceptable to defend the mixed economy but not to espouse it. The dominant attitude is one of resigned acceptance and 'true socialism' is still assessed against the yardstick of support for nationalization. Much of the deep-seated antagonism to the European Community within the Labour Party stems from its Clause 4 socialists who do not want the mixed economy that Community membership involves. It is now time for those in Britain who wish to identify with the form of socialism successfully practised by other European socialists boldly to proclaim their adherence to the traditions of social democracy and wear openly the label of Social Democrat. Social Democracy is not a consensus, watered down form of socialism. It has a record in Europe of pioneering socialist policies of welfare reform which have redistributed wealth and power, but it has not yet identified sufficiently with decentralization and in some countries has been too corporatist.

The best working definition of social democracy is that of Leszek Kolakowski: 'the trouble with the social democratic idea is that it does not stock and does not sell any of the exciting ideological commodities which various totalitarian movements — Communists, fascists or leftists — offer dream-hungry youth. It is no ultimate solution for all human misery and misfortunes. It has no prescription for the total salvation of mankind. It cannot promise the firework of the last revolution to settle definitely all conflicts and struggles. It invented no miraculous devices to bring about the perfect unity of man and universal brotherhood. It believes in no final victory over evil.

'It requires, in addition to commitment to a number of basic values, hard knowledge and rational calculation, since we need to be aware of and to investigate as exactly as possible, the historical and economic conditions in which these values are to be implemented. It is an obstinate will to erode by inches the conditions which produce avoidable suffering, oppression, hunger, wars, racial and national hatred, insatiable greed and vindictive envy.'[10]

It is the obstinate will to erode by inches which contrasts so sharply with the passionate will to jump by miles that reflects the divide between the realists and the idealists, the achievers and the dreamers. Most social democratic parties in Europe can point to a record of practical achievement which neither of the British Labour governments of the 1960s or 1970s could match – of specific welfare measures and economic success which have directly benefited the poorest people in their countries.

What Kolakowski describes is an approach. It is not a soft, middle of the road, flabby consensus, but a hard-headed realistic assessment of what is obtainable within the democratic constraints that are imposed on any government. It is an approach built neither on dreams nor on dogmas. In every social democratic country the social democrats have strong links with trade unionists. The politicians see themselves as speaking for the views of trade unionists but there is not the same tendency to an exclusive relationship which is detectable in Britain. The relationship with the Trade Unions as organizations are close but not all pervasive.

As Paterson and Campbell have pointed out[11] some political scientists have attempted to define labour parties, as opposed to social democratic parties, by the closeness of their relations with the trade union movement: social democratic parties, in contradistinction to labour parties, are friendly to labour but do not have direct trade union affiliation. But the Dutch Labour Party adopted its name in 1945 when it ceased to have direct union affiliation, and only the British Labour Party retains direct affiliation and organic links with trade unions. Most social democratic parties began as 'labour parties' but have loosened the organic connection. In Belgium the Workers' Party was largely responsible for the creation of a strong labour movement after the war; but while the General Federation of Labour of Belgium is socialist-led it contains many other elements besides socialists and while it generally works closely with, and supports, the socialist Party, it has at times been harshly critical of it. In Germany, too, the Weimar period saw close relations between the SPD and the trade union movement, but those who helped set up the reconstructed trade union movement after the war – who included a number of SPD leaders including the present leader of the SPD in parliament, Herbert Wehner – ensured that the trade union confederation, the DGB, should not take on a party political affiliation. The SPD rejected a proposal that it should become a German Labour Party in 1945. As in Belgium, relations have in practice been good and close, but in Germany the unions do not financially underwrite the SPD as the British unions do with the British Labour Party, neither is there the type of close institutional involvement which takes place in the bodies of the Labour Party. In late 1980 following the re-election of the SPD/FPD coalition tensions occurred between the two coalition partners because the unions, backed by the SPD but opposed by the FPD, wanted tougher measures to ensure worker participation in industry, particularly in the coal and steel industries. In France and Italy, meanwhile, the Communist party has dominated the largest trade union confederation, while in both countries social democrats, socialists, Christians and the extreme Left have competed for control of other confederations and unions. David Hine has contrasted the French and Italian pattern of labour movement with the British, in which 'the potential for inter-union conflict is very great, but in which formal commitment to the ideology of labour-movement unity prevents an organizational rupture at confederal level'. The TUC is not politically linked – but this is a formality to cover the position of those unions not affiliated to the Labour Party. It does not stop the TUC working on future policy with the Labour Party through a body called the Liaison Committee.

The Labour Party and the trade union movement have different jobs to do – the one may work closely with the other, but for both the disadvantages of too close an organic relationship can be considerable. The defects of the one may be visited upon the other: at the moment the argument that the British Labour Party is run by the trade unions is a criticism of the Labour Party. There are however many individual trade union members who are critical of the trade union movement's close relations with the Labour Party. The fact is – as the continental parties have recognized – that the interests of a broadly-based socialist party and those of the trade union movement do not always coincide as in the past. The task for the Social Democratic Party is to build a close working relationship with trade unionists and the managers of industry, based on a clear under-standing and sympathy with the respective roles of both.

There has been little public concern in Sweden, Austria, Germany, Holland or Denmark when the social democrats have been in power that the government is controlled by or in any sense dominated by the trade unions or that the trade union leaders have an overwhelming position of influence. Labour governments in Britain have in contrast frequently been subjected to this charge. It often has little justification but at times the exclusiveness of the relationship has been justly criticized. It has also damaged the trade unions, for their primary relationship has become increasingly with the Labour Party to the detriment of their relationship with the CBI and with any Conservative government. It is worrying aspect of the Labour Party's decline in membership and in organizational effi-ciency that this has thrust the Party into an ever closer financial relationship with the trade unions, fortifying a recent trend towards trade union dominance. It is essential that the Social Democratic Party that hopes to win the support of all sections of society should have a measure of financial independence so that it is never wholly dependent on trade union support. It is no part of social democracy to identify itself only with the interests of the trade union movement particularly when a growing number of trade unionists vote Con-servative. The present danger is that the Labour Party is identifying increasingly with the trade unions and the political leaders of the trade unions and less with individual trade unionists. This trend towards an isolation from the grass roots is another aspect of centralization and corporatism and is part of the explanation for the decline in the Labour Party membership and votes in successive elections. The approach of the Social Democratic Party is the way to rebuild a wider electoral appeal for a future government. Narrowing the appeal, reinforcing the financial and political links with trade unions as opposed to trade unionists, is likely only to speed the decline in the Labour Party's fortunes. The Labour Party's refusal to recognize the mood which wants to give every member the vote on crucial issues, the Labour Party's reluctance to move away from delegated democracy to a more genuine participatory democracy, is against the trend of social democratic parties in Europe and against the trend of public opinion. It is a profoundly conservative response, the response of a Party that will not face the future, will not contemplate the equivalent of an SPD Bad Godesberg conference. It is a response heavily influenced by those trade unionists who resist the introduction of ballots in their own union and fear that their supporting one member one vote for the Labour Party will carry implications for their own union's procedures. Some trade unions want delegated democracy to continue in the Labour Party for the same reason, and these support GMC decision-making and the introduction of mandatory re-selection. Some also want the trade union block vote to exert an increased influence in the Party, which is why they voted, unsuccessfully, at the 1980 Conference for the NEC to be solely responsible for the Manifesto in an attempt to remove the joint responsibility of the NEC and Cabinet or Shadow Cabinet; and it is why they voted for an electoral college, with the block vote, which includes Conservative and Communist levy payers, for the first time being able to influence the election of the Party Leader and Prime Minister. The Labour Party, unlike the German SPD which had a clear Marxist philosophy prior to the Bad Godesberg decisions, has a less defined ideology, summed up in the saying 'Socialism is what the Labour Party does', and this has made it harder for it to grapple with a decisive redirection of policy. The Labour Party is facing the 1980s in consequence with the old recipes: more nationalization, more state control, more centralization. The problems of the 1980s are very different from the challenge of recovery from the effects of the Second World War. The task now for Social Democrats in Britain is to develop a new approach, drawing on two traditions, decentralized socialism and social democracy; to develop a new political force in Britain which can hold public opinion for a sustained period of government. Social Democratic values and attitudes will only bear fruit in Britain, as in Continental Europe, with a sustained period of over ten years of government.

PART TWO

THE MIXED
ECONOMY

5

ECONOMIC
POLICY

In post-war British politics no subject has been more obsessively discussed than how to achieve economic growth. One of the country's leading economists, Sir Roy Harrod, summed it up correctly when he wrote in 1965, 'economic growth is the grand objective. It is the aim of economic policy as a whole'.[1] As successive governments have failed to achieve sustained economic growth, they have been deserted by a disillusioned electorate ready to turn in despair to an opposition espousing a carefully packaged and electorally attractive set of seemingly new policies for achieving a higher standard of living, more jobs, and a better balance in Britain's international trading figures. It is the combination of poor economic growth and inflation which makes the British experience unique; few other countries have faced a similar economic and political cycle. What is also unique is the extent of the political differences over the economy. Britain at the start of the 1980s faces yet another period of polarised debate over economic policy.

The Conservative government came to office in 1979 committed to a complete overturning of the economic policies of the previous thirty years. Its rejection of Keynesian demand-management and its total belief in monetarism led the Conservatives, at a time of world recession, to start immediately to reduce public expenditure, rule out an incomes policy and increase inflation by raising VAT. They believed that a strict control of the money supply – which some monetarist commentators soon criticized as being too tight – with high interest rates, would ensure, together with the unfettered impact of market forces, an eventual reduction in inflation. The consequences in terms of unemployment, industrial bankruptcies, closures and cutbacks were known to be formidable, but the extent of the damage to Britain's industrial base was judged to be tolerable. Yet one of the consequences which soon became apparent was the distortion and downgrading of other aspects of economic management which began, in turn, not only to discredit the valid case for keeping control of the money supply, but also to shake the belief of some people that a mixed economy could ever again generate economic growth. In the 1970s the monetarism of the Right began to emerge to challenge the Keynesian consensus and so did the so-called 'alternative strategy' of the Left.

The alternative strategy, a mix of protectionism and state intervention, is advocated, predictably, by those centralist socialists who have never reconciled themselves to the virtues of a thriving private sector within the mixed economy. What is more worrying is that it is becoming also the refuge of others who have been driven to despair by the failure of past policies and are tempted by the argument that everything else has been tried. It is necessary, first, to convince those who might vote Social Democrat that support for the success of the mixed economy is essential, that it is still possible to achieve a measure of economic growth even against the background of the lower world economic growth over the next decade and that it is only possible to do so within the framework of the mixed economy. It is hard to do this when the advocates of monetarism and the alternative strategy are linked together in an unholy alliance to propagate the belief that all else has failed as the ultimate justification of their differing viewpoints, and when ever higher unemployment figures sour the atmosphere and make rational debate very difficut.

Since the Second World War British economic policies have been adopted against a background of economic decline not found among our major economic competitors. This has been due in part to the severe problems of the legacy left by two World Wars and to the accompanying dismantlement of the Empire, which would have faced any model of the British economy. But it also reflects the nature of British politics. Alternating Labour and Conservative governments have sought, particularly over the last decade, to repeal the policies of their predecessors in the belief that this would deal with the fundamental problems facing the economy. In some policy areas the symbolic issues of importance to the party faithful of both the major parties have come to be elevated well beyond reason. The commitments and attitudes adopted in opposition, combined with the volatility of the money markets, have contributed to the major economic mistakes made in the early years of the life of most new governments. The Labour government's refusal to devalue in 1964, something clearly envisaged by Reginald Maudling if the Conservatives had been returned, bedevilled the possibility of achieving planned economic growth in 1964 and 1965; a Labour government in office after thirteen years of opposition and facing the necessity of another election because the majority was only five, sadly lacked the confidence and authority to devalue in order to pursue economic growth. The same excuse could not be used when, in July 1966, deflationary measures were taken even though there was a large parliamentary majority. In 1970 and 1971 the industrial relations' legislation, the decision to wind up the Prices and Incomes Board and the Industrial Reorganization Corporation, destroyed all feeling of a continuity of economic purpose across the parties. The 'market forces', 'stainless steel' approach, characterised by the Selsdon Park pre-election conference held by Conservative strategists, helped to destroy any chance of a sensible partnership between the TUC and the new Conservative government. In 1974 and 1975 the new Labour government inherited indexation commitments which it felt it could not break and which made a major contribution to inflation; this was then compounded by agreeing to high public sector pay settlements. It can be claimed in the Labour government's defence that in 1974 it was a minority government that had to face another election soon, and that the public mood after the miners' strike was very unsettled. It took, however, until the summer of 1975, after the EEC referendum had been held, before the government grappled with the spiralling inflation rate which by then was frighteningly near 27 per cent. But it was in opposition that the Labour Party had committed itself to the view that rising wages had little to do with inflation and this still hung round their neck in the first year of government. An albatross of unreality.

In 1979 inflation was already rising, but the new Conservative government, again partly because of unrealistic attitudes adopted in Opposition, decided unwisely virtually to double VAT. This was a consequence of their unwise pledges to cut direct tax and it was done despite party spokesmen having denied throughout the election campaign that an increase in VAT would be the result. But it was this decision, like the Health government's decision to index, which was the decisive factor in doubling inflation by the middle of 1980.

The structure of the nation's economic life cannot be switched and changed with the rapidity of the past without weakening the country's ability to compete in world markets or to serve the domestic market. For example, whatever the detailed criticisms about the management of the British steel industry since the war, no one can seriously question that the endless political uncertainty and debate about its structure has been a major debilitating factor contributing to its decline. 'It is high time the political parties sorted out the difference between the things which as a nation we can afford to disagree about and the things which we cannot'.[2] Perhaps this is a utopian hope, since it is precisely our economic decline which has contributed to the polarization.

It is hard to escape the conclusion that the British economy has suffered uniquely from this peculiarly polarized debate existing in Britain between the two governing parties about the relative roles of private and public enterprise. It is an oversimplification to trace all the swings of economic policy to this debate, but it has had a corrosive effect on the creation, in many sectors of the economy, of a working partnership between the private and public sector. While the debate has ranged between the extremes of Left and Right, the consensus that has emerged and has been labelled 'welfare capitalism' has itself made fatal compromises, eroding the virtues of both the private and state economy. Instead of recognizing that within the mixed economy the private sector and public sector, providing public services, need to be treated in different ways, there has been a tendency to meet the criticism from the extremes in a way which militates against any such differentiation. The non-commercial public sector has been expected to adopt many of the disciplines and attitudes of the private sector, to present its accounts in terms of a largely bogus profitability, to charge so-called market prices for services and to create market forces or pretend that they exist where they do not. The private sector has for its part been expected to take on many of the disciplines that the state applies to the public sector, their pricing structure and profit ratios have been subjected to detailed control, their employment practices expected to be modelled on the state sector and their salary and wage levels held down with an expectation that they will provide the same job security and pension entitlements as the public sector.

The most damning criticism of the socialist 'revisionist' case is in this area. They have tried to amalgamate the public and private sector while at the same time advocating the merits of a mixed economy. They have tried to have the best of both sectors by refusing to face the political difficulties of admitting that there are necessary differences between the sectors, and that one of these differences is that profits are the motive force of the private sector but that in the public sector these can conflict with the concept of public service. Fault can also be found with liberal conservatives who, while criticising the 'unacceptable face of capitalism', have listened too much to the interests of property, insurance and the stock market and have not given enough attention to the interest of producers, and particularly to that of the manufacturing exporter. They have, too, been reluctant to defend the public sector against their own Right wing, and have acquiesced in unfair criticism of the virtue of public services and necessary state involvement. The strengths and virtues of the mixed economy and much of its dynamism come from a sensitive understanding of the extent to which an amalgamation of public and private sector attitudes and policies is tolerable and a readiness to sense the point at which amalgamation destroys the dynamics of the system itself: when curbing profits really does limit investment, or when squeezing prices reaches the point when it does limit expansion, or when a movement towards average wages and job security impairs innovation and risk-taking and contributes to low productivity and inefficiency.

Britain has, unlike most of its Western European competitors, lurched between expansion and recession, between wage inflation and statutory freeze, between unrealistically high sterling exchange rates and precipitous falls in the value of the currency, and from the peaks and troughs of industrial investment to periods of intense property investment and speculation. It has a stock market where, compared with other countries, there is a uniquely high priority given to paying large annual dividends at the expense of capital growth, and a financial sector which will not lend long.

Over all these years it has also had a running dispute over the need for new industrial relations' legislation and both of the governing parties have swung with the pendulum of public opinion and fashionable comment as to the priority to be given to legislative control of the trade unions. Immense quantities of legislative time and political capital were expended on this issue in the 1960s and 1970s. Legislation has been introduced, bitterly fought, then repealed or replaced, with very little net benefit to anyone. If a fraction of this ministerial, opposition, parliamentary and departmental effort had been put instead into fashioning and promoting agreement over industrial relations, with the steady introduction of industrial democracy by negotiation, it could only have had a far greater effect on reducing industrial disruption and increasing productivity.

The condition for making the mixed economy work is the preservation of the degree of flexibility that allows for a swift market response to continuing changes in the world economy. There are those on both the extremes of British politics to whom a degree of consensus between the major parties on the policies which are adopted to reduce our economic problems is an anathema. They are content for the periodic lurches to Left and Right to continue unchecked. They know what to do. Doubt for them is a stranger, for dogma and doctrine provide their certainty.

The essence of the Social Democratic case is that no one economic policy can be pursued in isolation without distorting the other policies. It is a recognition in politics of an approach that is central to the behavioural sciences with their emphasis on inter-reaction and inter-relationships. Such an approach is not an argument for the status quo for tolerating current levels of economic inequality, or for being less concerned about the existing maldistribution of resources.

Any economic policy should be judged against a background in Britain of persistent class divisions and the widespread existence of poverty. Class divisions in Britain remain pronounced though it is less certain that they are more extreme than in most other Western countries and we need more comparative evidence. The difficult task of changing attitudes is best tackled by a variety of policies and the problems could be resolved quicker if we were able to achieve greater economic growth. The advocacy of low or zero growth as an alternative may appeal to conservationists but offers little hope for the poor and unemployed. Britain like other Western countries will have to adapt in future to a lower economic growth if we are to redistribute wealth within the world, quite apart from consciously deciding at times that the evironmental and social price of a particular high growth policy within Britain is unacceptable. Even as conventional a study as former President Carter's Global 2000 Report[3] suggests that current economic methods such as those used in agricultural production will have catastrophic consequences if they are pursued for another twenty years.

There is a major difference between adapting to low growth and adopting a low growth strategy as the most desirable course within present day Britain. Priorities for public spending are difficult enough when the need is to divide an expanding, albeit slowly expanding, national income. If in deciding where to put additional finance the question of where to reduce spending in order to cover that finance is also introduced, the arguments become fiercer and harsh choices are more likely to be avoided in favour of the status quo.

While economic growth produces a buoyant climate of well-being in which it is easier to ensure that some people's incomes increase relatively slower than others, that very same buoyant climate is one which often induces inertia in grappling with income distribution because most people are benefiting. Paradoxically it is in periods of low economic growth that the climate of opinion is more opposed to marked inequalities of income, and yet the resistance to income redistribution is then greatest as people hold hard to what they have. The market economy, in as much as it can be separated from the capitalist economy, is also criticized as impeding redistribution but the controlled planned economies have if anything a no better record on redistribution and certainly a worse record on overall economic prosperity.

The harsh fact is that there is no one set of circumstances which will guarantee a more equal income distribution with an increasing level of general prosperity. The trade union commitment to free collective bargaining works against any centralized income redistribution: decentralized bargaining by different unions representing different crafts and skills perpetuates and often increases differentials. Resistance to paying much higher child benefit does not just come from Conservatives; it is very strong within the trade union movement and amongst traditional Labour voters; and it is these people, who form the bulk of the population, who are the electoral target of all the political parties. The strength of the pressure from pensioners who vote for increases in the pension benefit level, is very strong. Pressures of this kind influence decisions which run counter to the factual basis of assessing need and real social priority for non voters such as children and the mentally handicapped.

The cumulative percentage shares of personal wealth of the richest groups have fallen since 1960 but this movement towards redistribution has not been marked, neither does it show any sign of accelerating. The reasons for the falling share of the top 1 per cent has not been the imposition of increased capital taxation by Labour governments but has been due to the slump in the market for shares and the erosion of the value of assets, apart from property, through inflation.[4] It remains a fair conclusion that inherited wealth is still responsible for a substantial degree of inequality and that large-scale inheritances still pay relatively little tax. The Vestey affair in 1980 in merely the tip of a very large iceberg.

It is apparent when analysing the inequality of incomes over time that a similar modest trend has reduced the extent of inequality but that, as with the distribution of wealth, great inequalities in the distribution of income remain. It is noticeable that the small amount of redistribution which did occur from 1949 to 1977–8[5] largely failed to help the very poorest, the bottom 30 per cent, and helped only the middle income groups at the expense of the very high earning groups. The lack of redistribution is also remarkable, given that, throughout the period, a progressive tax system with increasingly higher rates was in force. The UK tax system seems progressive, since marginal rates of tax are higher than the average, but the effect of inflation in the 1970s was to bring more low earners into the tax net during the long period when the tax allowances were not index-linked. The failure to raise tax allowances, the increase in indirect taxation and the small rises in universal benefits in the 1970s created the 'poverty trap', a social scandal whereby many families with children were better off not working. An examination of the poverty trap for the period of two governments from November 1978 to May 1980 (though many of the trends were inherited from the previous Labour government so the criticism of the disincentive effect and the inflationary effect have to be shared by both governments) shows that a family with four children has more spending power if the father earns £45 a week than if he earns £85 and in every case the spending power gain from extra earnings is less two years later. The poverty trap is even worse in 1981, primarily due to the refusal to index personal tax allowances and to inadequate child support and the poorest paid, particularly those with children, are paying much more in tax today than ever before.

The impact of tax on the traditional Labour Party voter is a recent phenomenon and one which carries immense electoral implications. In 1945 redistribution of income through tax was a popular policy and even in 1955 the average married male manual worker paid no income tax. But by 1967 he was paying the standard rate on his marginal earnings and by 1974 nearly half of his income was taxed at the full rate, a factor which is particularly important if the taxpayer does not enjoy the tax advantages of owner-occupation. The effects of fiscal drag, where people are pulled progressively into paying tax, account[6] for the political resistance to paying tax but it has also contributed to poverty for it has created a group where actual increases in poverty took place in the 1970s. This is shown clearly in the relationship between wages and the level of income at which supplementary benefit becomes payable.

The other alarming feature of the poverty trap is the extent to which it triggers inflationary wage pressures. Between May 1979 and May 1980 prices rose by 22 per cent so that in order for net weekly spending power to be maintained over the year a person's gross weekly earnings of £55, which was just over 60 per cent of average male earnings, had to rise from between 27 per cent to 73 per cent; the larger the family the greater the wage increase.[7]

Successive governments have adapted Beveridge, so instead of being the exception means-testing has become widespread, and ad hoc changes have brought about a system which is insensitive to the demands of some of the groups experiencing the worst poverty. Instead of using objective criteria for fixing benefit levels political choices are being made about who deserves extra benefit often quite unrelated to measured need.

Throughout the 1980s demographic changes will bring great pressure to bear on health and personal social services budgets to meet the increased costs of caring for an ageing population. The major challenge to the sensible development of social policy will be in adjusting to these demographic trends and relating cash provision with care provision, a particularly difficult match when public expenditure is being cut back and when increased care costs will fall on the health authorities' and local authorities' budgets. In a period of high unemployment there is the additional need to ensure a degree of equality between workers in secure well-paid jobs and those who are employed only intermittently or who face long periods of unemployment.

Another trend is that the number of one-parent families doubled between 1966–76. As a result the system of Supplementary Benefits, which Beveridge saw as being a safety-net only, has had to cope with providing for the needs of an increasing number of pensioners and young children. Furthermore, it was hoped by Beveridge that incomes from employment would be sufficient to support a one-child family, but this has not proved to be the case and the need has arisen for a state scheme which caters for those families in poverty even when the wage-earner is in full-time employment. The low level of 'take-up' for means-tested benefits has also meant that poverty has continued even when relief is theoretically available. Low take-up has been especially persistent among those groups most at risk, the elderly, and the large family.[8] The overall rise in the levels of unemployment in the 1960s and 1970s increased poverty among those of working age, and placed a heavier tax burden on the working population. Public expenditure constraints over the last five years have meant that social security, health, social services and housing budgets have all grown more slowly than was desirable in terms of proven need and restraining their growth has had a disproportionate effect on the poor. In addition the large increases in charges for services which usually went hand in hand with expenditure reductions have hit many on low incomes who do not enjoy statutory exemption. The Labour government of 1974–9 sought to protect spending on the social services but they still suffered when considered against the adverse demographic trends and the increased demands on child support services. Though social security expenditure increased during this period in real terms, as a proportion of public expenditure and as a proportion of Gross Domestic Product, the largest increases took place in the early years of the government when the economy was declining. Spending was relatively static towards the end of 1978 and the beginning of 1979 when the economy was growing more rapidly and this interesting discovery has prompted one author to write: 'whether, given this performance, it is true that redistribution can only take place when there is economic growth must be in some doubt' and that, 'in aggregate, to have achieved a shift to social security at a time when real incomes were static or declining was a major achievement.'[9]

Environmentalists also have serious arguments for challenging the automatic assumption that all economic growth is desirable. The sensible ones are now increasingly arguing the limits or counter effects of high economic growth rather than the desirability of low growth. They carry more conviction as they concentrate on those aspects of economic growth that produce specific and quantifiable damage to society, and pursue a selective growth strategy. This is the path for those who see the environment in the widest context of bad housing as well as of open cast mining and who worry about the values of a harsh, materialistic and market-dominated society.

It is understandable why some people have come to reject economic growth as they have become disillusioned by the acquisitive values of an affluent society, disheartened by the rapacious nature of a growth-orientated society with its emphasis on materialism, competition and money. In the past the emphasis of the revisionists on economic growth was not accompanied by a sufficient awareness of the degradation of values that would accompany growth and it was wrong to imply that more growth could of itself satisfy all the needs of our society. Growth increases the amount of resources at our disposal. Some of these resources can create greater freedom, but unless the society in which growth develops can also develop different attitudes to counter those associated with growth, it can create a divisively competitive and harshly acquisitive society.

In as much as one of the motivating forces of most people is to improve the standard of living of themselves and their families, we are seeing that people strive not just for a high salary, but also for prestige goods, unusual furniture, antiques, rare books and china. People want interesting creative jobs, they seek rural peace, even remoteness and seclusion, and these are all trends which increase with affluence. In some senses the rarity value is self-defeating if large numbers of people seek the same ends, for the appeal is related to its uniqueness, its exclusivity. Individual acquisition in these terms cannot satisfy everyone's needs and so the nation, city, town or village is driven to make collective provision and this is more equitable and allows more people to achieve their goals. However, this cannot satisfy everyone; the quest for exclusivity is one that simply cannot be satisfied, and we need to acknowledge that this tension will not disappear, 'to the extent that the mismatch between current expectations and resources is qualitative rather than quantitive, the restraint necessary would be not patience but stoicism, acceptance and social co-operation – qualities that are out of key with our culture of individualistic advance.'[10] Stoicism does not mean resigned pessimism, but realism and a readiness to relish diversity. The change in attitude that is needed is to moderate the abrasiveness and starkness of the ethos of the individual so that we seek harmony, by extolling the ethos of community, not by advocating the destruction of individualism or by compelling collectivism but by recognizing the value of co-operation. We need to work together, not on the basis of perfect equality but on the basis of searching for equality – something that cannot be achieved in a society riddled with inequalities.

The growth record of the British economy in the last decade has been very poor, both when compared with what has been achieved by other EEC countries and when compared with our immediate post-war record.[11] It is likely that in the 1980s growth will be even more difficult to achieve, given that world trade is growing far more slowly than in the 1960s and the 1970s. World trade in manufactures, of crucial importance for the British economy, is estimated to grow by 2–7 per cent per annum in the 1980s compared with an average for the 1960s of 9 per cent. A 1 per cent growth in world trade adds about a quarter per cent to British national output, so it is of the greatest significance for our rate of growth that the world economy will be sluggish: 'even on the most hopeful assumptions, the world trade environment suggests that growth in the economy will be much harder to achieve in the 1980s than it was in the 1960s.[12]

In this situation the export-orientated manufacturing industries will find it progressively more difficult to export and will face increasing competition from imports. The implications for employment if manufacturing industry faces a difficult world market situation are very serious since Britain, in common with other industrialized countries, still depends on the manufacturing sector to provide over a third of total employment. In the 1950s and 1960s shortages of skilled workers constituted a bottleneck and impeded growth, whereas in the 1980s the situation is very different as the number of people of working age is increasing rapidly and, with more women in employment, the proportion of the age group seeking work is increasing. In the early 1980s the workforce is likely to grow by 0.5–0.8 per cent per annum and, assuming an estimate of productivity rising by 1–1½ per cent per annum, then output will need to grow by 2–2½ per cent per annum just to produce a gradual reduction in unemployment.[13] These estimates are subject to a wide margin of error; the estimate of the rise in productivity may, for instance, be too optimistic. They indicate, however, the scale of the problem of providing sufficient jobs for an expanding workforce which will require a level of growth above that which has been achieved in recent years.

There is, in addition, the further problem presented by new technology bringing a serious mismatch between the available jobs in new industries and the old skills or a total lack of skills. The disparities between regional rates of unemployment could increase dramatically with the industrial north, Scotland and Northern Ireland declining and falling further behind the relatively more prosperous southern England, where it seems likely that many of the new industries will be located. Youth and inner city unemployment could rise even further and threaten a generation with long periods of enforced stagnation and consequential alienation.

Job sharing schemes and reductions in working hours could help to reduce unemployment provided they are introduced in a way which keeps British unit costs broadly in line with those of our major competitors. This proviso is crucial. Job sharing and other such techniques provide an answer only if people are willing to accept lower real incomes in return for fewer hours of work. The trouble is that by and large people are not willing to accept this and it will require a major effort to persuade people to do so and to agree that this is a technique which must be used to ease unemployment.

Steady growth will remain necessary to provide, and pay for, full-time secure jobs for all those seeking work. If a period of a high rate of growth can be achieved the service industries will increase their share of total employment; this should not be decried for it is an inevitable trend. Jobs in manufacturing can possibly increase if investment in new plant and machinery is sufficient to offset the reduction of jobs implicit in the introduction of new technology. The manufacturing sector must, above all, ensure that it is competitive in world markets; only this will guarantee steady employment and earn foreign exchange to pay for our imports. At present the service industries, including government and defence, provide about 69 per cent of employment, while manufacturing employs 31 per cent. The numbers employed in manufacturing have fallen by 17 per cent or nearly 1½ million in the last fifteen years, and serious unemployment cannot be avoided if this rate of rundown continues. The service industries, such as retailing and administration, owe their ability to provide jobs to the continued existence of a healthy manufacturing sector, while the ability of the government to provide jobs in education, health and the social services also depends to a large extent on the revenues generated by industry.

In the United States, where the concept of a post-industrial society has been under discussion for longer than in Britain, manufacturing industry has increased its productivity and been able to compete in world markets, having moved into new technological growth products more successfully than in Britain. Manufacturing industry in Britain is a large and important sector of the economy, earning 50 per cent of our total foreign exchange and constituting 60 per cent of our exports of goods and services. Britain's share of world trade in manufactures fell from 24.6 per cent in 1950 to below 9 per cent in 1974. Since then it has stabilized at a level of 9–10 per cent and this represents a real achievement. At the beginning of the 1980s, with a world economic recession and Britain appearing to be worst hit, the prospect is that our share of world markets will decline even further; this possibility is strengthened by some disturbing evidence that the 'technology component' of United Kingdom exports is not as high as that of the United States, Japan and West Germany and that Britain's performance has been weak in rapidly growing, high technology markets.

Import penetration of British markets has shown a long-term tendency to increase which, in part, reflects the post-war liberalization of trade and an increase in the division of labour on a world scale. Similar trends towards an increasing dependence on imports can be observed in all developed countries, but in the case of the United Kingdom this process has gone much further, and has increased more rapidly than in all other developed countries except Italy.[14]

In the United Kingdom imports met 17 per cent of total demand in 1970 for manufactures, but by 1979 imports had risen to 26 per cent, while this trend has shown an alarming acceleration with imports of finished manufactures rising by 20 per cent in 1978–9.[15]

Our growing dependence on imports has not been due to Britain being 'flooded' by cheap goods from the low wage developing countries or the newly industrializing countries. In 1979 there was a £2.1 billion surplus in our balance of trade with the low wage developing countries and a surplus on manufacturing goods of £1.2 billion in trade with South Korea, Taiwan and Mexico. Our manufacturing deficit is with the EEC and Japan, a trend that reveals the type of goods that we are making and the growing technological gap between Britain and the other industrial countries.

We have done better in trading with the European Community since joining it than we have with the rest of the world. Exports increased by 350 per cent to the EEC in the first seven years as opposed to an increase of 200 per cent elsewhere. Before entry to the EEC our trade balance with EEC countries was deteriorating and now the trade deficit is narrowing markedly in real terms. The increase in UK oil exports to the EEC is speeding the improvement but even excluding oil the eight other member states in 1980 were providing 39 per cent of the total market for British exporters. Britain's export growth in the 1970s was rapid, with the proportion of GDP being exported rising from one-quarter in the mid 1970s to one third by 1980. This was a major achievement but while the value of exports rose by 334 per cent between 1970–8, the value of imports rose by 458 per cent to more than counterbalance it.

In the 1970s manufacturing industry was also subjected to an unprecedented profits' squeeze, which was both a cause and a consequence of the declining ability to compete internationally and one of the more serious effects of the successive prices and incomes policies operated during that period.[16]

In the early 1980s overall profitability figures are only likely to be maintained by the build-up of profits from North Sea oil. The challenge will be to achieve the right combination of channelling North Sea profits into productive investment in manufacturing industry at home and investment in overseas assets rather than into home consumption. North Sea oil introduces a major new factor in the handling of the British economy and its significance can hardly be overestimated. It has direct effect on those who work in or have invested in the oil and gas fields, it spreads out from them into the offshore industries and above all it provides the British government throughout the 1980s with substantial revenues from taxes and royalties. Oil exports will make a major contribution to the balance of payments; but that does not mean, as some have argued, that the expanding oil contribution must be offset by a decreasing contribution from manufactured products. Some of the balance of payments benefit will and should flow out again so as to increase Britain's foreign currency income when the oil income declines; some of the balance of payments benefit could and should be spent increasing our imports of raw materials and semi-manufactured goods so as to make it easier to expand economic activity within the UK and boost the level of manufactured goods.

There is no case for accepting the view that other countries who import our oil must export more to us and therefore boost our import bill, or that our net exports of other goods will have to fall by an equivalent amount if we are to keep the same target for our balance of payments.[17] According to this view, we can allow the size of the manufacturing sector to shrink and we should reinvest virtually all the profits from oil abroad, producing a restructuring of the economy due to the effects of oil and a high exchange rate. The problem with this analysis is that it offers little help in reducing unemployment in the industrial sector in the short to medium term and simply assumes both that a restructuring of the economy can create sufficient new jobs outside the manufacturing sector, and that Britain will be competitive in new industries when the flow of oil dries up. It would be wrong to argue that North Sea oil does not entail a restructuring of the economy, but what is very damaging is the extent to which oil is contributing to keeping the exchange rate at a level which is destroying the country's manufacturing sector. Even if interest rates are the major influence on the exchange rate, we shall have to cope with the oil factor when interest rates fall in line with those of other countries. If oil revenues were used to remove the balance of payments constraint facing the government they would allow the economy to be reflated through investment in key sectors of industry that have been identified as core industries that must be maintained, through higher public spending in selected areas which have a high employment content, through reducing insurance contributions to encourage employers to retain their labour force, and through tax reductions to ease the burden on those least able to bear it, which would also stimulate the economy through increased spending power. If we were to increase our import bill, this would decrease our balance of payments surplus, but would also allow the exchange rate to fall, which should increase the competitiveness of British industry. In 1980 the trade weighted index was near to 80 after a sustained rise in the exchange rate. In the autumn of 1977 within the Labour government I was arguing that the trade weighted index should be kept around 62. The handling of the exchange rate has been wrong ever since 1978.

What is needed is a balance of policies, a mix in the allocation of oil revenue. There is a need to assert, however, that the prime objective is to preserve our industrial base if Britain is to continue as a manufacturing nation. To rely only on income from overseas investment would be to make the British economy deeply vulnerable to external events beyond our control. While some revenue could be invested abroad and achieve a good return, we must reinvest the major portion of the profits from oil in Britain rather than abroad. Additionally a tougher oil depletion policy would decrease the rate of extraction of the oil and spread the revenues over a longer period. This would prevent the distorting effects that would accompany a few years of massive revenues, much of which would find its way not into industrial regeneration but into consumer spending. This is why there are important psychological arguments for devising a special Oil Fund so as to achieve at least a theoretical separation of oil revenues from the normal revenues available to government, rather than putting oil revenues directly into the Treasury. In practice, of course, all revenue is effectively within the control of the Exchequer, but the case for treating oil revenues differently is that not only are they 'one-off' revenues coming from a finite resource, but all experience shows that if we treat revenues in the normal way as we did with North Sea gas we shall do what the Dutch Government did: use the revenues for short-to-medium term economic management and leave behind a legacy of industrial decline. A special Fund will not guarantee that the revenue will be prudently used, but it at least will ensure that governments are held specifically accountable and the pressure is maintained to increase investment in manufacturing.

Manufacturing investment has been at a level very much lower than in other countries for some time; gross fixed capital formation per head in manufacturing 1970–74 was £240 in the UK compared with £450 in Germany, £540 in France and £740 in the USA.[18] As a result, in part, of low investment, the rate of productivity growth has declined from its long-term trend rate of 2.5 per cent per annum, 1950–73, to 0.7 per cent per annum, 1974–80, a level which is well below that of the rest of the EEC which was on average in 1974–80 2.5 per cent. The prolonged recession of the 1970s, with low or negative growth since 1973, did not have the consequence of controlling the rate of inflation. The decade witnessed a succession of increasingly severe policy measures designed to control inflation with a cycle of stop-go reducing business confidence and investment. The performance of the British economy in the 1970s was described in 1978 by some Cambridge economists in the following terms: 'Events have so far confirmed our worst fears. Manufacturing product is barely higher than 7 years ago, while the volume of imports of finished manufactures over the same period has risen two-and-a-half fold; unemployment has risen from 600,000 to nearly 1,500,000 – a figure that would not have been believed 10 years ago. Inflation is now at about the same rate as it was in 1970–71.'[19]

There is every indication that the adverse trends of profitability, investment, employment and competitiveness are not temporary phenomena and that they are likely to continue.

Designing an industrial strategy which will arrest the decline and provide a base for future expansion will require flair, imagination and a major shift in attitudes towards co-operation in industry. One thing is certain; co-operation will not be achieved on the basis of the simplistic polarized dogma of the Conservative government, with their animus against the public sector and their belief that there is no useful role for the state in stimulating industrial activity. But neither will it be achieved by replacing the present dogma by an equal, but opposite, animus against the private sector and a belief that only state intervention can stimulate industrial activity. Such a swing of political opinion and government decision-making in the 1980s would be an unmitigated disaster from which Britain's present industrial decline might never recover.

In 1968 the Washington-based Brookings Institution, in an analysis of the British economy, highlighted the slow rate of economic growth and poor productivity in comparison with other countries. If anything, the report was too sanguine; the decline continued over the next twelve years. In 1980 when they produced a new study, *Britain's Economic Performance*, the Institution's researchers concluded more strongly that the economic difficulties derived from poor productivity, the origins of which lay deep in the country's social system. The authors believe that our productivity problem needs to be tackled by improving industrial relations and increasing industrial incentives. It is difficult, but essential, for politicians to absorb the research findings of such studies and start to make policy on the basis of similar research and facts. The central focus must be the failure of managers and workers to trust each other and to co-operate effectively, together with the apparent inability in Britain to develop a commercially-orientated social climate within industry.

In the post-war development of an industrial strategy for Britain the obsessive debate about the role of the state – privatization versus state nationalization – has been destructive and damaging. But it is fundamental that interventionism is not allowed to become the dominant thrust of an industrial strategy or its marginal benefits exaggerated. Far greater importance must be given to creating changes in attitude in industry rather than embarking again on a state nationalization programme on the scale of 1945–51. The centralized-corporatist incomes policies of the past must now be rejected in favour of a more modest, and, one hopes, more sustainable decentralized approach, where commercial realities in the market sector of industry are not obscured by overall national norms and centrally imposed pay rigidities.

It may be too harsh a criticism, but one of the country's foremost scientists, Sir Alan Cottrell, in the 25th Fawley Foundation Lecture in November 1979, attacked successive governments for choosing to play God with industry: 'in the Conservative government, to take but one example, there were the crazy directives given to British Rail in 1972. The order in June was *economize*, by saving £15 m. a year. By July it had changed to *keep fares steady*, even if this meant losing money! But September brought more golden fruit: a new policy, *spend* as much as possible! That is the policy, not of Marx, but of the Marx Brothers. The Labour government were not to be outdone in commercial ineptitude, however. Thus by the mid-1970s we had Mr Benn blithely bestowing taxpayers' money on commercially hopeless private firms, to convert them into commercially hopeless workers' co-operatives, on the curious principle that the way to mend a broken-down car is simply to change its owner.

'But these are minor examples. Much more serious was the overall effect of frenetic governmental actions on industry generally: of stifling success by various financial and other controls; and of propping up failure by handouts from the public purse. The industrial policies of the governments in the 1970s thus ended up as a "reverse-carrot-and-stick" policy. Stick for the winners and carrot for the losers. This was one of the ways in which the actions of government undermined British industry; by destroying incentive.'[20]

How important is incentive? There has been a strange reluctance to consider the disincentive effect of the 'poverty trap' where tax acts harshly on people who receive a low wage for a full week's work, and puts them only just above the level for claiming a variety of means-tested benefits. The debate has concentrated instead only on the disincentive effect of taxation on the middle to higher incomes. It is absurd to deny that incentive is a source of motivation; but it is not the only motivation, and not always even the most important motivation. There are real problems relating to our present tax structure, particularly for the low wage earner and at the level of middle management in motivating someone to move or undertake more responsibilities. There are problems, too, associated with low profitability and the general dampening down of the adventurous and innovative spirit which cannot be dismissed as of no consequence. The levels of tax have to be fixed to take account of how people behave as well as according to criteria of social justice. Politicians need to approach the subject with a greater readiness to initiate research, to take note of comparative evidence from other countries, and generally to act on evidence not prejudice.

In developing a distinctive approach to British industry best suited to the British political and cultural tradition, we cannot expect to mirror exactly either Japanese–French commercial *dirigisme* or German–American benign *laissez-faire*, for the UK industrial base is different from either that of Japan, France, West Germany or the USA. We do not necessarily need the same tax system in terms of rates or allowances, though the extent to which British management at quite low levels is able to claim fringe benefits, with company cars and special allowances, is unique. Nor do we need the same profit ratios, but if profitability is to be restored to increase investment, it must be accompanied by a review of corporation tax, which has virtually ceased to exist as a revenue-raising tax, and a review of corporate tax. What Britain cannot ignore is that our industrial strength depends on our ability to compete and sell our goods in world markets. We must learn from the experience of France and Germany and start to put a far greater emphasis on winning markets than hitherto and on recognizing throughout British society the commercial and competitive imperatives on which our prosperity depends. This does not mean an emphasis on unrestrained market forces. The two decades of low economic growth before 1973 were wasted years; and even then our growth rates were sluggish by comparison with those of other countries. Intervention by governments is taking place in the wake of a world recession in most countries, and is increasing in all countries in the European Community, even in West Germany, and in the USA the government intervenes to help Chrysler and Lockheed.

What government must learn, however, is to judge when to intervene and when not to intervene, on the basis of a disciplined, scientific and thoughtful approach, not on the basis of dogma, doctrine or prejudice. Improving our commercial orientation must come from a change in attitude and this can in part come from an extension of industrial democracy, and where possible from industrial co-operatives. It will not be enough to improve industrial relations in the conventional sense, for this will not of itself achieve the orientation of the whole workforce towards the market place or a basic understanding of the need to compete commercially. Britain also requires a greater emphasis on the application of science and technology, on good management, the encouragement of small business with the recognition of its importance to the economy and a readiness to respond more rapidly to changing technologies. It means economic policies aimed at steady even if modest economic growth and increasing the demand for industrial goods supported by increased industrial investment. Above all, what is required is the development of an industrial policy which can be operated over a sustained period with the reasonable hope that it will not be chopped and changed about. Within a stable but market-orientated climate there is undoubted scope for more government intervention: for a new state-funded investment facility, for the National Enterprise Board to diversify and put in risk capital in support of high technology, and support regional policy in association with Regional Development Agencies. There is also a case for much tougher monopoly legislation. One of the effects of the corporatist trend has been to allow a steady increase in monopoly provisions and to pay too little attention to trust busting, and generally to accommodate too easily to the monopolies within the mixed economy.

The problem facing those who merely advocate a further extension of state monopoly nationalization is that it is widely realized that past experience of most nationalized concerns has been that it no longer commands immediate uncritical support, even among Labour activists, let alone among Labour voters. Some nationalized industries have done well, particularly those which provide predominantly a service to the public. British Gas has a good record, and so now, after five years of much needed sustained investment, has the National Coal Board. Germany, Belgium and France all subsidize their coal industry far more than British governments do and we are still doctrinally hesitant to do the same. British Railways have struggled against inadequate investment and the failure to produce an integrated transport policy. It is inescapable that any rail network will need a public subsidy; such a subsidy can be justified on energy, environmental and social grounds and we should stop being so defensive about the need for and the desirability of a rail subsidy where again other member states in the European Community see it as inevitable and right to provide large subsidies.

It is in the commercial sector that nationalization has a much poorer record. Essentially it has suffered from ill-considered governmental intervention in support of regional industrial policies, as well as a poor commercial orientation and a political reluctance to face up the need for faster adjustment in the face of very stiff international competition. The record of British Steel is depressing, despite every allowance for the distortion of its performance by its critics. British Shipbuilders faced a dramatic decline in the world market for ships on being nationalized but have made a reasonably good start in rationalizing wage rates and in improving productivity. With Defence contracts playing such an important role the shipbuilding industry is bound, whether in private or public ownership, to have an interlocking relationship with government, and denationalizing the profitable warship-building yards is no answer to the industry's difficulties. The case for state involvement in the ship repair yards was always dubious; they are probably best left to operate within the private sector, particularly since the government already has the four large naval dockyards. The argument for the nationalization of British Aerospace was that the state was a major purchaser, it had a continuing close interest because of Defence, and on projects like the European Airbus other governments were playing a leading role in their national industries. In this industry the introduction of mixed finance between public and private investment need not necessarily be a bad policy and there is little justification for the automatic assumption that it must be wholly government financed and owned. The same argument may apply to British Airways – although their financial difficulties are such that few would wish to purchase private equity at a time when airlines all over the world are facing economic difficulties.

There is considerable disillusionment about the practical working of the nationalized industries under the model arrangements conceived by Herbert Morrison, but the disadvantages which he foresaw of their day-to-day management being subject to detailed ministerial and parliamentary scrutiny are even more real today, as their complexity has increased. There are two possible evolutions of the Morrison model. Firstly, to try to split the nationalized industries such as railways, coal, gas and electricity into smaller management units. The other is to bring in alternative sources of finance, not through equity shares but through public bonds. Ending the dogmatic polarity between privatization and nationalization is an essential national interest and an acceptance of some degree of mixed financing might help. It would also help to make a clearer distinction between the public sector which operates commercially – British Aerospace, British Airways, British Steel and British Shipbuilders – and those which provide a service – British Rail, British Gas, the Electricity Boards and the National Coal Board.

The Labour Party is already pledged to repeal all the legislation introduced by the Conservatives to bring private equity capital into the public sector, whereas adaptation of this legislation would be a more sensible course. If state industries have a mixed source of finance they may become accepted as politically neutral and be given the necessary stability by all governments to concentrate on producing higher standards of service and becoming more efficient.

The main concentration of the minds of Ministers and parliament should be on the techniques for developing an integrated policy in the two areas of major public service covered by nationalized industries: transport and energy. A more effective role for Ministers is essential in all the areas of transport and energy but it is unrealistic to believe that the mere act of legislating for the nationalization of the ports, road haulage or buses, of the nuclear power industry or North Sea oil will integrate policy in these areas.

Pricing is the key to an effective integration of policy in relation to rail and road transport for industry, or to car, rail and bus for passengers. In transport the need is for an investment strategy, and a tax and pricing structure which balances the economic, social and environmental costs, and the advantages and disadvantages of an integrated transport system. There is a need for rationalization between rail, air, ship and road transport and for a socially sensitive policy for rural and urban transportation.

The issues are extremely complex and cannot be resolved by concentrating on ownership. In transport central government is not always the dominating presence. The role of local government, particularly in the major cities, is in many respects more influential than that of central government. Private decision in terms of the motor car ensures that no policy wholly based on state intervention can carry conviction. The more policy is developed within the context of the regions rather than centrally the more likely it is to serve local needs and adapt to local circumstances. This is a task which could be overseen by the regional assemblies advocated in Chapter 9 as part of the reform of the constitution.

The pseudo competition between gas and electricity with different showrooms, different policies and incoherent pricing policy militates against any integrated energy policy. Energy policy is influenced substantially by the OPEC cartel fixing oil prices, so to talk about market forces and market prices in the energy field is grossly misleading, and has worked against the rational wish for consumer choice.

A further problem is the organization of the electricity supply industry. The case for regional all-purpose electricity boards along the lines of the proven and efficiently run Board in Scotland, would be worth a fresh appraisal for England and Wales, now that the government in 1980 has rejected the Plowden Report's recommendation for reorganizing the electricity supply industry on a more centralized pattern.

The development of natural gas, the home conversion programme, and the transition from town gas was helped by a centralized British Gas organization. But there is a case for examining the establishment of autonomous Regional Gas Boards for the future, when the gas industry starts adapting to the situation which will exist in the early part of the next century. Then, as North Sea gas declines, while we will not return to the old pattern of small town gas plants, area synthetic gas plants will have to be developed, initially making up for, and eventually replacing, natural gas. There is at least a strong argument for considering afresh greater regional autonomy in the future.

Slowly over the next few decades, driven by cost and anxiety about availability, a much more diverse energy supply situation will be developing, with householders investing in solar power, wind power and even, where available, water power as additional energy sources for the future. Rationalizing energy prices against these trends with the need for a far more active conservation strategy and the need to encourage the use of the most efficient energy source will present major conceptual as well as practical difficulties for central, regional and local government.

Conservation is still not seen within central government as a source of energy. Government has a decision-making structure which absorbs easily a multi-million pound decision to build an individual power station, but has as yet no mechanism to offset the value of such an investment to increase electricity supply with a range of smaller investment decisions in conservation – which cumulatively should add up to a multi-million pound programme to reduce the demand for electricity. Investing in conservation would also provide a major source of employment in the 1980s when unemployment is certain to be distressingly high. Yet also there is a necessity for a steady ordering programme for new power stations in order to maintain a viable industry for the future. A pricing structure which discourages the use, particularly in daytime, of electricity as a source of heating would, for example, have to be sensitive enough to allow for the situation where the householder or industry has no access to the preferred alternative of gas or coal. A pricing structure for industry is also needed which encourages the use of coal but which discourages the use of gas except for those industries where gas is essential. It is also important that a pricing structure ensures that Britain's industries' energy costs are certainly no higher and preferably lower than the international average, so as to help reduce manufacturing unit costs in comparison with those of our main industrial competitors. This is an area where industry can be helped without breaching international trading agreements and where other countries are already doing far more than Britain.

The amazing complexity of developing an integrated transport and energy policy, is one which has as yet been barely touched on by successive governments, bogged down by detail and dogma. Indecisive and incoherent, this lack of integration represents government at its worst. In both energy and transport, the believers in market forces, if they are honest, soon discover that there is not a true market, and that playing around with privatization and talking about beating monopoly power are irrelevant. The task of national government, and in some of these areas also the European Community, is to try to bring different strands of policy together into an integrated whole. In some senses the continuing debate in the last few decades over nationalization has been an excuse to avoid grappling, in energy and transport, with the much harder task of developing an integrated policy. Clarifying the different roles and the different techniques of managing and controlling the private market-dominated industrial sector and the public service-dominated industrial sector is the essential prelude to achieving greater coherence.

Coherence also demands that politicians accept an even more formidable discipline: they should be very reluctant to implement structural industrial changes which appear to have no long-term hope of being accepted, and will only be reversed. That is not to exclude imposing structural changes against the view of an official opposition party, or of vested interests, but to shift the onus of proof for making such a change in a way that gives a far higher priority to ensuring continuity than has been done hitherto.

For some, on both the Right and the Left, this will be the hardest discipline of all to accept. It will be argued that this is a prescription for 'middle-of-the-road', consensus politics and that the same arguments could thus be applied in education, health and social policy. To some extent this objection is valid, but it is also true that in the areas of social policy in post-war Britain there has been a greater degree of continuity across governments, particularly over the last decade, than there has been over industrial policy. Yet it is our industrial success which determines the national wealth which alone can support, extend and improve our education, health and social services. We cannot continue to conduct ill-judged political experiments with our industrial strategy, whether by taking non-intervention by the state to an extreme or state interventionist policies to an extreme. Our industrial base is crumbling, and far faster than in other comparable countries. We can best alleviate this, not by violent shifts of policy, but by the steady, firm and resolute application of a variety of policies directed towards modernization and greater efficiency. We cannot afford to spend the 1980s with major industries like ship-building, aerospace, aero engines, air, road and sea transport, gas and oil, oscillating between private and public ownership.

The trend towards industrial discontinuity as an article of political faith was started by the Conservative government of 1970, the yo-yo effect has continued ever since and the 1980s promise to be worse. Automatic repeal of the legislation of previous governments besides being very disruptive and negative when it is accompanied by threats to renationalize without compensation, is also wrong. Politicians out of government would be wise to pause, consider carefully all aspects of industry, and nearer the election decide what should be the overall strategy. Politicians should also consider whether attitudinal change is more important than structural change. A measured response over reversing privatization and extending state ownership if combined with a radical commitment to introduce industrial democracy is a more credible programme, also with a better chance of acceptance. There are strong grounds for believing that industrial democracy and co-operatives by emphasizing a change of attitudes would bring a far better return. It would help to increase awareness of the need for increased productivity, improved industrial relations, and add to the commercial orientation of industry, which is so essential to increase national wealth.

Planning is another aspect of an industrial strategy which can contribute to attitudinal changes. The saddest aspect of policy development in Britain has been the decline over the last fifteen years in the politicians' confidence and belief in the potential contribution that planning can make to the development of an industrial strategy. Planning is not just concerned with obtaining an information base, though this is an essential prerequisite. It is also concerned with anticipating trends and taking action to prevent or mitigate situations which may be foreseeable, and then trying to develop policy which is not just reactive but ahead of its time. If new products are developed at the start of the world recession they can alleviate some of the worst consequences in terms of unemployment and industrial decline.

The arguments for Ministers having a personal policy advisory team as well as a political advisory team are developed in Chapter 8 on Parliamentary Government. Such a team will have little effect, however, unless politicians can also be convinced of the need to restore planning to an important position at both political and bureaucratic level, in the European Community, Whitehall and local government. There is no contradiction in deploying the case for greater decentralization nationally and at the same time recognizing the need for more highly developed centralized planning; planning and decision making are different though the two run logically in harness. Sensible decision-making necessitates a careful assessment of the right level at which decisions should be made, and in a decentralized system it is even more necessary to establish planning links so that information and experience are carried back from a wide spread of decision points.

The European Community, and in particular the Commission, also has a modest planning role on broad international strategic issues covering monetary policy, forward trading patterns, industrial adjustment, agricultural balance and energy self-sufficiency which cannot be considered only within a national framework. The Commission often fails to cover these areas adequately because the European Community has allowed itself to become deluged in the detail of harmonization and of policy implementation. The Community has commissioned over the years many valuable medium- to longer-term reports which contain interesting ideas and projections, but the systematic monitoring of national states' performance towards agreed goals is still in its early stages.

The climate of opinion in most other European Community countries is more receptive than it is in Britain to the concept of planning and even to interventionism by government. In the European Community at present the use of subsidies in Germany, France, Italy and Belgium is quite widespread, with increasing reliance on state aid in many areas of the new technologies of telecommunications, microchips and robots. In France the National Plan has been given perhaps too much of the credit for their industrial revival, but it has been of some value, and planning has helped to maintain continuity in Italy despite its uncertain political history; even West Germany, hitherto hostile to planning because of its identification with state control in East Germany, has changed its position over the last few years, and the case for planning is put now much more strongly within the SPD.

In Britain, the ghosts of past failure are still strong; the collapse of the National Plan, the slow dismembering of the Department of Economic Affairs, still arouse painful memories. But if the Labour government in 1964 had devalued and put growth as its priority policy, its whole planning initiative might have been a success. The 1974–9 Labour government tried to develop planning through the sector working parties as part of a less ambitious overall industrial strategy developed within the framework of the National Economic Development Organization. Some valuable work was done but the structure, by concentrating on ensuring sectoral representation, tended to encourage a fragmented approach to planning, with a high degree of special pleading.

Another aspect of industrial planning is retraining and the up-grading and updating of skills. In many European countries this has been given a far higher priority than in Britain. In Sweden 2 per cent of the workforce is being retrained at any one time; in Britain the same proportion would mean retraining 400,000 people. In West Germany nine out of ten school leavers are trained for two years or more in a professional skill of their choice, whereas in Britain nearly half our school leavers get no further training or education at all. We have an appalling record, and our reluctance to introduce educational maintenance allowances to encourage children to continue with educational training beyond the age of sixteen simply demonstrates our lack of commitment. Imaginative policies towards employment planning are more important in the long term than many of the changes relating to structure, for without skilled employees no company, private or public, can compete.

The British record in this sphere is lamentable, falling far below that achieved elsewhere in Europe, and it is symptomatic of our preoccupation with much less crucial factors that this failing has rarely been discussed by civil servants or by politicians. Britain has not attempted wide-ranging employment planning since the National Plan and more recently under the last Labour government when policies were adopted more as a reaction to rising unemployment than as a conscious attempt to plan and to make the best use of the workforce. Industrial decline in Britain is related to our inadequate and outmoded educational and training systems, which have failed to produce skilled workers in sufficient numbers and with the right kind of skills. Education and training are also important, in a wider political perspective, in helping to break down class barriers, to create a more socially mobile population and in educating workers for a wider democracy in which they will be better equipped to participate more fully in decisions which affect them most directly. The acquisition of skills, especially by those from poor backgrounds who are at present badly served by the education system, can help in reducing social tensions arising from unemployment among ethnic minorities, inner-city youth and in easing the transition to new technology.

Training and retraining will need heavy investment by future governments in order not only to contribute to economic growth but as a socially just measure to allow manual workers to share in the benefits of new technology. The immediate, short-term challenge can be judged by the fact that the proportion of manual jobs is projected to decline below 50 per cent by 1985 from the 1978 level of 56 per cent. A recent report, *Education, Training and Industrial Performance*, came to the alarming conclusion that : 'the delivery of training in the UK has two major weaknesses. The first is the concentration on initial training at the expense of upgrading and retraining later in life. Secondly, training is concentrated on a relatively narrow range of jobs, for reasons which are as much to do with tradition and collective bargaining as with the intrinsic needs of the occupation. Women and unskilled workers suffer particularly. As a result of these two factors, the system of training is rigid, conservative and slow to respond to new industrial requirements.'[21]

The report went on to note that as many as 15 per cent of young people leave school with no formal qualifications and that nearly two-thirds of young people leave school at the age of sixteen and do not go into full-time further education. A Manpower Services Commission study found that Britain's performance contrasted badly with that of other members of the EEC and that Britain has the lowest proportion of young people in industrial training or full-time vocational training within the EEC, with the deficiency being marked between Britain and our major industrial competitors in Europe.[22] The Finniston Report made suggestions for policy changes and noted 'that by the late 1980s a serious shortfall is likely in the supply of new engineers relative to the continuing high demands from employers.'[23] A significant fall in the numbers taking apprenticeships and other kinds of formal training within industry has also taken place in recent years, with a decline from 450,000 (or 5.6 per cent of the industrial workforce) in 1968 to 240,000 (3.6 per cent) in 1980.

It is to the credit of the last Labour government that employment and training schemes were given an enhanced role during a period of severe financial restraints. A wide series of measures sought to protect jobs and to retrain workers, with the emphasis being on job preservation rather than on training and job creation. The Temporary Employment Subsidy saved over 400,000 jobs between 1975 and 1978 and the Young Employment Subsidy and the Small Firms Employment Subsidy saved several thousand more jobs from 1977 to 1979. The government increased training opportunities for adults sixfold from 1971 to 1977 and the most important of these schemes, the Youth Opportunities Programme, had catered for 203,000 young people by July 1980.[24]

The employment subsidies had a very direct social benefit and they have been found to be a cost-effective solution to rising unemployment. It has been found that the amount of revenue lost through lower tax collection and the increase in social security payments by the government when a worker becomes unemployed, is equal to 89–105 per cent of average male earnings in manufacturing industry for a single man and 89–96 per cent for a married man with two children. Therefore, subsidies of up to 90 per cent of the average industrial wage are likely to reduce the budget deficit.[25]

It is a task of central government to develop a comprehensive programme of retraining and job protection, integrating these two aspects to avoid the indefinite protection of jobs which are in uncompetitive industries. Retraining should be encouraged by the adoption of training boards which will estimate future labour needs in the expanding industries and which will be allowed attractive rates of pay to workers undergoing retraining. We should aim to provide training for those young people – a majority of young people – who at present leave school with meagre qualifications.

The crucial area for government is in setting the most beneficial economic climate for industry. A major truism over any industrial policy is how marginal is the beneficial effect of government action. Yet even if government can exert only a minor influence it should not be disparaged merely because it is minor, for cumulatively every positive development adds up. The danger comes from pretending that government action can have a major impact and from the disproportionate effect of ill-judged and damaging action.

No government can ignore the need to control the money supply, but any government should be prepared to learn from experience rather than theory which are the variables that are most necessary to control, and any government should recognize that, given the imperfect state of economic knowledge, rigid and dogmatic adherence to keeping only one variable under control is too risky a policy. The same fundamental lesson can be applied to other aspects of policy, controlling inflation through a prices and incomes policy and to maintaining the level of public expenditure. The natural scientist operating within all the limitations of behavioural science would never seek such certainties or apply remedies with such single-minded determination. One of the tragedies of much post-war economic practice is its rigidity, its search for solutions, its inability to learn from experience and to operate for any sustained period a mix of policies. The 1979 Conservative government, far from being pragmatists as some claim them to be, adopted new economic theories with all the uncritical fervour of the convert. At least the Left who adopt the alternative strategy have never wished to be associated with pragmatism; they have always had the inner certainty of knowing what must be done and want to impose it.

It is wrong and mistaken to abandon all policies of the last thirty years and to attempt an economic 'experiment', whether from the 'protectionist' or the 'monetarist' viewpoint. There is no evidence to support the view that such a drastic switch of policy at a time when Britain's economic position is extremely weak will do anything but further debilitate the economy. Past policies have failed to deliver the same levels of economic growth as many of the economies of other Western countries, but we have nevertheless maintained – at least until recently – reasonably full employment and, in the majority of post-war years, an annual improvement in people's standard of living. The failure of our economy has not been because the analysis of what was wrong was essentially flawed or because anyone lacked the economic tools to implement the correct policies. Analysis of the last few decades shows rather that failure in most cases was because the economic policies were applied too late and with a timidity and reluctance to initiate sustainable change against the resistance of individuals and institutions. Any economic strategy aiming at a revival of the British economy should be accompanied by changes in the operations of our powerful financial institutions and of the markets for investment finance. The stark alternatives of the protectionists and the monetarists aim at macro-economic variables and neglect the scope for reforms of micro-economic markets and institutions in order to improve resource allocation. The low level of industrial investment in the British economy and the age structure of our industrial plant and machinery clearly place our industry at a competitive disadvantage when it is compared to Western Europe, Japan and the United States. In addressing itself to the major problems facing British industry the Wilson Committee,[26] set up to review the functioning of financial institutions, stated that: 'A higher level of worthwhile private investment will only be achieved if a number of conditions are satisfied. First, managements will have to have the incentive to seek out viable projects and, in appropriate cases, to maintain their existing operations. Secondly, there will have to be changes in attitude on the part of both managements and employees about making the most efficient use of existing financial assets. Thirdly, finance of the right type, price and maturity must be available.' The problem of the provision of finance for industry was regarded as not being one of a shortage of funds, for the Wilson Committee noted: 'we have received no evidence of any general shortage of finance for industry at prevailing rates of interest and levels of demand, and with present perceptions of the risks involved in real investment. Industry has not felt that it has been held back by an inability to obtain external funds provided it was prepared to pay the price asked.' This view was qualified by saying that the existing financial mechanisms 'seem to have a degree of difficulty in meeting the demands of small, especially new, firms', and that the dominance of financial markets by cautious portfolio managers of pension funds and life assurance funds has served to inhibit investment in high-risk areas. It can be argued that there is no shortage of investment funds and instead there is a shortage of worthwhile projects in Britain, with a high enough rate of return. This neglects the important point that the supply of funds must be of the 'right type, price and maturity' in order that potential investment projects will be regarded as being economically viable.

The commercial banks in Britain lend money to industry for shorter periods than do banks in Japan and in the EEC and they attach more stringent borrowing conditions to the loans. A result has been that investment is curtailed by the need to repay interest on loans in a short period, before a project has begun to generate a return on the investment. Businessmen are reluctant to consider long-term investments, when faced with short-term loans, or large investments when banks are unwilling to advance a large proportion of the cost of a project. A cautious and unenterprising attitude is instilled which, in part, serves to justify cautious lending policies by the banks. This is in marked contrast to the confidence shown by European businessmen and the institutions from which they borrow.

There is a need in Britain to foster a set of attitudes which accepts risk-taking by entrepreneurs and by financial institutions. For socialists this means recognizing that a market economy is founded on a readiness to take risks, which can bring also high rewards. This is not to advocate or extol unfettered capitalism. The City – which advocates the uninhibited operation of the market system for everyone else – was extremely reluctant to see its rigours applied to its own secondary banking system in the early 1970s. No depositors with any of those banks lost their deposits – the banks concerned being rescued by the lifeboat fund operated at the request of the Bank of England. Sir Leslie Murphy who supported the operation, which was mounted to sustain the integrity and credit of the City, has commented that, 'it is an odd result that those who received higher interest rates on their deposits because of the lower security involved in depositing with a secondary bank were not penalized when those banks got into difficulties. The City is, it seems, not always in favour of the unfettered operation of market forces.' What is needed is a better balance. A role for government is in trying to encourage less restrictive lending policies by the commercial banks in order to help to stimulate industrial investment and risk-taking and to break into the vicious downward cycle of confidence-sapping economic decline. A limit should be reimposed on the total of bank lending, in order to prevent bank credit financing consumption of imports, and the government should make it clear that an increasing proportion of the total is to be used to finance productive investment. The banks could also be persuaded to increase the length of loans, from the present low average level of three years to the continental level of five years or more. To meet these needs the banks will require an increasing proportion of personal savings to be deposited with them instead of with the building societies and to do so the banks should be allowed to offer more attractive terms to depositors. It will not be easy to achieve these changes since radical reforms are perceived as being more difficult during an economic decline and caution is preferred to risk-taking. There is a need to establish a totally new concept of mixed private and publicly funded investment facility to channel oil company and government North Sea oil revenues into productive investments in the United Kingdom. At present too much of the revenues of the oil companies goes abroad and government revenues have been used to finance tax cuts and could well be used to stimulate consumption of imported manufactures. The management of the fund being mixed would make it more entrepreneurial, since it is vital that it is a risk-taking investment facility. The existing financial institutions, such as the pension funds and life assurance funds, could lend a proportion of their funds to such a new investment institution and would receive in return a guaranteed minimum rate of return to equal that for gilt edged stock. This could encourage the trade unions to be less conservative in the investment decisions of their own pension funds. Finance could be offered by the investment bank at a variety of interest rates and it would be expected that, as the note of dissent to the Wilson Committee Report noted, 'the ability to offer finance on favourable terms would have a major effect on the number of new projects being put forward.'

The fact that sensible economic policies have been applied for too short a period to achieve results has been due in particular to the discontinuity between governments which started most markedly with the change of government in 1970. Since then a succession of ideologically-motivated governments has ensured little or no economic continuity other than that forced on them after a period in office by the realities of a world economy. The exchange rate in particular has for long periods been too high and has been instrumental in undermining our manufacturing base.

It is clear that the 1980s show every sign of continuing this trend. Instead of there being a gradual depreciation of sterling, a high exchange rate will be maintained under the influence of high interest rates and the possession of North Sea oil, and it will severely damage industry. Selective import controls will be necessary where penetration is having damaging effects and support is likely to grow within the EEC for a more detailed policy for managing trade – or, as it is called by the French, more 'orderly marketing arrangements'. If severe import penetration takes place, the already high unemployment figures risk reaching levels which would not be tolerated by other Community countries. We should use our membership of the

EEC to negotiate specific import restrictions: if Britain could demonstrate that real disruption was occurring, some arrangement might even be negotiated for intra-Community trade. Unilaterally introduced controls, however, should be a last desperate remedy. Before they were to be instigated there should be seen to have been serious international negotiations in a genuine attempt to reach agreement. Presenting our trading partners in the EEC and GATT with a *fait accompli* would incur the same hostility as we encountered in 1964 by our EFTA partners. To argue that Britain can easily act alone is dangerously chauvinistic and unrealistic. In any serious negotiation a readiness to act unilaterally in the last resort has to be a negotiating counter but it has to be used with skill and understanding. Unilateral protectionism would receive a very hostile reception from our Community partners if they assumed it was merely a prelude to our withdrawing from the European Community or if we appeared to care little for our obligations to other nations under GATT or under our membership of the IMF.

Above all, Britain's economic policy needs to be approached with a greater intellectual humility and political sensitivity, a willingness to learn from our past mistakes. A position of economic weakness nationally and internationally is not a time either to espouse an economic ideology hostile to the working of the mixed economy – which would be seen by a significant section of those who work within our economy as being harmful to achieving the goals of full employment and a rising standard of living – or to adopt a policy which cannot be made broadly tolerable to all who work in the public sector, to management and to unions. To pretend that any British government can impose its will in economic issues on important sections of the national community or international economic institutions without any serious counter-balancing consequences is fundamentally to misunderstand the limitations of democracy within Britain and the interdependence of the world economy.

6

INCOMES
POLICY

The history of the last thirty-five years suggests that full employment, reasonable price stability and free collective bargaining are mutually incompatible. All governments which aspire to economic growth have tended at various times to concentrate on incomes policy and to challenge the principle of free collective bargaining, but they have rarely followed a consistent line. It is impossible to challenge the corporatist trend of the past while endorsing the centralizing trend of post-war incomes policies and, as has been argued in Chapter 3, on corporatism, the issue of decentralization within the trade union movement cannot be ignored by socialist politicians when they come to grapple with the problem of influencing free collective bargaining.

All the policies that have been tried have failed in a number of respects: they have not substantially held down wage inflation except in the short run; they have not reduced the problem of low pay; and they have not markedly improved industrial relations. These failings can be attributed to lack of flexibility, to inability to take account of 'special cases', and to neglect of grass roots' pressure. The policies, though initially often popular, have not been regarded as fair in practice, particularly those that started with cut-off anomalies and were then increasingly circumvented. As a result, trade unions have not been able to restrain their members' demands, even though opinion polls may still have been indicating popular support. Moreover, when the results are retrospectively assessed over a five-year period and all the economic consequences are averaged out, including what happens when the policy ceases to operate, it is clear that the real economic effect is open to question. The problem is that no one can calculate the effect of what would have happened if there had been no incomes policy. There are some who argue for a statutory policy and claim that only if the full weight of parliament is brought to bear can there be sufficient democratic authority to maintain the policy. But this is to ignore changes in the structure of British society and the patterns of wage bargaining that call for a more flexible, decentralized approach.

Governments have generally felt that, if they can be confident that wages will rise within certain percentage limits, they can more easily plan for a higher overall level of demand in the economy without risking a high rate of inflation or damaging the balance of payments. 'The need for incomes policy arises when it appears that a tolerable degree of price stability cannot be achieved by reducing the level of demand, or can be achieved only at an unacceptably high cost in terms of unemployment, loss of real output, and interference with growth. Hence, incomes policy is often presented as a means of improving the trade-off between unemployment and price stability.'[1] Governments have tried, therefore, to show workers that the lower the earnings figure in its economic projections then the higher will be the growth and employment figures that the government can aim for without failing to contain inflation and the balance of payments deficit.

This has been the thinking behind the policies worked out by the social democratic governments of Scandinavia, the Federal Republic of Germany, and Austria, with fiscal policies and incomes policies being linked in various ways. Some have involved a form of social contract which is agreed by the national trade union organizations, the employers' federations and the government.[2] The unions have agreed to limit wages in return for government action to secure full employment and certain social benefits. For instance, in Norway in 1975 the unions agreed to accept only 80 per cent compensation for the rise in the cost of living over the previous year, with only 30 per cent out of the 80 per cent being taken in wage rises and the remainder in increased family allowances, income tax cuts, pension rises and a price freeze.[3] A similar policy was achieved in Ireland in August 1979 with a 15-month pay deal. The package was made up of separate agreements on pay, taxation and employment, with the pay policy being agreed between the Irish Confederation of Trade Unions and the employers, but with the implementation of each policy closely linked to the observance of the other two.[4] These policies have been very successful, both in securing social goals and in containing inflation. 'For more than a decade after 1956, the Swedish system of centralized wage bargaining . . . constituted an important element in the realization of the policy goals of minimal unemployment, moderate price inflation, rapid growth of productivity, and rising real income, and greater equality of income distribution, especially through the provision of pension benefits and the health insurance. In Norway, incomes policy based on similarly centralized bargaining, but with direct participation by the government in the process, enabled the authorities to keep the rate of unemployment generally below the European average and to secure steady and rapid economic growth.'[5]

One reason for Britiain's failure to achieve a similar success is our different insititutional framework. In Scandinavia, the national trade union organizations, the equivalents of the TUC, have authority vested in them by their constituent unions to negotiate with the government and employers and they have the power to deliver their side of the bargain by limiting wage increases. This is not so in Britain, where the TUC is weak and unable to control strong unions such as the miners or engineers and where individual unions are unable to control shop-floor organizations of their own members. The Donovan Commission found that in the 1960s the level of effective decision-making moved downwards from the national trade union officers to committees of shop stewards, a trend caused by comparatively full employment, which enhanced the ability of the shop-floor to demand increases, and by increasing shop-floor frustration with the acquiescence of the unions in incomes policies. The rise of shop-floor power created a dual system of industrial relations, with national wage agreements being supplemented by local pay rises. Some unions responded to this by formally decentralizing.

It is interesting that the Donovan report stated that 'it is often wide of the mark to describe shop stewards as troublemakers . . . Quite commonly they are supporters of order exercising a restraining influence on their members.'[6] Four major changes took place within the unions in the 1970s: a movement from national level to lower level bargaining, changes in the scope of lower-level bargaining, an increase in lay involvement on negotiating bodies and the extension, or introduction, of reference-back procedures. An example of lower-level bargaining was the withdrawal of the T&GWU from the Road Haulage Wages Council in December 1975. Other examples were the Liverpool Dockers' secession from national negotiations in 1967, and the Confederation of Shipbuilders and Engineering Union's withdrawal in 1971. This movement has also been influenced by companies either leaving an employers' association and/or withdrawing from industry-wide negotiations. Metal Box withdrew from the Tin Box Joint Industrial Committee (JIC) in 1969 and 1970 and moved to individual factory bargaining. Cadbury-Schweppes left a JIC in 1968 and introduced plant bargaining. A change in the scope of lowest level bargaining was of greater significance and represented what Donovan called the 'two-system pattern', where national negotiations set minimum rates and hours and substantial increases are obtained at the local level via productivity deals. T&GWU annual reports increasingly show the union's involvement in productivity deals. By 1975 the scope of discussions at National Joint Industrial Committee level was considerably reduced and over 50 per cent of all wage increases were obtained at the local level.

Devolved bargaining has also produced a marked change in the structure of the T&GWU, largely because, if the union had sought to retain the involvement of full-time officials in local bargaining, a large increase in the number of officials would have been needed. The number of full-time officials declined from 530 to 485 between 1968 and 1975, while the ratio of members to senior shop stewards and conveners fell from 637:1 in 1965 to 433:1 in 1975. There is also evidence that shop stewards were replaced less often and hence numbers of full-time and senior stewards rose. Obviously more local bargaining will lead to increasing involvement by lay unionists, as a result of increases both in the number of local negotiating bodies and in the scope of local discussions. However, there has also been an increase in lay involvement in bodies above the local level.

In the Scandinavian countries there are fewer unions and all the major negotiations take place at the same time of the year, the synchro-pay day; it is, therefore, easier for the national union bodies to achieve agreement from the individual unions, since the latter do not have to worry that other unions will achieve higher settlements in the current pay round. The Scandinavians have in consequence to some extent avoided the leapfrogging that is endemic in Britain. But in the 1970s, when world inflation rates rose and Scandinavia was particularly vulnerable to oil price increases, the system of centralized wage bargaining began to break down; it may be that the success of the past was possible because of sustained growth and low inflation and that a centralized incomes policy cannot withstand the strains imposed by world economic recession and high inflation. Although British trade unions have a far more decentralized structure than do the Scandinavian, successive British governments have attempted to instigate a very similar pattern of centralized incomes policies. National norms have been either agreed with a reluctant TUC or imposed on them and, in most cases, later abandoned as being either unrealistic or too inflexible to withstand growing pressure from the shop-floor or the challenge of a major union.

The most successful period of prices and incomes' policy was from 1940 to 1945, when Ernest Bevin, as Minister of Labour, introduced a statutory policy which resulted in the only redistributive five-year period in British history. The problem of continually rising prices was foreseen even then in the 1944 White Paper *Employment Policy*, which stated that, 'Action taken by the Government to maintain expenditure will be fruitless unless wages and prices are kept reasonably stable'. Sir Stafford Cripps in 1948–9 had a policy which simply asked for moderation, and for those two years it worked, but it was undermined by the growing power of shop stewards and by devaluation in September 1949 and the Korean War in June 1950. Moreover, as prices began to rise faster than wages it lost the appearance of equity which had been so carefully preserved during the war years. Interestingly, Aubrey Jones argues that, 'the 1948 White Paper had shown little awareness of the fact that shop stewards in the factory were moving out of the control of the national trade union leaders.'[7]

The next attempt was by Harold Macmillan when, as Chancellor of the Exchequer in 1956, he set a 'plateau' for public sector prices but with direct control of wages. Then, in August 1957, Peter Thorneycroft set up the Council on Prices, Productivity and Incomes to create a greater awareness of the need to limit rises in prices and wages. On 25 July 1961 the then Chancellor, Selwyn Lloyd, announced a 'wage pause' for government employees, later extended to workers covered by Wage Councils; it was not backed by statute and existing commitments were honoured. The pause ended on 1 April 1962 when the National Economic Development Council was set up.

In 1962–3 a 'voluntary restriction' was set of 2–2.5 per cent and then 3–3.5 per cent. This allowed exceptions for high productivity, labour mobility and certain adjustments found to be in the national interest. In November 1962 a National Incomes Commission was founded to set future targets. In 1965–6 a new Labour government evolved a voluntary 3–3.5 per cent policy with the same exceptions but with an additional provision for low pay, and set up a Prices and Incomes Commission, later to become a Statutory Board. This was followed in July 1966 by a compulsory six months' 'freeze'. In 1967–8 the 'zero norm' was introduced, and a voluntary policy adopted, though the government retained powers of delay. The exceptions were for productivity, low pay, labour mobility and adjustments in the national interest. By 1969 a 3.5 per cent ceiling on rises in exceptional cases was permitted. In 1969–70 a 2.5–4.5 per cent 'voluntary band' was agreed, but there were no statutory powers, for example, to delay wage rise, and wage levels soon began to exceed the limits. In 1971–2 the 'n – 1 formula' was a voluntary guideline, but it was imposed by the government on its own employees. In the private sector, however, free collective bargaining pushed wages far ahead in advance of productivity, and unit costs rose. In 1972–3 there was a statutory freeze, no exceptions were allowed; this was followed in 1973 by the 'one pound plus 4 per cent formula' and a '12-month rule'. This was again a compulsory policy, the only exception being for moves to equal pay and for settlements deferred by the freeze. In 1973–4, a system of 7 per cent or '£2.35 flat rate plus threshold payments' was introduced as a compulsory scheme. It had a 1 per cent margin to deal with pay structures. Genuine productivity schemes and payments for unsocial hours were the only exceptions allowed. The productivity element was a deliberate loophole to cope with the miners, but because of bad handling and more by accident than design, a major confrontation followed, leading to the 1974 election defeat.

In 1974–5 inflation soared, fed by the threshold payments provision that the new Labour government had inherited. This compensation for price changes between the main settlements was an inbuilt escalator and, as a result of the social contract, exceptions were allowed for low pay and equal pay, which in turn led to large increases for nurses under the Halsbury award and for teachers under the Houghton award. In the summer of 1975, with inflation running at 27 per cent, a '£6 maximum' with some exceptions for low pay and equal pay was agreed, together with a 12-month rule; there was no statutory back-up on wages, though a statutory price restraint introduced by the previous government had been maintained. In 1976 a 5 per cent policy with a minimum of £2.50 and a maximum of £4.00 was again agreed with the TUC, but no exceptions were allowed. In 1977 a 10 per cent maximum with exceptions for productivity was introduced and, though not agreed by the TUC, it was acquiesced in, though in the early stages it did involve the government withstanding industrial action from the firemen.

All these policies have been challenged by workers in profitable industries demanding a share of those profits. In 1977 Ford workers achieved an 11 per cent settlement which, with other provisions, was well above the government's 10 per cent maximum and very nearly broke the whole policy. In 1978 it was again Ford who, with a 27 per cent settlement, not only substantially broke the then attempt to agree a 5 per cent pay guideline, but was also the test case which led to the parliamentary rejection of government sanctions, to the abandonment of the pay policy and the famous 'winter of discontent' in January and February 1979 which led, in turn, to the fall of the Labour government in May 1979.

This is a sombre tale, and before embarking on the same course again, it is very necessary to analyse objectively the record of incomes policies in affecting the economy and to see if there are lessons for the future.

Successive British incomes policies have in fact failed to achieve the social goals that have been for many their chief purpose. They have, notably, not affected the hoped-for redistribution of income in favour of the lower-paid. The spread of differentials has not been substantially narrowed by the flat rate policies of 1973–4 and 1975–7, except at the very top of the incomes spread. A certain amount of caution is necessary in drawing any conclusions about the effects of policies on differentials, since not all the information is available, but the evidence shows that what slight narrowing in differentials did take place between 1970 and 1977 was not confined to the periods of flat-rate policies. It is noticeable that, during the period of the Labour government's £6 per week policy, there was no movement in favour of the lower-paid. Much larger changes occurred between April 1976 and April 1977 when a percentage policy was in operation. Stages II and III of the Conservative government's policy between April 1973 and April 1974, which were only partly flat-rate policies, appear to have had as much redistributive effect as other pay policy periods.

Figures available for the top 1 per cent of men in full-time employment show that there was a substantial narrowing of the gap between the top percentile and the median between 1970 and 1976, but that this took place between 1970 and 1974 and was actually reversed under the Labour government between April 1975 and April 1976 – a period during which the Stage I policy permitted in theory no increases for those earning over £8,500. These results are disappointing, but they can probably be explained by the considerable potential for evasion through promotions, job changes and circumvention of the limits.

Differentials can also be studied by looking at the wages structure within companies These figures show long periods when differentials stayed fairly constant followed by short periods of narrowing. In engineering a large compression took place between June 1974 and June 1975, the period of the original social contract, which was effectively a period of free collective bargaining when compared to later policies. A further narrowing did take place during the year of the £6 policy but this was not as great as the previous movement. None of the policies of the 1960s had very much effect. On shipbuilding a National Institute of Economic and Social Research study said that, 'There is certainly no evidence therefore that the skill differential in shipbuilding has been eroded at an industry-wide level during periods of incomes policy.'[8]

Differentials have been decreasing over the last twenty years in manufacturing industry, but there is further evidence that this has not been a result of incomes policies but a reflection of influence of long-term changes in the labour market and the rate of inflation. A study by the University of Aberdeen concluded that, 'the narrowing [of differentials] was under way well before the most recent incomes policies, so that the explanation of this significant development must be sought elsewhere.'[9] Another study found that the narrowing of differentials had occurred because of rapid inflation and equal pay legislation. A National Institute study of 1978 concluded that, 'we can find little evidence, apart from the highest income groups, that there has been a strong compression of pay brought about directly by incomes policies.'[10] A 1976 study came to the surprising conclusion that after the policies of 1972–4 the restoration of free collective bargaining reduced differentials further instead of returning them to their pre-policy level.[11] The problem of low pay and the poverty trap on this evidence is not likely to be solved through the marginal changes that a pay policy can make, but will require major reforms of the taxation and benefits system and a resolute commitment to redistributive patterns within such reforms.

It is also arguable that all policies have failed to limit wages in the long term, because catching up takes place after the end of a policy. A recent major study concluded that, 'whilst some incomes policies have reduced the rate of wage inflation during the period in which they operated, this reduction has only been temporary. Wage increases in the period immediately following the ending of the policies were higher than they would otherwise have been, and these increases match losses incurred during the operation of the incomes policy.'[12] And a series of econometric tests carried out by the Department of Employment for the period 1951–69 found that the 1965 Labour policy had some effect in its first two years, but that in the next two years pay rose by about the same amount that it would have done without the policy.[13] Some people would argue, however, that anything can be proved with econometrics, and the 1967 devaluation, which allowed inflation to be 'imported', may have affected the econometric model used. The net effect of incomes policy in the 1960s was merely to alter the timing of the onset of inflation, though it should not be forgotten that in some circumstances such an influence can be very important, as it was after the 1973 oil price rise. Overall, it has been claimed that the effects of all the policies up to 1972 had been 'derisory' and that 'incomes policies have repeatedly failed to achieve any of their . . . stated objectives'.[14]

The first major issue to resolve in the 1980s is the extent to which any prices and incomes policy, as opposed to general tax and social security policy, should contribute to a redistribution of income. There is a strong case, in the light of the evidence, for leaving redistribution to tax and social security policy. Only if the economic circumstances were so bad that incomes needed to fall in real terms would there be a case for attempting a redistributive formula, and even then there are grounds for believing that the tax and social security system is a better vehicle for protecting the low paid. The redistributive argument is often used to justify an incomes policy, but there is very little hard evidence for the assertion that free collective bargaining itself produces low pay. It is impossible to ignore the record of the Wages Council in perpetuating low pay, or the appalling situation of the unskilled employees of central and local government. In equity there is a strong case for a formula that seeks to allocate more to the lowest paid than the market economy will allow, but this needs to be negotiated since it will be resisted if it is imposed, and will eventually undermine the other more worthwhile benefits of an agreed pay policy. Statutory minimum wage legislation phased in, as was done for equal pay, may help, and could be imposed, but the difficulties are considerable.

One of the keys to developing an agreed long term incomes policy is to accept that a greater measure of decentralization is inevitable and that past failures have been due to excessive centralization. The issue underlying the centralized or decentralized argument is very basic: should wages relate to the task the employee does or to the ability of the employer to pay? In theory, the most socialist wages policy and the one which should lead to a more equal wage distribution is one which relates to the nature of the work. This pattern could emerge in centrally controlled economies and broadly does, even though they also retain very considerable pay differentials. But in a mixed economy the issue is far more complicated. If the profitable company which can easily pay more has its wage levels controlled or influenced to a level below that which it could pay, it merely increases its profitability. As a consequence, those who want free collective bargaining point to the inconsistencies of interference in wages. The centralized Left, who most frequently argue for no interference, often square their socialist conscience by saying that until the state owns all the means of production there is no alternative to playing the market game. Although this position is escapist and patently absurd, it is nevertheless used to counter the charge that there is nothing socialist about free collective bargaining. The danger of the centralized approach to all these issues is that its very strength – its across-the-board nature, its apparent fairness, its ease of implementation – contains the seeds of its own destruction: an inability to discriminate and adapt flexibly to circumstances, the creation of anomalies, and the possibility of circumvention which will threaten its overall credibility.

The question of how to handle profits during a period of incomes restraint is a substantive issue. So far the only way it has been tackled is by calls for dividend restraint – which only postpones an eventual pay-out to shareholders. It is interesting how, in the commercial state industries, wage claims are increasingly related to arguments about profitability, rather than forcusing on the nature of the task. Trade unionists are often the strongest advocates of nationalized industries adopting a pricing structure which produces profit, since it is easier for them to argue for higher wages against a profit than against a loss. One of the stresses to which the prices and incomes policies of 1975–9 eventually succumbed was the ability of many sections of the private sector to pay high wage claims and their readiness to do so either of their own volition or under industrial pressure. Ford was only the most publicized case, no doubt because it always comes early in the pay round, but also because the car industry is seen to be a pace-setter. Where were Ford's profits to go if not in wages or benefits to the Ford workers? How, if Ford could offer both to pay higher wages and to keep within the Prices Code, could one justify depriving Ford workers of the benefits of the company's commercial success? The same was also being argued for British Oxygen, for the oil tanker drivers, and many other private companies. This issue must be tackled as part of a credible long-term policy for prices and incomes.

There is also the vexed problem of productivity. If wage increases are related to productivity increases, or wages to levels of productivity, then one has the problem of high wages or big wage increases in sectors such as petrochemicals, where productivity is very high because the process is very capital intensive, or in sectors where increases in productivity can be very big because of technical progress. This can easily produce enormous discrepancies in the wages of people doing very similar kinds of jobs, dependent only on the area in which they work. Centrally imposed flat-rate or percentage increases may last a year or more at a time of economic crisis, but the real need is for a policy which operates before an economic crisis occurs, and stops the crisis from happening. The first essential in the private sector and in the public commercial sector, such as NEB companies and some industries like steel, shipbuilding and aerospace, must be a readiness by unions and employers to negotiate within the particular parameters of profit and productivity that relate to the specific firm. This will mean more realistic bargaining in some private sector industries than hitherto and a greater readiness by trade unions and employers to face up to market realities. Yet even if this is achieved and the average wage increase for the private sector does not put unit costs above what can be justified in the market place there is likely to be a very wide difference in wage increases. The evidence is that these wide differences add significantly to pressure for higher increases in other sectors where they cannot be so justified. So in countries like the Federal Republic of Germany and Austria, employers and trade unions have come together in a loose arrangement with the government to concert the general guidelines within which free collective bargaining will take place.

Such a concertation procedure accepts in very general terms that people are going to be paid for what they do and that the profitability or losses of the company will determine wage levels, but argues that a nationally-agreed margin for manoeuvre in wage bargaining helps control national inflation. It could be linked to a vetting and scrutiny procedure similar to that operated for productivity deals at one stage by the Prices and Incomes Board. Yet some firms' profitability will allow for wage increases considerably in excess of the agreed margin for manoeuvre. If the firm pays up, the national margin is widened and a drift upwards in wage levels will soon follow. The value of concerting nationally is that it is a way of neutralizing or dampening down this otherwise very wide margin of wage negotiations.

Yet some way is needed of ensuring that the worker in the profitable concern shares in its success, and sees any excess profits used creatively and constructively for the good of the firm, and its future work prospects as well as improving working conditions and fringe benefits. It is here that a measure of genuine industrial democracy is so crucial, so that the workpeople are involved in decisions about the reinvestment of wage increases foregone because of national wage guidelines. This is much more realistic than a national investment fund which would be remote from the workers on a particular shop floor. Trade unionists cannot be expected to support a wages policy if they feel that their restraint simply provides higher dividends for shareholders. Unless they see a wages policy in the broad framework of an acceptable industrial and social policy for their particular workplace, not just for the nation as a whole, they will act as exploiters of market forces. It has been a major failure in all prices and incomes policies that have ever operated in the UK that they have not really grappled with this problem. To last, any incomes policy must relate to the individual and the individual firm; it must cover investment in the particular industry and the effect on jobs and conditions of service for employees. The government may decide to intervene to control key prices as part of their contribution to creating the climate for concertation, but the distortion effect on the market needs to be carefully weighed and the extent and scope of the intervention must be agreed as part of the concertation process. Past national prices policies, like incomes policies, have been far too centralized. An overall percentage price ceiling can result in bankruptcies or lack of investment, particularly when world commodity prices are rising fast. The powers and structure of the Price Commission as they stood in 1979 were a better compromise with all the conflicting pressures.

The hardest question, particularly for those who wish to rely on a voluntary policy, is the extent to which sanctions should be used. Arbitrary power is disliked and if any sanctions are to be used for any period, then some form of appeal machinery is essential. But it is necessary to be able to challenge price increases or dividend distribution by a company which has exceeded a pay ceiling voluntarily agreed by unions and management, even where the particular company was not directly party to the agreement. Similarly, the government's role as purchaser should be able to take account of breaches of the pay guideline. It can be argued that these are not statutory sanctions in the conventional sense; but the devotees of free collective bargaining on the Left and Right oppose them, seeing a precedent for introducing statutory wage curbs on employees: if there cannot be agreement, then the case for statutory control may have to be faced. Recent Labour governments have been virtually committed to never introducing a statutory policy, which has the effect of gravely weakening their bargaining power in trying to establish a voluntary policy. Yet it is hard to see why parliament should not intervene if negotiations fail; democratic imposition is far preferable to the arbitrary use of executive power for which there is no formal legislative authority. But voluntary agreement, such as has been negotiated in Austria and the Federal Republic of Germany, is far preferable.

The dilemma in those parts of the public sector that are financed by consumers through price tariffs is well illustrated in the understandable wish of gas workers to benefit from the huge profits of their industry, and by the water workers who want to be compared with those key public service supply workers in the gas and electricity industries. Yet to what extent can we accept ability to pay as the only criterion that should dictate wage levels? How do we compare gas workers' wages with those of the miners, traditionally high industrial earners? Society needs both gas and coal, and the profitability of the industries depends on accounting conventions, subsidy policies and other factors in a managed energy market – to say nothing of decisions made by the OPEC cartel – as well as on efficiency and productivity. The tripartite structure of government, National Coal Board and mining unions being involved in a planning agreement forum, where wages are discussed but not negotiated, along with investment and conditions of work, is a good augury for the future and a valuable manifestation of industrial democracy where the particular unions do not wish to be represented formally on the National Coal Board.

If a margin for manoeuvre in the consultation process for the private sector is inevitable, why, it will be argued, should this not cover the public sector as well? It probably can cover the price-linked public sector, but in the purely public service sector, where the service is financed by central taxation or rates, free collective bargaining cannot involve arguments relating to profitability, and here even productivity is hard to assess. Comparability in the public service sector means a guarantee that the public service employee will not fall behind the movement in earnings in the private sector and the commercial public sector. Provided it is honestly and objectively applied and takes account of such factors as fringe benefits, it should not lead to the leap frogging and inflationary pressure that it has generated in the past. The plethora of public sector pay arrangements that have operated in the past cannot continue. The Armed Forces Pay Review Body, Doctors and Dentists Review Body, Top Salaries Review Body, Civil Service Pay Research

Unit, and other ad hoc bodies – all need to be brought together into a single Comparability Commission. Without such a safety valve, workers in areas where profits are not measurable will seek to demonstrate their indispensability by industrial action, as health and local government employees did in 1979 and civil servants did in 1981 following the unilateral suspension by the government of their agreed arbitration procedures.

A prices, investment and incomes policy must not be asked to bear the strain of acting as short-term manipulator of the economy, for this will discredit it in the long term. It needs to start out with the objective of being sustainable over the minimum time scale of a four to five year parliament. This requires a new understanding of the limitations as well as the potential of such policies. It means that trade unionists in the private sector must have access to a level of information about profitability and investment that is not at present widely available, and that collective bargaining must take place in a wider context of the firm's future than at present. This will benefit from the introduction of industrial democracy, in the context of which it should be possible to achieve a trade union commitment to concertation and to establishing national wage guidelines. Trade unions in the public services would have to represent their members' interests less in direct negotiation with employers and more in marshalling their evidence to a Comparability Commission. The safeguard that they would be able to offer their members is that their incomes would move with the overall movement of incomes and be directly influenced by free collective bargaining in the private sector. In 1979 the public sector trade unions thought their interests were best served by breaking free from an incomes policy which at least attempted to cover both public and private sectors. In 1980 after a year of free-for-all the government began to apply a purely public sector pay policy. Again, as in 1962, a Conservative government was attempting to operate a discriminatory incomes policy, with restraint in the public sector. But all past experience shows that the social price of this type of incomes policy is a growing discontent as the public sector falls behind the private, and that such a one-sided policy is no longer compatible with the industrial strength of the public services, whose power to disrupt society is now very strong. One of the tragedies of the 1979 'winter of discontent' was that the establishment, in the Clegg Commission, of comparability machinery for the public sector, which was eventually the basis for a return to work, had actually been offered to the relevant trade unions by the government in the November 1978 renegotiated package.

Public service trade unions do not share the view of many commentators that the Clegg Commission gave inflationary awards; in some sectors they felt the awards were not generous enough, and they are becoming more hostile to the concept of comparability. True comparability will allow both private and public sector working conditions and fringe benefits to be compared. If any of these are improved by negotiation, with profitable companies coming up against the ceiling of any overall nationally-agreed margin for manoeuvre over incomes, then this will be taken into account and reflected back in public sector wage awards, but where public sector conditions and fringe benefits are in advance of those of the comparable private sector they will not be able to obtain much improvement. Such a combination of bargaining within agreed limits for the private sector and comparability for the public sector based on realistic criteria reflects the pattern, if not the exact formulation, that was emerging by November 1978. The government was then within a hair's-breadth of agreeing the crucial fourth year for a flexible prices and incomes policy. The offer was of comparability for the public sector, an extra weighting for the low paid and flexible arrangements to cover productivity, skill shortages and other marginal improvements. The offer was not 5 per cent, but between 8 and 9 per cent, which with drift would have had an out-turn nearer 12 per cent. Inflation was 8 per cent when, in October 1978, negotiations restarted over the 5 per cent limit which had been rejected by the TUC and Labour Party Conference. The renegotiated package, itself the result of a three-year learning process, was lost by one vote in the TUC General Council on 14 November 1978. Yet even had it been won by one vote, the crucial will to make an agreement stick was missing. The two key figures in the trade union movement who had helped to make the 1975 agreement work, Jack Jones and Huge Scanlon, were retiring and it was the public service unions, like NUPE, that were setting the pace. By 1981 most trade union leaders knew that failure to reach agreement in 1978 had worked against the interests of their members. The Conservative government in 1980–1 imposed a pay policy for the public sector, which was designed to cut living standards, and relied on unemployment and recession to moderate wage claims in the public sector.

The arbitrary nature of the decisions, the unfairness, bitterness, and disruption in the public sector demonstrate yet again all the problems of abandoning the search for an incomes policy. A clear commitment by all political parties to try to establish an agreed framework is urgently needed: 'It is not only that each party in turn has abolished the institutions of its predecessor, so that none of the bodies set up during the past two decades – the National Incomes Commission, the National Board for Prices and Incomes, or the Pay Board – had a chance to establish itself. In addition, each party in turn has changed sides on this matter, opposing income policy when out of power and adopting it when in power.'[15]

A new policy will require a more realistic and specific framework than previous generalized social contract agreements. It must accept that the pace of wage movements cannot be fixed centrally, but must reflect, at least initially, market realities in the private sector and a disaggregated wage bargaining pattern. It will also need to be concerned with prices and dividends, with limits being agreed with the consent of the trade unions and employers' organizations. A one-sided bargain which limited only wages and not other sources of income would be seen as unfair and merely as a way of forcing one group to bear the brunt of the struggle against inflation. In accepting that past prices policies have been over-centralized, based on either a freeze or an inflexible set of criteria for price rises, it must be recognized that a flexible price policy needs to be supplemented by a competition policy which limits the powers of monopolies to pass on price rises to a captive market. The virtual absence of serious anti-trust and monopoly legislation in Britain is in marked contrast to the powers that exist and are being extended in the USA and that were introduced by a social democratic government in Sweden.

Any incomes policy should also be supplemented by an active employment and rehousing policy to enable the labour market to work more efficiently. For instance, skill shortages in certain areas of the country have been responsible for bidding up wages, while unemployed labour with suitable skills has existed in other areas. If in this process other occupations demand wage rises to maintain some past pay relationship, then general inflation occurs, relative wages do not change rapidly and shortages of labour tend to persist.

A decentralized incomes policy cannot be expected to halt wage inflation in its tracks, since it would not attempt to freeze wages or rigidly to contain all wage rises within a certain percentage figure. However, it would offer a better chance of eventually keeping inflation under control than would a series of ad hoc, centralized policies that eventually collapse and allow inflation to rise again until other draconian measures are adopted. And it should reduce the need for trade unions to demand large rises to compensate for inflation in advance, which has contributed to previous inflationary spirals.

A decentralized policy that relies on a mixture of market forces, controls and comparability should be able to be maintained by successive governments of whatever party. A Left government's approach would temper market forces and agree social goals with the trade unions, in the realization that the pure free market alternative was likely to protect against both inflation and unemployment. A Right government would by contrast place a greater faith in the working of market forces and give less weight to the trade unions, hoping that market disciplines would prevail and would tolerate higher levels of unemployment. Yet all governments would at least be rejecting the stop-go policies of the past and recognizing that curing inflation by deflation has serious medium-term effects which in their turn have dangerous implications for our longer-term industrial strength.

Deflation brought inflation down from its 1980 peak of nearly 22 per cent but large firms that were semi-monopolists were able to pass on higher wage costs, whereas small firms who could not were then pressed by large firms for payment, with the alternative of bankruptcy. Large firms also secured loans at more favourable rates than small firms, so that the credit squeeze was not impartial in its effects. Most companies reduced investment before they laid off workers or refused to pay wage claims, since they were generally reluctant to interrupt production as a result of a strike, knowing that they could lose markets and that their extra capacity would no longer be needed. Making workers unemployed hitherto has been an option that tended to be considered only as a last resort: most firms conceded wage demands before laying off skilled workers since they knew that there would be difficulties in recruiting those workers back once the economy picked up. But as the economic prospects in the 1980s worsen more firms will be ready to shed labour.

The economy is dominated by large firms able to secure finance from banks, to finance claims themselves, or to pass on cost increases. It is uncertain whether the 1980s free-market squeeze will bring inflation down below that of our major industrial competitors; but the medium-term effects on unemployment and some industries have been drastic. The challenge for Social Democrats is neither to ignore the lessons of successive governments nor to reject the need for an incomes policy. What must be developed is a policy for incomes, investment, prices, profit and productivity which is geared to the actual working of a mixed economy and realistic enough to be sustainable over a number of years.

7

INDUSTRIAL DEMOCRACY

Industrial democracy must be an essential element in any serious attempt to move towards a more decentralized democratic society. It is not surprising, therefore, that it was the ideal of workers' control that lay behind much of the debate between socialist centralists and the decentralists before the First World War, an argument which was briefly traced in Chapter 2 on the Decentralist Tradition. Nor is it anything other than inevitable that if the growing corporatism and its manifestations are rejected (see Chapter 3), the natural replacement of corporatism will be a revival of the power of parliamentary democracy and the extension of democracy into the place of work.

Centralism and corporation flourish on the mix of an Executive unchecked by Members of Parliament, on employers' organizations unable to reflect the specific views of individual companies, and trade union leaders unable fully to reflect the differing shades of the wide spectrum of views within very different unions. The arguments against corporatism do not seek to undermine 'tripartism' and the considerable value of management, unions and government reaching agreements and understandings. For industrial democracy itself is concerned with the means whereby such agreement and understanding can be reached at different levels, affecting people's working life, embracing far more than wages or salaries, or even pension or sickness benefits or health and safety arrangements. It covers the range of issues which affect the running of the country's economic and industrial affairs and the decisions of individual companies on their own economic and industrial activity. It is a considerable extension of the process of free collective bargaining, but complementary to it. Industrial democracy also seeks to do more than merely widen the subjects of discussion between management and workers, since its aim is to increase participation as of right by the workforce at all levels. Democracy means the number of workers having a say in decisions that affect them being greatly increased

and the process of decision-making being seen to be openly democratic with the widespread use of secret ballots.

To be effective and radical industrial democracy needs to do much
more than transfer power from managers to trade union officials or
shop stewards. To succeed it needs to involve individual workers on
a wide range of issues. It will be argued that this carries a cost in
terms of money and slower decision-making. Some have attempted
to quantify this, citing the Works Council and Co-Determination
Laws in West Germany. But what also carries a cost is industrial
disputes, avoidable alienation, and poor productivity stemming
from boredom and lack of interest. By relying on agreement through
open democratic procedures or openly agreed arbitration, industrial
democracy represents consensus in the sense that democracy itself is
in part a consensual process. But the essence of democracy is that
it allows the majority view to prevail, so that industrial democracy
does not have the limitations imposed by consensus arrangements,
whereby everyone has to agree and where unrepresentative minority viewpoints can inhibit agreement, or when industrial action
cannot be taken until there is an agreement. Balloting the workforce
allows for a decisive decision to be taken in circumstances where the
minority finds it acceptable to go along with the view of the
majority.

The Bullock Report found widespread recognition for what the
European Community Green Paper called a 'democratic imperative'
that 'those who will be substantially affected by decisions made by
social and political institutions must be involved in the making of
those decisions.'[1] The Report found that in the last twenty years
giant industrial enterprises have come to predominate, placing
economic power in fewer hands and resulting in decision-making
becoming increasingly remote from the people who will be affected
by the decisions. The pace of change has also accelerated with the
introduction of new technologies. In increasingly competitive world
markets, managers have found that they need to be responsive to
change if they are to survive. Such changes have been frequently
resisted by employees and it is now more widely recognized that not
only have employees a legitimate right to be involved in the taking
of decisions which vitally affect the continued existence of their jobs,
but that if they are not involved their resistance to change is
invariably greater. The ailing economy of Britain has often been
compared unfavourably with the growth record of the German
economy and it has been asked whether the existence of forms of
industrial democracy in West Germany has contributed to its

success. It would be unwise to attribute too much to the existence of varying manifestations of industrial democracy there, but some significance should be attached to their contribution. The West German system, dating from 1950–1, has meant good industrial relations and a strong realization of commercial realities by trade unionists, of the importance of maintaining existing markets and winning new orders.

Rising standards of education and a higher standard of living have produced less deferential workers who are unwilling to tolerate old-fashioned autocratic management methods and who feel able to participate in making decisions. Management has also realized that such workers can make a very real contribution if their energy and experience is harnessed to constructive ends. In a letter to his managing directors Sir Arnold Weinstock of GEC, where management techniques are controversial though arguably successful, admitted that 'if the skills, experience and intelligence of workers can be harnessed constructively in the operation of industry, if the attitudes of management and workers can be brought together in effective co-operation, then there would follow a great upsurge in industrial efficiency and a general atmosphere of relative satisfaction.'[2]

The argument is over how best such a harnessing can be achieved. GEC does not support legislation imposing industrial democracy but favours informational exchange. Yet it has been widely recognized by many managers in British industry that some form of industrial democracy will bring substantial benefits to all concerned. For the Social Democrat the additional attraction is that industrial democracy is an end in itself; the making accountable of concentrations of economic power, whether that power is found in the public or the private sectors. The fundamental question is the method to be used to introduce industrial democracy – persuasion or legislation.

The revival of interest in industrial democracy began in the 1960s; in part it reflected the direct outcome of frustrations felt by many trade unionists at the workings of various prices and incomes policies. This in turn highlighted the limitations of narrowly circumscribing the range issues to be included in collective discussions and agreements. Yet despite various working party reports, the Labour Party's commitment in the October 1974 Election Manifesto was general: 'to introduce new legislation to help forward our plans for a radical extension of industrial democracy in both the private and public sectors.' There was no commitment to single-channel representation. No action was taken by the Labour government until it was forced to do so by the success of a Private Member's Bill sponsored by Giles Radice in 1975, providing for workers' representation. The result was the by now traditional response of all governments to radical change, to set up a Committee of Enquiry. Those who believed that industrial democracy must be introduced on the basis of trade union representation fought hard for terms of reference which would not allow the Committee to re-open what they saw as being essentially political decisions. After a Cabinet struggle they eventually did succeed in ensuring that their views were covered in the words of the terms of reference: 'Accepting the need for a radical extension of industrial democracy in the control of companies by means of representation on boards of directors, and accepting the essential role of trade union organizations in this process.'

Under the Chairmanship of Lord Bullock the Committee reported quickly and presented their report[3] in January 1977, a few months before the Labour government, in order to maintain a reasonably stable parliamentary majority, entered into an arrangement with the Liberal Party. The majority within the Committee proposed that its worker director system should apply to groups of companies and subsidiaries with 2,000 and more employees. A $2x + y$ formula would mean that shareholders and employee representatives would have equal representation and the two groups would jointly choose the 'y' group which would be an odd number smaller than 'x'. The shareholders and employee representatives would have equal rights and duties and would not be mandated delegates of their constituents. Shareholders would be left with a right to veto crucial matters such as acquisitions and sales of assets, although in future takeovers would not be allowed without the consent of the board being taken over. Employee representatives would be chosen by a method determined by a new body called a Joint Representation Committee (JRC). A union-run ballot of all employees would be held to determine whether worker directors were wanted and the scheme would only go ahead if there was a majority in favour and the vote in favour was that of more than one-third of the full-time workforce. All the unions recognized in the company would set up a JRC which would then decide how the worker directors would be chosen.

The Bullock Report was met with well-orchestrated hostility by the Confederation of British Industry. Some of it was genuine, but there was also a strong political element. The CBI, sensing an early election, was becoming daily more politicized and more closely identified than for some time with the Conservative Party. The trade unions were also shown to be split in their attitude, reflecting all their historic ambivalence over the issue. The Liberal Party was not prepared to support many of the Report's key recommendations in relation to the role of the trade unions. To have attempted to implement the Bullock Report immediately would have brought certain humiliating parliamentary defeat on the Second Reading. The Labour government responded instead by trying to achieve a sufficient measure of agreement to be able to legislate by the next year. The majority of the Cabinet, however, realized that even if the proposals were supported by parliament, legislation would need to be able to command far more widespread support in industry than was possible if the government stuck rigidly to the majority view in the Bullock Report. The suggested y component was not supported by German experience, and many were rightly sceptical of giving a decisive voice in any situation of conflicting views to the least knowledgeable and least committed members of the Board.

The Labour government's White Paper published in May 1978[4] satisfied few people, mainly because the political climate of opinion was by then heightened as an election grew closer. Differences of view in the Cabinet were covered in the White Paper by setting out both sides of the arguments on key controversial issues and avoiding reaching a firm conclusion. It proposed that the law should require employers in companies employing more than 500 people to discuss company strategy. Members of the Joint Representation Committee, JRC, under these proposals were to be given the statutory fall-back right to require the board to discuss company strategy. Members of the JRC would consist of employees of the company broadly representative of the independent trade unions in the company. If any trade union considered that the composition of the JRC was inequitable then it could appeal either to the existing Advisory Conciliation and Arbitration Service, ACAS, or to an Industrial Democracy Commission, IDC, if such a new body were to be established. The statutory obligation was to cover all major decisions affecting employees of the business before decisions were made over investment plans, mergers, takeovers, expansion or contraction of establishment and all major organizational changes. This would need a Code of Practice. If the JRC was dissatisfied by the company's failure to fulfil its obligations they were to have the right to appeal, and the suggested way of dealing with this was to use an existing body, the Central Arbitration Committee, CAS, which already had powers concerning complaints about failure to disclose information for collective bargaining purposes.

This part of the legislation was not as controversial. Much of the information, if made available to government, could have also provided the data necessary for the development of more systematic national planning. The case for reducing the number of employees from 500 to 100 for firms required to discuss company strategy is strong. Initially 500 was chosen to avoid putting a burden on small firms. But that argument is dangerous for it accepts that industrial democracy does not give a return to the employer as well as to the employees. Also 500 is a large company in many towns and cities and there is a need to involve many more smaller companies particularly in the range with 200–300 employees. Concentrating first on the statutory revealing of information and providing for discussion of company strategy, was deliberate in the hope that progress would be achieved by agreement in this area and that gradually the best existing industrial relations practice would become universal and that the worker director issue could be dealt with in a less political climate of opinion. The 1978 White Paper dealt with the worker director issue by proposing a statutory right to have representatives on the board in companies employing 2,000 or more in the UK. The statutory right was to be exercised as over company strategy by the JRC after a ballot of all the company's employees. It was proposed, however, in part to show an evolutionary approach, that a period of three to four years from the date of establishment of the JRC would elapse before the statutory right to board-level representation came into operation. This was also done because of the unresolved controversy about the single channel, not so vital in terms of discussion of company strategy, but an issue of more fundamental importance in terms of board representation.

It needs to be asked why such an obvious extension of democracy has had to wait such a long time to be implemented in Britain although it is common in other countries. An answer is that 'History suggests that movements for industrial democracy well up every so often, only to founder on the four rocks of conceptual ambiguity, trade union and official Labour ambivalence, employer hostility and rank and file apathy. Add to that unpredictable changes in the economic weather (pushing the issue down the list of priorities) and in the political climate (changes of government) and you have a recipe for repeated shipwrecks.'[5] It is hard to fault this perceptive and succinct summary. Industrial democracy will be shipwrecked again if there is not a better understanding among its proponents about the overriding need to legislate for the basic right and then let the schemes develop at differing speeds and in different ways.

Democracy is an evolutionary process. A legislative framework can provide the right to participate but cannot provide the will. There must be a freedom for the workpeople most concerned to choose at all stages what, if any, pattern of industrial democracy is to apply in their place of work. It is because trade union leaders' voices favouring a rigid all-or-nothing trade union dominated solution have been loudest and have been listened to that progress has been negligible. It is perfectly understandable that they should have sought to enshrine in legislation the trade union movement's natural desire for predominance and that they have not been content for this position of predominance to emerge as an inevitable development. This insistence on what has been called the 'single channel' approach, whereby trade unionists alone would elect their repre- sentatives, underplays the fact that in the vast majority of cases the trade union voice would win acceptance as spokesman, and in only a very few situations would a workforce as a whole demonstrate its independence of the trade unions. The issue has been elevated to one of principle by powerful voices in the trade union movement. The effect has been to ensure that the introduction of industrial democracy has been dominated by an argument about the role and power of trade unions rather than by the issue of the rights and powers in a democracy of every individual at his or her place of work. Public sympathy which could perhaps have been won for the essentials of industrial democracy will not so readily be engaged for what is presented by the opponents of industrial democracy as a further entrenchment of the power of trade unions.

An extraordinary paradox is that in the main those trade unionists most in favour of free collective bargaining and who reject industrial relations legislation have been those most keen to advocate a pattern of industrial democracy by legislation which could not be either collectively negotiated or even tolerated by most employers. It is a position as illogical as it is paradoxical. The fact that the argument that industrial relations legislation is essential to reform the working of the trade unions is not advocated as part of the democratic reforms discussed in this and other chapters is not because the case has not been carefully considered: few subjects have been more discussed and have taken up more legislative time in parliament since 1966. It is because after weighing the evidence and taking account of past experience it is felt that the gains from any such legislation would be slight. A Social Democratic government would find that its influence with the trade unions even while legislating for industrial democracy would be reduced if it introduced industrial

relations legislation, any gains being far outweighed by the disadvantages of a period of severely strained political relations.

It may be that some parts of the 1980 legislative package on
industrial relations will be proved by experience to have merit. The
proposals to encourage trade union balloting are certainly right, but
they would have been likely to have commanded more support if
they had been part of separate legislation to encourage balloting for
all democratic organizations, whether political, trade union or
charitable. After the self-inflicted though nevertheless real trauma
that followed the argument and discussion over the fairly mild
proposals envisaged by the Labour government in 1978 in the
publication of *In Place of Strife*,[6] any socialist politician will hesitate
before embarking on a similar course. The evidence is that a
reforming government can achieve far more by persuasion than by
legislation. The case for industrial relations legislation has always
suffered from the grossly exaggerated claims that have been made
about its proposed benefits. Few would deny that at times the
bargaining power of trade unions has been used irresponsibly and
that at times it has fed inflationary pressures. But the damage has
often arisen from trade union weakness and that is as much the
responsibility or fault of employers whether in the private or public
sector, as of the workers. Legislation will not of itself provide
employers with resolve, nor can it do much to alter the balance of
power, except in the case of mass picketing which has recently
emerged as an area needing control. The organization and coverage
of secondary picketing has admittedly become far more effective and
this has changed the balance of power to strengthen forces outside
the particular company, but it is still an open question as to whether
persuading the TUC to wield its influence on the basis of agreed
Codes of Conduct, which will obviously at various times be ignored,
will not prove to be more effective in the longer term than the
legislation introduced in 1980.

The broad general principle which argues that legislation for
human behaviour has severe limitations and needs to be applied
sparingly and with sensitivity has considerable weight. Yet if one
accepts these arguments and supports the cogent case put forward
in the Donovan Report on trade unions, it is impossible to justify
imposing a form of industrial democracy favoured by some trade
union leaders against the bitter resentment and hostility of employers. It is on issues like these, well demonstrated in the arguments over the effects of the 1975 trade union legislation on the
freedom of the press that any politician faces a dilemma between his

or her commitment to democratic liberties and the commitment to and support for the important interests of trade unionism. The trade union interest – wholly legitimately upheld by socialists in keeping with their recognition of the values of collective action – is nevertheless a sectional interest. There is no justification for allowing this interest to override the fundamental wider democratic interest of putting first the maintenance of an individual's liberty, where it does not critically affect the liberty of others, and this is what underlies the controversy over single channel representation.

The trade union movement expressed its views in a letter to the government in 1977 from the General Secretary of the TUC stating, 'The single channel of trade union representation is a central principle of the trade union movement . . . any statutory expression of collective rights must be related to the trade union movement if it is to lead to stable industrial relationships and is to be compatible with collective bargaining arrangement.' It is, however, for parliament to determine the balance of democratic rights for the citizen, not for the trade unions or for employers' organizations. Any democrat wisely accepts that legislation in this field must be related to the trade unions' concerns and to managers' concerns too, but above all it must be related to the rights of the individual citizen. In practice the trade unions will be the channel for representation in almost all cases and their nominee will be accepted by the workforce balloting in secret, and so the controversy tends to exaggerate the practical significance of the issue. Democracy hinges on principle and the arguments of principle on this issue are strong, correct, and cannot be dismissed on grounds of convenience or practicality.

The 1978 White Paper stated the problem rather than offering a solution, saying, 'there is a clear dilemma. One view is that industrial democracy should mean that every employee has a right to be directly involved in selecting representatives on the board. The other view is that any arrangement should be consistent with the established system of collective representation of employees in British industry.' In the co-operative movement democratic involvement of all members is the essential principle and in some trade unions this is becoming accepted practice. The member states of the European Community would never accept single channel representation and the trade unions in the member states would regard it as undemocratic. The sooner British trade unions accept this too, the easier it will be to make progress.

Trade unions cannot insulate themselves from the underlying movement within the country for democratic participation. Their resistance to balloting must be overcome and it is no part of socialism to identify itself as reluctantly democratic – preaching democracy on the basis of one person, one vote everywhere except within the Labour Party and the trade unions. In most large factories and enterprises there already exists a closed shop that is recognized by the workers and management as rightfully existing. In such cases the trade union machinery will be used for the election of its nominees as worker directors but a secret ballot of the workforce is the only way to safeguard the rights of individuals to reject the trade union nominee. Trade unionists individually have rights that have to be weighed with the right of trade unions as organizations. Where the unions are strong the trade unions are likely to resent any by-passing of their industrial relations' machinery and the system could lose the benefit of having the unions working together in the Joint Representation Committee. In the interests of industrial harmony it is also unlikely that many managers would wish to see the established forms of industrial relations upset by new structures. It is therefore extremely unlikely that there would be any wish on the part of the JRC to exercise their statutory rights to call for board representation if they felt it would provoke a challenge to the position of the trade unions. 'The JRC would have the right to determine how the employee seats on the board should be filled, but if any trade union considered that the methods or results of the system proposed was inequitable it could appeal to the IDC/ACAS. The IDC/ACAS could delay the implementation of the scheme until it was satisfied of its fairness, but could not impose a solution.'[7] In effect, no scheme for board representation could be introduced without either the agreement of the trade unions in the firm or the approval of an independent body if appealed to by a dissatisfied trade union, or any substantial homogeneous group of employees. The concept of the group is necessary to guard against the vexatious or mavericks.

It is not sufficient to confine the right to appeal to an individual union. This right for a group of employees will be controversial though very rarely exercised, but if the legislation is not to offend basic concepts of democratic rights, then it must make specific provision for a right of appeal to be extended to a substantial homogeneous group of employees. This is in Britain the price that has to be paid by the trade unions if parliament decided to introduce legislation for industrial democracy. The statute should set out the criteria by which any appeal would be judged. These could cover the geographical and occupational distribution of employees in the company; and in the event of successful appeal there could also be a requirement for elections based on nominations of candidates by trade unions and by groups of at least 100 employees, whether or not they are members of trade unions. Given a firm legislative commitment on these lines it would be hard for even its more vehement critics to challenge the democratic basis of the proposals, though such a compromise would be a particularly difficult one for many trade unions.

The White Paper proposal of waiting three to four years for implementation of board representation meant that any legislation would not achieve board representation within the lifetime of one parliament. Delay as a tactical judgement was understandable in 1978, for any legislation would have been coming at the tail end of the parliament.

Industrial democracy legislation to succeed should be given the highest legislative priority and introduced in the first session of a new parliament. It could then be timetabled so that within the first year of enactment JRCs should have been established, and where they invoked their statutory right, an agreed procedure for the discussion of company strategy would have been started. Within the second year of enactment board level representation should be established where the JRCs invoked their statutory right. This would then normally mean the new legislation would be fully operating within three years of the general election. This would be a very tight timetable, and given the considerable resistance to implementation that there would be within such a timetable, it would be wise to match it by taking some politically sensitive decisions to reduce the resistance from employers. There is a case for making changes in existing company law so that companies who wanted to do so could adopt the less controversial two-tier board structure with separate policy and management boards, and have their employee representatives serving on the policy board. It would be open to keep and appoint representatives to a unitary board. A policy board would, besides taking the major decisions in the company, also be responsible for promoting participation agreements throughout the Company. It would certainly be necessary to prohibit the mandating of employee representatives though encouraging them to keep in close touch with the employees and trade union.

It would also be wise to accept that parity of representation is too radical a change for the present. The 1978 White Paper proposed that while not ultimately excluding parity of representation on the board, the statutory obligation would initially be to appoint one-third of the members of the policy board. As in the case of the unitary board, companies would be free to appoint a higher proportion of employees to the board. Though there will be considerable reluctance to accept one-third initially, the trade unionists who have served already on boards such as the NEB and BNOC know that numbers on the board are not as crucial as the ability to influence, and that this depends on the quality not just the quantity of the workers' representatives. A board which was putting every issue to the vote would soon cease to contribute constructively in any area.

These proposals will need to be argued for with trade unionists, industrialists, and above all the general public, for they are likely to be resisted on a number of grounds. Critics from the left will argue that separating policy and management boards will result in all major decisions being taken by the management board, with the policy board and its worker directors being little more than a rubber stamp. To guard against this it would be useful for the worker directors and their fellow directors to agree in advance the precise division of decision-making between the two boards. The worker directors must have financial support to develop quickly sufficient expert advice and research facilities to be able to understand and influence decisions. Some industrialists hope that industrial democracy will fade away; other industrialists have always feared that trade union bargaining would be transferred from the shop floor into the boardroom and that this would inhibit discussion and the making of decisions which were in the long term interests of the company. This danger will be reduced if it is made clear that the worker directors are not delegates of their union or workforce, although there is a vital need for worker directors to keep their electorate informed of their participation. The worker directors may also find it difficult to endorse all the decisions of their board, though at times like any democratic leaders they will be in conflict with the workforce they are representing. There is a case for all directors being given the opportunity to indicate dissent from a decision in the minutes of the meetings. But the legislation will succeed or fail on whether worker directors contribute to changing attitudes on both the shop floor and within the boardroom.

Some will decry such a package of measures as too cautious, others as forcing the pace far too quickly. Britain will soon come under pressure from the European Community to implement some form of industrial democracy. The long discussed Statute for European Companies and the Fifth Directive cannot be ignored, even by a government hostile to the whole concept. Statutory provision for workers to participate in industrial decision-making already exists in four Community countries, the Netherlands, West Germany, Belgium and Denmark. It also exists in Norway, Sweden and Austria. It has become a necessary element in the efficient and acceptable working of the mixed economy. It is an issue on which the time is overdue for decision. Few can expect to achieve a package with which they will agree, but the essential is to move from discussion of theory to legislation and then from actual experience to build on practice and later to bring in further legislation. In the nationalized industries, following the same procedures, there is scope for quicker and bolder action, since trade union membership is widespread and the government has the role of shareholder being able to dismiss and appoint the chairman. Where it represents the wish of the workforce, which is clearly the case for Post Office workers though not for mineworkers, workers could be given 50 per cent representation on the main board. The chairman would in case of deadlock be the final decision-maker and the safeguarder of the public interest.

The ambivalence of central government and the hostility of local government have not helped the movement towards industrial democracy. There has been only half-hearted implementation in the nationalized industries, the best scheme being for the Post Office in 1977, now abandoned. The corporatist tendency on this issue, as on so many others, predominates. Ministers and civil servants have tended to use the accountability to parliament of nationalized industries as an argument against introducing industrial democracy. The alliance between the Executive and the Bureaucracy manifests itself in an ability to obfuscate the issue. Both perceive a mutual interest in obstructing and circumventing existing parliamentary control of their handling of the nationalized industries, but they unashamedly invoke the notion of parliamentary control to avoid any reductions in their own powers that they feel may well come from strong employee representation on the boards. Hitherto nationalized boards have operated under the weakness that as all are appointees of the government they have no independent status. Unless the public sector gives the right to its employees to participate fully on their boards, it will mean keeping them wholly dependent on Whitehall civil servants and Ministers. Industrial democracy in the public sector is a potentially liberating force. The accountability of Ministers responsible to parliament for the industries is not an adequate reason for resisting the appointment of worker directors. To have worker directors is a right to make the industries accountable to their workers and it must apply in logic to the public sector just as much as to the private sector. Ministers will rightly retain a substantial measure of control, in the public interest, by the ability to appoint half of the boards, other than the worker directors, and will expect the Chairman to hold the balance in favour of the wider interest of consumers or of national priorities within the existing framework of parliamentary accountability.

Worker directors do not seem likely in the civil service, with its advisory role reaching up to private offices of Ministers. In theory there is no reason why civil servants should be deprived of the right to participate in civil service management decision-making. It may be possible to identify policy relating to the civil service within the Civil Service Department itself and in other areas where the civil service fulfils some of the functions of boards of directors in industry. The Board of the Inland Revenue and the Property Services Agency are boards which could have worker directors on the same basis as in nationalized industries.

The greatest problem over worker directors is likely to be encountered in their extension to local government. In local councils it would be possible to identify policy relating to local government service matters where representatives of workers could be given a proportion of seats on the relevant committee, if not in the main council chamber. The traditions of local government, however, strongly favour consultation and not direct representation of their workforce, and given the need to preserve their own democratic autonomy it might be better to let them adopt their own procedures and to exclude them from mandatory legislation.

Legislation will benefit not just from the co-operation but also from the commitment of the trade union movement, where opinion is at present deeply divided. There are some enthusiastic supporters of industrial democracy, as there are for industrial co-operatives, yet some trade unionists are still suspicious of both concepts. The trade union leadership needs to rethink its attitudes fundamentally. It could find that industrial democracy offers a new positive role, not on the basis of automatic rights but on winning democratically through the ballot the right to speak for the workforce on issues far beyond the narrow confines of free collective bargaining. Legislation for industrial democracy may have to come against the resistance of the trade union movement's leaders, but its introduction could be as substantial an extension of democracy as the introduction of the universal franchise. It represents a fundamental and far reaching reform and a major challenge for Social Democrats, to act in the best interests of all the workforce and of the nation.

PART THREE

REPRESENTATIVE DEMOCRACY

8

PARLIAMENTARY GOVERNMENT

Looking at the development of parliamentary democracy over the last century it is hard to disagree with the judgement that, 'the House of Commons has steadily lost influence over the executive because of the increasing strength of the party system. In the nineteenth century, the House had dismissed governments without having to face a general election, it had sacked individual ministers and had introduced and carried bills against the government and had taken government measures and defeated or rewritten them.'[1] The size and scope of British government was relatively steady between 1790 and 1910 when parliament's power was greatest and the proportion of Gross National Product devoted to public expenditure each year averaged about 13 per cent. The growth of government has continued steadily since 1911, its expenditure never falling below 36 per cent of GNP since 1946. The numbers in government employment probably doubled between 1850 and 1890 at a time when the working population increased by around 40 per cent. Between 1890 and 1950 government employment increased by 1,000 per cent while the working population rose by 57 per cent. The proportion of the working population in government employment increased from 2.4 per cent in 1850 to 3.6 per cent in 1890 to 24.3 per cent in 1950.[2] The growth has accelerated very rapidly in the post-war years reaching 28.3 per cent of the workforce in 1979. Because of differing classifications it is hard to make an exact comparison with the pre-war years. Together with the increase in size of the civil service went an increase in its powers, a process encouraged by political leaders of both main parties. Ministers preferred to see the civil service hold the powers which they as Ministers could not hope to exercise physically, believing they could influence the use of those powers more easily than if they were passed to parliament.

In 1967 the Fulton Committee on the civil service was set up by a Labour government whose concern was not primarily the size or powers of the civil service but an anxiety that the generalist administrator was not able to deal with a technological society. The civil service was not then criticised as a political obstacle to the effective implementation of specifically socialist policies, but was seen rather as a technical obstacle to the technologically based policies of that government. Political criticism of the civil service began to increase after the 1970 election defeat. This criticism was triggered off by a series of published diaries and memoirs by former Ministers, revealing clashes of personality between themselves and their civil servants. The importance of Richard Crossman's diaries[3] was initially largely overshadowed by such titbits of personal information. In fact their real message is that Ministers confront an appallingly detailed workload and an amazing range of activity, and that the extent of ministerial discretion is matched only by the irrelevance of most of the supposed parliamentary controls on the Executive. It is an absurd distortion of reality that now depicts the wicked machinations of politically-motivated civil servants out to flout the direction of 'true socialism' as the reason for the failures of past Labour governments.

Some in the Labour Party now claim they want to ensure that, as they describe it, the whole Party takes power when Labour wins an election. This sounds superficially democratic and they argue that what they advocate is not contrary to parliamentary democracy and that what they are putting forward should not lead anyone to argue that their proposed system replaces parliamentary democracy. They are correct to refer to it as a system: it is a carefully constructed, interlocking arrangement. Abolition of the House of Lords, the unelected half of parliament; mandatory reselection, even of MPs whose constituency parties wish to retain them; every Labour MP to sign a pledge of support for the Manifesto; an electoral college to elect the Leader of the Party and sometimes the Prime Minister; the election of the Cabinet, as in Opposition when there are elections for the Parliamentary Committee by all MPs; minutes and votes of all meetings of the parliamentary Party to be published; and all with the aim of extending formal accountability to the movement as a whole for all decisions taken by MPs, with the implicit threat of reselection by the General Management Committee.

Similar changes to those advocated for parliamentary procedure are advocated to apply to local councillors. The objective is clear: to pressurize MPs and councillors, rather than to compel them – since this is known to be unacceptable – to bring them ever closer to becoming delegates of the Party. It is a far-reaching change which, it is claimed, is not designed to replace parliamentary or local government democracy; yet its effect would be that every time an MP or a councillor faced the choice whether to exercise his or her judgement or to follow the party line, the present balance – already weighted towards the Party – would be shifted even further. The scales would be tipped decisively to toeing the Party line. This is, of course, the object: delegated democracy would replace existing parliamentary and local democratic practice within the Labour Party.

Edmund Burke was right when he said, 'authoritative instructions, mandates issued, which the member is bound blindly and implicitly to obey, to vote and to argue for, though contrary to the clearest conviction of his judgement and conscience – these are things utterly unknown to the laws of this land and which arise from a fundamental mistake of the whole order and tenor of our Constitution.'[4] He also said, 'Parliament is a deliberative assembly of one nation with one interest, that of the whole, where not local purposes, not local prejudices, ought to guide, but the general good, resulting from the general reason of the whole. You choose a member indeed, but when you have chosen him, he is not a member of Bristol but he is a member of Parliament.' This is not an old-fashioned élitist concept, as is sometimes claimed. Any political party is itself an élite simply because its members are activists and skilled advocates of a particular set of policies. They are seen by the apolitical majority as a narrow and powerful clique. Taking account of active members of political parties in the constituencies, on a generous estimate, no more than 25,000 people are actively involved in politics in this country.

Judging the national interest is not a matter just for Party activists to determine. The wider electorate do not consider the notion of the national interest a narrow or old-fashioned concept. A radical change was made with the introduction of the referendum to determine the destiny of the country within or outside the European Community in 1975. It was designed on a divisive but vital issue to reach beyond party politics and to attempt to judge the national mood. The use of national referenda in Northern Ireland in 1972 and over devolution in 1979 was justified on the grounds that a constitutional change was being considered. The Left's hesitation to adopt referenda more widely reflects that on some issues, such as the abolition of the death penalty or trade union reform, a national referendum would produce results which they would not favour. In law, the use of referenda has not challenged parliamentary democracy to the extent that in all cases the referenda were explicitly

134 *Representative Democracy*

made dependent on parliament's final decision; and in fact, in the case of the referendum over Scottish devolution, parliament decided that an arithmetical majority on a low poll was insufficient to justify major constitutional change. Originally the referenda were portrayed as an extension of democratic choice, but from the beginning there were those who warned that their use would favour the conservative, no-change attitude in society and would reduce the ability of parliament to judge the national interest, sometimes against the trend of public opinion. Certainly the move towards referenda runs counter to the trend towards delegated democracy, though this has not prevented some socialists from advocating both, without an attempt to explain the contradictions. On constitutional issues referenda provide a protection against governments elected by a minority of the population forcing through fundamental legislation, and are therefore a safeguard; but they should be used sparingly for other political issues. They can only represent a snapshot of public opinion which changes rapidly on many subjects. On constitutional issues the knowledge that there has to be a referendum is a discipline for the government actively to seek out a consensus.

Another way of extending democracy is to give tenants greater participation and involvement in the running of their housing estates or blocks of flats. Greater participation and involvement of parents in the running of schools is another extension of democracy, yet both contain within them the seeds of conflict, either with the views of individual councillors or, even more, with the decisions of the Party caucus. But despite its limitations, and its possible use as a brake on radical reform, the referendum is a way of extending democracy, and its use in some States in America will doubtless increase and it may well be used on occasions by Local Authorities in the United Kingdom. But simultaneously to endorse the shift towards participatory democracy and delegated democracy, with all its authoritarian and even totalitarian overtones, is to move in opposite directions. It is a sad commentary on the present state of the Labour Party that that is exactly what it is doing, and few wish to face up to the contradiction.

Similarly, opposition to the use of secret ballots within organizations usually comes from ruling élites – who also oppose the release of information to allow for informed debate. A party which claims to be committed to an increase and extension of democratic decision-making should not resist any extension of democracy within its own ranks to give its own members the right to be involved in the taking of key decisions. This is the only legitimate way forward to extend the practice of political democracy: it is humbug to advocate greater democracy in a political party and yet to flinch from the really key reform of giving voting rights to every paid-up member of the Party. One member, one vote, should choose a Prime Minister or Leader of the Party not block votes or delegates from the party in an arbitrarily chosen formula of an electoral college. It is wrong also to allow the sacking of an MP without giving him the chance to appeal against any decision by the delegates to the paid-up membership of the constituency Party. Once the Labour Party wanted to widen the franchise for choosing the leader and no longer trusted the judgement of its MPs then the only true option was to trust the judgement of every Party member. The Social Democratic Party by founding itself on the principle of one member one vote is ensuring that it will be the most democratic party in Britain.

What is right and wholly within the spirit of parliamentary democracy is for the Party decision-making process to be fully respected by Members of Parliament, who should strive to fulfill these policies bearing in mind their judgement of whether the national, overall, interest imposes any restraints on the policy. This requires any political party to approach its policy-making role on the basis of detailed information, careful thought and open debate. Money from parliament for research staff for the parliamentary spokesmen from Opposition parties needs to be increased, and, to reduce the information gap between Government and Opposition, there is a case for seconding civil servants to assist official Opposition spokesmen for a period; this would also help to improve Opposition decision-making and give its members a greater awareness of the implications and relevance of their alternative policies – something which could be crucially important to an Opposition out of power for as long as thirteen years. The decision by parliament to vote financial help for the Opposition is itself a recognition of the national interest in building-up an informed Opposition. An extension of this is to implement the finding of the Houghton Committee on State Financing for Political Parties. It concluded that a 'modest injection of state aid is the best, and perhaps the only, way of arresting the run-down of the parties, and of starting the process by which their effectiveness can be raised to an adequate level.'[5] But the level of aid must be pitched so as to strengthen Opposition political parties but not to sustain them against a decline in membership. It should be fixed as a percentage of the total of membership subscriptions.

It is the relationships between politicians in government and civil servants which are crucial for understanding the nature of modern government. The permanent civil service, facing incoming Ministers, has initially the weapon of accumulated knowledge and expertise to set alongside what is often only a superficial knowledge or no past involvement on the part of the Minister. The civil service has a whole series of conventions about the confidentiality of government business which can ensure that Ministers take decisions outside the glare of publicity and beyond the scrutiny of the informed public. Most information available to Ministers is not made available to the general public: the criteria used by government departments even in quite routine decision-making procedures are still not published despite a worthwhile attempt by the last Labour government to make more information available. Ministers, anxious to avoid too many embarrassing questions, often shelter behind the civil service doctrine of secrecy, finding it all too easy to invoke lightly the national interest. The result is the complete absence of any informed debate. The holding back of the vital information on which government takes its decisions has contributed to the present tendency for all political parties to espouse simple ideological slogans or to take refuge in generalities. The political activists in all the political parties out in the constituencies would find it much easier to accept the abandonment or reversal of a Manifesto commitment if they could sense that the decision had been openly argued through and all the facts that had contributed to the decision made available. Nothing is more frustrating for active Party workers than to see policy commitments overturned but to know none of the reasons. To shut interested people out of the process of decision-making is to encourage hostility to and suspicion of the system of government.

One cannot extol the merits of representative democracy without being conscious of the limits of the representatives themselves. It is fair comment that, 'A combination of thrustful and strong-minded senior civil servants, complex issues demanding both a substantial body of factual knowledge and an appreciation of the personal qualities of persons with whom the Department has to deal, and an inexperienced, indolent, ill-endowed or indecisive Minister, will sometimes lead to a situation in which a Minister dwindles to a political mouthpiece of his civil servants.'[6] The late Richard Crossman likened himself to 'a person who is suddenly certified a lunatic and put safely into this great, vast room, cut off from real life and surrounded by male and female trained nurses and attendants.'[7] The chauffeur-driven cars, the salary differential between Ministers and MPs, the cocooning the cosseting – the fact that a politician is addressed formally as 'Secretary of State' or 'Minister' – are part of the insidious bureaucratic embrace.

The most dangerous embrace of all is the growing reliance by Ministers on committee decision-making which ensures that the Whitehall view is inserted into every meeting. Far too many decisions are made collectively by Ministers and the degree of Ministerial discretion is being eroded on the seemingly unobjectionable grounds of democratic control and Departmental views. The weekly meeting of Permanent Under Secretaries which is a relatively recent development, ensures the co-ordination of attitudes. It is claimed that no decisions are made at these meetings but it is here that the co-ordinated civil service view is evolved and a sense of direction maintained. It is commonplace for Departments clandestinely to pass copies of briefs prepared for their own Ministers to other Departments, and a Department will prepare for its Minister a brief which refers to the expected position of another Minister and make it clear that his or her views are different from the views of the Department. This fosters the concept of a departmental view distinct from the minister's viewpoint and the 'departmental' view continues across different governments. A powerful civil service, with its own ethos, can easily incorporate Ministers and drag them further away from their political party, parliament and their constituents. It is this bureaucratic embrace which a politician has most to fear. Some Ministers who serve in the Ministry of Defence 'join up' and wholly identify with one service. The Army, Air Force and Navy have developed a system of service indoctrination for their junior Ministers which can make a Parliamentary Under Secretary for the Royal Navy feel like a First Lord of the Admiralty in the old days. Some Ministers in the Foreign Office can become so engrossed in foreign travel that they are strangers in their own country, let alone in their own party.

The civil service is not, however, a single monolithic entity. Many of the major Departments have developed over the years their own particular identity, attitudes and style which continues irrespective of which party is in power. The Ministry of Labour has a seventy-year-old tradition of emphasizing conciliation and arbitration within the framework of collective bargaining. The Ministry of Health has a tradition of standing up to the British Medical Association in defence of the National Health Service that would stir the heart of all believers in the NHS. Health Department officials demonstrated this in their support in 1975 for a Labour government facing a three-month strike by hospital consultants trying to force through an 'item by service contract'. This was their constitutional duty – but it was also clear that the very idea of paying for every operation or procedure was anathema to many civil servants who supported the principles of the NHS and to many of the doctors in the Ministry who were resolute in their conviction that these payments would damage patient care and should be resisted in the longer term interest of the NHS. The free trade attitudes of the old Board of Trade still live on with a Messianic fervour in the Department of Trade's resistance to all forms of protectionism. They still champion free trade with scant regard for the change in Britain's international trading position: resist the more flexible interpretation of the various international rules and decry any covert protectionism or moves to design regulations to inhibit imports. Even measures which run no risk of retaliation and which are put forward as being in Britain's own interest are fought hard on the principle that Britain must be the purest of all nations. The Foreign and Commonwealth Office too is influenced by a small group of intelligent and single-minded people who in the negotiations to join the European Community developed a political role in influencing public opinion – sanctioned by Ministers at the time – which they now find difficult to abandon even though we have joined the EEC; they tend to adopt political attitudes of their own to the conduct of the negotiations, often in defiance of ministerial views, and brief the press independently. Yet this resistance is not party political; the evidence points to Mrs Thatcher as Prime Minister encountering the same resistance from officials in the Foreign Office as I did as Foreign Secretary when demanding a tougher negotiating stance with the EEC. The problem is that some Foreign Office officials regard their own views as according with the national interest and feel that they should let those views become known to a wider audience, in much the same way as the admirals and generals justify their independent view-point, invoking their wider responsibility to the security of the state.

The Ministry of Defence still continues to display many of the old attitudes of the old War Office and Admiralty – though the younger Air Force Department is markedly more flexible. The controversial reforms recommended by the Headquarters Organization Committee in 1970 to downgrade the three service Boards were master-minded by the very able Permanent Secretary at the time, but sadly, the incoming Conservative government, supported by the Service Chiefs and the more traditional civil servants with 'single service' Departmental loyalties, decided to drop them. In effect the three

Services still virtually split the Defence Budget up each year into a third for each service. They rotate the position of Chief of Defence Staff on such a strict basis that it may not even alter following the premature death of a Service Chief. The consequence is a defence strategy which is rigidly structured and based more on trade-offs between the Services than on rational choices on inter-Service priorities. The single services also maintain a direct link with defence correspondents through a press department manned, in the main, by service personnel, having a loyalty to their service. The decision in 1981 to abolish single service Ministers is a welcome first step.

The Fulton Report's main recommendations barely touched these complex issues. They covered the recruitment and career structure of the civil service, including the merging of the Administrative and Executive classes into a single 'Administration Group'. Implementation has been slow and criticized for circumventing many of the reforms that were thought to be fundamental.[8] On secrecy, openness and civil service accountability, the Fulton Report simply advocated another enquiry. Undoubtedly the generalist bias in the civil service and the low priority given to scientific and technical expertise can be most speedily countered by outside expertise. Yet there is a long tradition of civil service hostility to outside appointments in anything other than a temporary and advisory capacity. The Diplomatic Service reluctantly acquiesce in the appointment of outsiders but only to be Ambassador to Washington or Paris and as the UK Permanent Representative to the UN. At every level there is a case for more outside appointments. Since the war no permanent secretary or deputy secretary has been brought into the civil service from outside. Yet at this level it is quite common for civil servants to leave before their retirement age of 60 or to start a job within the two year time-limit of retirement in important and influential positions in industry and the city. The fact that a former Head of the Civil Service, Sir William Armstrong, went to the Midland Bank in 1974 within a year of retirement and that the former Secretary to the Cabinet, Sir John Hunt, went in 1980 to the Banque Nationale de Paris, makes it now very hard to justify the continuation of the two-year rule on grounds of propriety. There are few important commercial or financial secrets in government to which these two civil servants were not privy. The Committee of outsiders vetting civil servants who take sensitive appointments within two years of leaving should have their powers and decisions investigated by parliament, which should either reassert criteria for the two-year limit following its erosion by prime ministers responsible for the civil service, or there should be no rule and individuals should be trusted. I refused requests from Ambassadors to take certain jobs, on one occasion putting the reasons myself in writing to Lord Diamond's Committee which upheld my decision. Criteria need to be sensibly applied because it is desirable to encourage more interchange but there is also a need to insist that senior civil servants maintain in some areas a degree of separation. This issue raises the wider question: what attitude should parliament and politicians take to administrators?

Administrators are an essential part of democracy, not a race apart to be denigrated as 'bureaucrats'. Good administration need not be bureaucratic. The paradox is that those politicians who most criticize the civil service tend to be those who most want to legislate for and proliferate its growth. The present tension in the relationsip between civil servants and politicians reflects in part the disappointment and frustration of Britain's post-war decline. Personality clashes or disagreements occur in any organization. What is unique about the civil service is that it is almost impossible for Ministers or the civil service to sack incompetent officials or remove those whom Ministers find hold views incompatible with their own. Voluntary redundancy is available but compulsory redundancy is virtually non-existent. This is particularly serious at the most senior levels; lower down in the hierarchy it is possible to transfer an offical to a departmental backwater. Yet the civil service is not slow in recommending redundancies for others and reports written by officials are bespattered with the advocacy of redundancies in British Steel, British Shipbuilders, the power generating industry and elsewhere.

Whatever the policies of Ministers' parties or the inclinations of the Ministers themselves, it is widely believed that the 'Whitehall view' tends to prevail. Why is this so? Is it the growing complexity of government? The frequency of ministerial reshuffles? Or is it – as I believe – fundamentally a question of ministerial workload, competence, confidence, courage and willpower? The constitutional position is that civil servants are crown servants employed to advise the Ministers of the Crown. Yet in practice vast numbers of decisions are made every day in which Ministers knowingly delegate the decision-making to officials. Such decisions are in some cases delegated by legislation to specific classes of officials, such as immigration officers, or inspectors at planning enquiries. Yet the tradition is still maintained that the Minister is individually responsible for every decision taken by the Department. This is not a worthless fiction, as some allege. For only if it is felt in the last analysis to be a reality will the individual civil servants feel obliged to take controversial and important policy decisions to Ministers, and thereby will ministerial accountability be upheld. This is particularly important given the fact that civil servants are intelligent, opinionated people who enjoy greater security of tenure than Ministers. Similarly, retaining the neutrality of the civil service so that different governments can be served creates a grey area between policy and practice in which civil servants are usually concerned not to impair their own ability to implement different policies. The issue of accountability to Ministers remains the most complex and important of all. It is unrealistic to believe in the absolute purity of the principle accepted by Sir Thomas Dugdale, in the famous Crichel Down case, of responsibility for the conduct of the Department. The principle is not one, however, which can be or should be totally abandoned. It is a myth, yet to some extent it is a necessary myth, if parliamentary government is to be realized. Of course twenty-four Cabinet Ministers cannot possibly control or answer for the detailed decision-making of an administrative structure that, in 1980, twelve years after the Fulton Report, employed 548,600 non-industrial servants. Ministers are not 'running the country' in the sense of taking every decision. The ultimate responsibility of Ministers simply does not provide justice for individuals, save in the most exceptional cases, and for individual cases there is an important role for accountability before the law, through developing and reviewing our existing administrative law and jurisprudence. Parliamentary scrutiny and public scrutiny should focus on a specific Minister responsible for a decision and on named civil servants responsible for decisions that are not referred to the Minister. The practice of blurring accountability by Ministers being able to retreat behind a cabinet decision, or civil servants being able to avoid responsibility by claiming it was a committee decision, should be systematically challenged by Select Committee investigation. Yet in some areas of departmental work the blurring is inevitable and there can be no real distinction. Where the area is politically sensitive then an outside political appointment should be made, for example in immigration control, private medicine in the NHS, and policy towards South Africa. The individual appointment should be justified to parliament and the person held accountable by it.

The top echelons of the civil service numbered, in 1980, twelve years after Fulton, 42 permanent secretaries, and 158 deputy secretaries and ambassadors. The names of these senior officials and what they do was unknown to the general public and even to most

Members of Parliament. While the overall civil service numbers have increased in the ten years by 7 per cent, the increase in under-secretaries and above has been 35 per cent. It is the growth in senior appointments which represents the important potential drain of talent from productive industry. These are the people who could and with a more active redundancy programme should be re-deployed in any systematic attempt to reduce the size of the civil service. Yet what has happened in previous cutbacks is that cuts are applied across the board and fall on disabled doorkeepers who can find no other job, while the recent increase in under-secretaries and the top-heavy structure remains largely unchanged.

Critics of the civil service usually focus on salary levels, pension entitlements and relative job security compared with other posi-tions. The top layer of salaries in government and state industries has been fixed, since 1971, by a Review Body chaired by Lord Boyle. This has not however insulated the issue from public comment or criticism but it is wrong to criticize the fact that civil servants are paid more than Ministers. In the past, at times when they have been advocating pay restraint, politicians have refused large salary in-creases. They do not need to be paid more than top civil servants to exercise control. For senior politicians to stand aside from the spiralling salary race marginally reduces the value of salary as a status symbol of power and influence and checks the belief that pay is the only reward for service. It is a healthy trend, which would be reinforced by paying Ministers very little more than MPs.

The most worrying aspect of the corporatism that has developed in Britain is the circumvention of parliament when important decisions about the future of society can be made by Ministers with little or no democratic control by parliament. Powerful groups can also bypass Ministers completely to take decisions in concert with the permanent civil service. The bypassing of parliament is most evident in two areas: industrial relations and collective bargaining. While there is a sensible reluctance on the part of many politicians to legislate in those two areas, an antipathy to legislation has become an article of faith within the Labour Party to the extent that many members now rule out any form of statutory involvement. This is worrying not only because it implies granting a special immunity to the TUC but also because it has in the past led to a transfer of decision-making in an important area of policy from parliament to the TUC and CBI, reinforcing the corporatist trend. Parliament cannot cease to be the forum for the representation of a wide variety of views and must never accept being the endorser of decisions curbing the individual rights of citizens that are taken by departments or Ministers without specific parliamentary authority. The constitutional propriety of administrative sanctions was rightly challenged by the House of Commons in 1978 over the imposition of sanctions in public purchasing policy against, in particular, Ford to secure compliance with the non-statutory incomes policy. But over thousands of smaller issues civil servants reflect, in their advice to Ministers, the consensus which emerges from their discussions with outside parties. Since many matters are connected with trade, industry, tax, social policy and international affairs, vested interests are strong or preconceptions and doctrines well entrenched, the advice to Ministers, reflecting the views of those interests, are very rarely published or separately tabulated so they can be examined independently of the Department's advice. Often the viewpoint has itself been hammered out in the matching official Cabinet Committees which have developed an identity of their own, further entrenching the move towards civil service government. The outcome is a mass of advice which is most frequently endorsed by Ministers without serious challenge. This is why the doctrine of ministerial responsibility looks jaded.

The more parliament and the public hear and see all these private arguments fully exposed before decisions have to be made, the more likely it is that ministerial decisions will reflect the wider debate. Already, where decisions are highly complex and ministerial involvement slight, but where the possibility of public or parliamentary scrutiny always exists, the civil service has a tendency to avoid from the start any policy option likely to be controversial: it may even exclude certain options, before any ministerial involvement has occurred, by saying that it might be potentially embarrassing for Ministers. Too often Ministers themselves refer issues to inter-departmental committees without any political guidance being given. Not surprisingly the result is an amorphous amalgam of conventional, safe, views always tending to the status quo. Bureaucratic procedure itself has become a source of stultification. Short-term economic considerations may be used to rule out an option which a Minister might well be prepared to fight for, despite the cost, had it been known that it was being considered. A fundamental fact which can hardly be over-stressed is that in the existing system there is no substitute for ministerial activism, for intervention early in the consideration of a problem, for being sufficiently well informed to challenge the Department, tough enough to insist on using outside expertise, and for being seen to control the Department. The combination of weak Ministers and too much collective decision-making is a recipe for inaction and is the source of much of Britain's lack of drive and initiative and of its resistance to change. In the United States the tension between the President and Congress is positive, but in Britain there is a danger that there is no productive tension between the Executive and parliament, within the Executive, or between Ministers and civil servants.

The advice which eventually reaches Ministers, and on which they take their decisions, will often have already been considered by a large number of officials, and anything unorthodox or thought to be too controversial will probably have been ironed out. If there are options it will involve a choice between safe, conventional proposals. The existing structure favours but does not guarantee civil service government. It will manifest itself where there is a weakening of ministerial control of the civil service and too little public and parliamentary scrutiny of the Executive. Parliamentary scrutiny must operate a delicate balance to prevent the inhibition of thinking; and the fear of making a mistake or taking a risk which breeds a stultifying caution. It is worth giving one specific example of the way in which official committees, preparing the ground for ministerial meetings, can present an apolitical Whitehall consensus, an amalgam of Departmental interest which, once allowed to take root, can be very difficult to alter.

When the last Labour government was giving serious consideration to the options for economic and trade sanctions against South Africa the usual bureaucratic procedure was followed and a committee of officials matching a special Cabinet Sub-Committee was established. Whitehall was adamantly opposed to the application of any sanctions. The only way of ensuring that the Departmental view represented the views of the Foreign Secretary was to see the minutes of the official committee circulated to the Foreign Office participants, and to discuss with my officials their views, and even at times writing as well as approving their evidence for that committee. The issues were clearly political, and I felt the Department view needed to reflect the view of the Foreign Secretary. The debate between the diplomats and myself took place within the Department before I could have been confronted by a paper agreed by Whitehall with which I might disagree. This was thought by some officials to be a very unusual procedure, though others welcomed my intervention. Clearly time does not allow a similar pattern to be followed on every issue but there is a need for officials to come back to Ministers for political guidance in sensitive political areas of policy. Few things are more damaging to ministerial control than to hear a Minister in Cabinet refer to what 'my Department thinks . . .' as something distinct from their own views. The Department should have a view and should challenge the ministerial view but once the Minister has decided within the Department their views constitutionally should become identical. The formal acceptance of the concept of separation is new and very corrosive of the principle of democratic ministerial control, and tends to legitimize the concept of a civil service policy as distinct from government policy. Of course civil servants have views and they should express them; their views are often correct and the Minister's wrong; retaining their expertise across governments of different parties has advantages and the case for moving to the American 'spoils system', where each Administration appoints its own civil service, is not strong enough to abandon the concept of neutral civil service; but that neutrality imposes restraints as well as bringing considerable power to civil servants.

The elected politician is not an expert, and, particularly in the early months of taking office, a new Minister will need good advice, and one hopes it will be taken. Many of the major mistakes made by government involves decisions taken in the first few months. Even after a year in office the Minister in charge will simply not have the time to master all the many subjects which require his attention. Whitehall, with some justice, argues that the early mistakes are when their influence is least and the Party's greatest.

Nothing is more nauseating than the spate of stories from ex-Cabinet Ministers about how they were thwarted by officials. A Cabinet Minister who knows his own mind, and can persuade his colleagues, can force his policies through. Any bureaucracy will resist change, but only in rare cases is that resistance politically motivated. The virtues of continuity, incorruptibility and bipartisanship which are broadly reflected within the civil service should not be decried. Any radical government will need to challenge and at times kick against the inaction of the machine. On occasion the civil service will itself put up radical proposals and some politicians are, in comparison to some civil servants, highly conservative. Permanent secretaries relish argument but most loyally support decisions once taken. Conflict between Ministers and civil servants does exist but it is no more than a reflection of the realities and difficulty of decision-making in any large organization. The civil service has not unnaturally tended to react to the criticism of its political motivation with a cynicism about politicians and their ability to insist on their policies. This has sadly reinforced in the general public a sense of distance and alienation about the whole government process. The 'gentleman in Whitehall' is not always fairly seen as the man responsible for various planning disasters, for remote insensitive decisions and endless red tape and for wastage in the spending of public money. It is in the interests of politicians to re-establish the image of government as something in which people have a stake and which they can influence. It is not in the politicians' interest or the broad national interest to perpetuate this unfavourable image of the civil service and government generally.

But some redefinition of these different jobs is undoubtedly needed. The Labour Party, in its evidence to the Fulton Committee, had put forward the proposal that Ministers should be able to recruit personal staff to work with them as in the French *cabinet* system. It was, however, the Conservative government which in 1970 first began to include, in major Departments like the Foreign Office and the Treasury, a number of politically appointed officials working for the Secretaries of State personally. Some of them, in accordance with the fashion of time and of that government, were businessmen. When Labour returned to power in 1974 Cabinet Ministers were somewhat grudgingly allowed to appoint up to two personal advisers. Many did not, and the total of politically appointed officials never exceeded thirty. They were appointed to Departments for the duration of the Administration, the appointments automatically lapsing on the day after the following general election.

It is important to evaluate this experiment, though the role of the advisers seems to have been different in almost every case. Some took on a 'very' political role, seeing it as their duty to ensure that Manifesto policies were carried out, maintaining contact with local parties and with the Parliamentary Labour Party. Others provided Ministers with a personal confidant who knew the intimate details of the Department's business but did not have the divided loyalties of those who, while endeavouring to help the Minister, nevertheless had their own career and standing in the civil service to think about. Yet others became actively involved in the Department's work, acting as an extra pair of arms and eyes for the Minister – sometimes in this role clashing with junior Ministers. In some departments the political appointees were virtually frozen out, while in others they became part, albeit a special part, of the normal functioning of the administrative machine.

My adviser for 1977–9 in the Foreign and Commonwealth Office went on four missions abroad that would not have had the same value if undertaken by an official. He visited Namibia to speak to all the internal nationalist leaders, visiting Ovamboland right up to the Namibian/Angolan border, which ensured an up-to-date account of a country where, for UN and other reasons, we had no diplomatic mission. He was also able to go beyond the British government's relations with the South African government by talking directly to key black African leaders. He visited the colony of Belize at a time where there was considerable tension between the Government and Opposition parties there and went to Maputo in Mozambique to talk to ZANU and improve relations at a time when ZANU felt the British government was favouring ZAPU, based in Lusaka. Finally, he went to India and Bangladesh to examine all the circumstances behind any medical examinations being conducted on women intending to emigrate to Britain and on the reasons for the long waiting-lists and delays in making appointments, something which was understandably a matter of concern.

In the Foreign Office, despite travelling commitments, the five Ministers, two special advisers and the two Parliamentary Private Secretaries used to meet once a week over lunch to discuss issues which were likely to come up at Cabinet and party politics. Issues which were frequently discussed in a party political context were the European Community, a range of African policies, and sensitive issues like the Falkland Islands, Gibraltar or Belize. The Private Secretary came to all the meetings; the Private Office were part of a team with the politicians. They managed to put their departmental loyalties into suspense for their period in the private office, and worked massive hours, but were free to criticize or suggest anything. They often felt the full brunt of the pressures and tensions that flowed through the Foreign Secretary's office but they could not have been more dedicated. It is necessary that a wider public should understand the intimacy and the confidence of most Ministers' relations with their Private Office – very well described by Barbara Castle in her Diaries.

The introduction of specialist political advisers is a valuable innovation. But it is no substitute for the more systematic development in Britain of the Continental *cabinet* system. A Minister also needs support over policy development. The Foreign Office has, like some other Ministries, a separate planning staff, set up in 1964 after the Plowden Report had highlighted the deficiencies of Foreign Office policy development saying 'Some of the most intractable international issues in which we have been involved in the last two decades could, in our view, have been handled better if their implications had been explored more fully in advance'.[9] 'It is alleged that the planning unit was quickly cobbled together in 1964 when the Foreign Office saw the proofs of the Plowden Report a month before it was made public.'[10] Whatever its origins, by 1977 the planning staff had become insufficiently independent of the Department and did not appear to be challenging the accepted wisdom from within the Department. To change the system would have necessitated a change in personnel and for the staff to work directly to myself as Foreign Secretary and not to the Department through the Permanent Secretary. This would have meant a major upheaval. For many reasons, not least that with a parliamentary majority so fragile one never knew how long the government would survive, I decided to circumvent rather than change the existing system. This was quicker and less traumatic and left everyone reasonably satisfied. In order not to engender the suspicion aroused by Denis Healey's establishment of a Programme Evaluation Group in the Ministry of Defence in the middle 1960s no formal announcement was made but, with the full co-operation of the Permanent Under-Secretary, it was arranged to transfer two people nominally to the staff of the Planning Department, a young diplomat with experience of defence policy and a young economist. These two, working closely with an existing member of that Department who had already had experience of co-ordinating work for speeches, then formed a separate policy unit working direct to myself as Foreign Secretary. At times they liaised with the Prime Minister's own policy unit and my Special Economic Adviser supervised any work involving economics.

The unit concentrated on defence issues and disarmament and also on the scope for selective import controls and their effect on the Third World and relations with the EEC and OECD. It soon developed an independent view and analysis. Its most important achievement was in challenging the accepted wisdom of the Ministry of Defence on Mutual and Balanced Force Reductions and challenging the Cabinet Secretariat on the detailed arguments over the Chevaline nuclear warhead programme. It also considered the strategic and political arguments against Trident as a possible Polaris replacement and prepared research on an alternative option to the Trident missile, the submarine-launched Tomahawk cruise missile. On none of these issues could the Foreign Office as such have made so effective a contribution. The unit was able independently to gather considerable information from the US Administration with the help of the ambassador in Washington, Peter Jay. Much of the information on Trident and on cruise missiles classified as 'Top Secret UK eyes only' in Whitehall was to be found openly in the Congressional record and amongst academics in the United States. A small expert personal policy unit is as vital for a Minister in making an informed judgement on departmental policy and advice as is the creation of a small political advisory unit. Both can work with the Department while being independent of it. Provided the units speak with the authority of the Minister through the Private Secretary there is no risk of any constitutional impropriety or unnecessary and wasteful duplication of effort, but it should be a formally accepted *cabinet* and should not have to be constructed in this way.

Expertise is a crucial element in checking and investigating government decisions. Nowadays a single official, perhaps an able graduate in his or her early thirties, concentrates on mastering relatively small areas of the department's policy, and can deal with all policy matters affecting his or her field of responsibility, working with the main outside or non-governmental bodies connected with the subject, briefing Ministers and drafting replies to questions from Members of Parliament. The involvement of outside experts and of a dialogue between government and academics, which is so strong in America, is still comparatively much less developed in Britain.

No sensible person expects one Cabinet Minister effectively to monitor everything that goes on in a Department. The very clear constitutional position which holds that Ministers are accountable to parliament, will remain a myth while very little detail of what the Department does is even known about by Members of Parliament. The decision in 1979 to establish after the initial experiment Departmental Select Committees is important, but the danger is that if they are inadequately staffed they will become dependent on and literally creatures of the Department. Given the laws and practices now governing secrecy the withholding of information can obstruct accountability to parliament yet be used as the excuse to prevent disclosure of information to the press or the public on the grounds that such a practice would diminish the accountability of Ministers to the House of Commons. It is a bogus argument: the scrutiny is all the more effective if parliament has the information on which the Ministers based their decision. So there exists a double lock on making information available. Leaks by officials to journalists often reveal far more about what is going on inside government than what is said in answer to Parliamentary Questions. As the Conservative government's ill-fated Protection of Official Information Bill demonstrated, once again, government collectively was more concerned to protect itself against leaks than to allow the public greater access to information about what those who govern are actually doing. But it is not use blaming officials. It is well in the power of government and politicians to open the system up. The fact is that successive Labour Cabinets have not had a sufficient majority within them to over-throw old prejudices and cross-party conservatism, and there has been little difference between Labour and Conservative govern-ments. Members of Parliament, unless they specialize, are most unlikely to be able to master any but the general outlines of the subject, and, lacking expert guidance, may be unable to ask the pertinent questions. Select Committees are now appointing expert advisers but there are still considerable financial constraints on the building-up of their expertise.

However, the growth of pressure groups and activist charities, covering fields such as mental health, housing, the old, or race relations, has fortunately provided a 'counter civil service' of experts who subject every move of the government machine in their specialist field to very close scrutiny. Many of these groups have built close ties with friendly Members of Parliament. But pressure groups, even those whose scrutiny of government is consistent and independent, cannot do the job of parliament: they do not have to balance different priorities. An important task of the Select Commit-tees is to lead an informed public discussion about what government is about to do, or has failed to do, or ought to be doing. In this area a readiness to publish more working papers prior to decision-making is very valuable. It was easier than many people thought to publish Foreign Office departmental papers and policy option papers in 1978 when the decision was taken to reveal more information. Gradually, the way government works is becoming better known. The publica-tion of the Castle and Crossman diaries has given the general public a unique description of the work of a Cabinet Minister as seen through the eyes of those Ministers. It has also meant a greater realization among academics and pressure groups of what goes on inside government and exactly how it works. Ex-Ministers and former political advisers have also spoken freely, in some cases at least concentrating only on past battles, but in doing so they have revealed something of how the civil service and the Cabinet system of government works. The Bingham Report on Rhodesian sanctions policy disclosed how the inner decision-making processes work when it published an internal memorandum with the circulation list at the bottom. This revealed which Ministers' Private Offices had known about the oil swap arrangement. What a further special parliamentary enquiry which the government had advocated in 1978 would have looked at, if it had not been rejected by the House of Lords, would have been why the Ministers and offficials concerned did not recognize, and advise Ministers about, the important constitutional issue involved on which Ministers could be open to challenge for having condoned past illegalities. Why were the issues not presented specifically by the Ministers involved to the relevant Cabinet Sub-Committee? Another more general issue which ought still to be considered is whether a procedure of copying the minutes of a meeting to Ministers' Private Offices is a sufficient safeguard, or is part of a bureaucratic machinery which gives a blanket coverage of ministerial involvement through a mass of unread paper circulating around Whitehall.

The Cabinet Committee structure is something which successive Prime Ministers have refused to publish for no very good reason. Their membership is an important source of prime ministerial power as was shown by the existence of a small Ministerial Committee of four Ministers which under the Labour government discussed some sensitive nuclear issues in 1977 and 1978 such as whether to cancel the Chevaline programme for improving the Polaris warhead which had been accepted by the full Labour Cabinet in 1974.

In this context what is important is that the existence of this Committee was not known to all the Cabinet. Neither was the membership of the small economic seminars which discussed exchange rate policy and other sensitive monetary matters widely known, until it was revealed in a newspaper. This is, however, not unusual since many Prime Ministers have used unofficial groups for political discussion and have justified the practice by saying that actual decision-making remained formally with the Cabinet Sub-Committees whose membership has always been a Prime Ministerial prerogative. No formal register or details of the membership is ever circulated to parliament, although senior civil servants working in the Cabinet Office know the structure of the Cabinet Committees and the knowledge spreads out in Whitehall. There is no escaping the fact that Prime Ministers have used this freedom to ensure limited discussion as well as to reinforce their authority. There is a strong case for confining the number of Cabinet Ministers involved in issues like nuclear or exchange rate policy but no justification for not informing the Cabinet formally of the existence of all such groups, or the wider public through parliament of the membership of the formal Cabinet Sub-Committees.

Within the Labour Party there are some who have said that the Chevaline programme conflicted with the Labour Party's 1974 Manifesto pledge not to replace Polaris. It was in fact a programme to harden the existing system so that it could withstand ballistic missile explosions. There was no real security case for withholding information about the existence of the project since most informed defence commentators had been writing about the modernization ever since it had first been decided by the Heath government – I had myself mentioned it in a book published in 1972 calling for more open defence decision making and drawing attention to the oil going to Rhodesia from South Africa through Laurenço Marques at the time of the Beira Patrol.[11] But because of the feeling that there had been a government cover-up, when the issue became public through the formal Chevaline announcement by the Conservative Secretary of State for Defence in 1979, and by the revelations prior to the Bingham Report and when it was published, there was a massive public outcry. The reason was a public feeling, largely created by journalists, that they had been cheated of information – even though the facts were already fairly well known. A Select Committee on Defence should and could have been given far more details about Chevaline, as could a Select Committee investigation of Rhodesian sanctions. The conspiracy of silence to avoid discussion about defence has only served to build up pressures within the Labour Party in favour of unilateralism and of hostility to NATO which feed on suspicion and fear. There is a price to be paid for avoiding open debate on any issue, particularly when the Labour Party goes into Opposition, when it is much harder to ensure rational informed debate. Law and order issues affect the Conservatives in much the same way, when in government they keep debate about such issues as the death penalty, corporal punishment or penal policy low key and then have to pay a price when strident demands are made to commit to hanging and flogging when they are in Opposition. The art of politics is to harness public and party opinion so that they keep broadly in step.

Paradoxically, the corporate state itself has added to the demands for greater openness because pressure groups have developed direct relationships with civil servants and have, in the course of what has become their normal work, forged a relationship with the official machine which has in turn spread knowledge about how it all works. Some of these pressure groups acquire an intimate knowledge of the work done by different officials at different levels in the departments concerned, of how their work is co-ordinated, and even of how the official machine is briefing Ministers and when Ministerial Committees will meet. Symptomatic of the corporate society is the lobbying which can be unleashed by industry, private and public, before a Cabinet or Cabinet Committee Meeting to discuss important industrial issues, or the release by the Child Poverty Action Group of a memorandum on child endowment just before key decisions are to be made. The parallel within government is the sudden arrival of telegrams from Ambassadors in European capitals to the Foreign Secretary when Britain's negotiating position in the EEC is due to be decided by Ministers. If the vested interests can be mobilized to put pressure on the decision-making, why cannot public opinion be mobilized as well?

The essential key to an effective parliamentary democracy is knowledge. Knowledge is power. The growth of corporatism has thrived on the complexity of modern life and the inability of parliament to adapt itself to grappling with that complexity by building up a countervailing expertise. Parliament's attempt to develop an independent source of knowledge and expertise has been deliberately blocked by successive Cabinets, often encouraged by the civil service. Parliament's resolve to wrestle from the political parties the power to decide when to vote has been weakened because of the rigid demarcation which many insist on retaining between Government and Opposition. Parliament has been constrained too by the rigid whipping system reinforced by the ability of the Whips to determine the membership of committees and the mechanics of voting. To some extent this is inevitable in the two-party system but one of the most welcome changes in the 1974–9 parliament was the readiness of backbench MPs to exercise their voting rights in a more independent way, while the Labour/Liberal arrangement in 1977 and 1978 showed that parliament could adapt to a situation where no party had an overall majority. It is now in the interests of democracy for parliament to insist that there should be fuller disclosure about what goes on in government, not only to its own Select Committees but also to the wider public, but this will necessitate a conflict with the Whips and traditional parliamentary leaders.

The argument about official disclosure of information quite rightly centres on demands for a legislatively-backed 'right to know'. This expresses the wish for the responsibility to be put on government to inform the public about what it is doing: yet in practice the subject has become inextricably bound up with what to government is the other side of the coin – the protection of official information from unauthorized or damaging disclosure. The debate has centred on the question of the reform of the Official Secrets Acts. The present debate about the reform of those Acts goes back to 1967 when the Labour government caused prosecutions to be brought against Jonathan Aitken and the Editor of the *Sunday Telegraph* for allegedly breaking the law in an article about the Biafran War. Both men were acquitted, but the whole episode led to the setting up of the Franks Committee on official secrecy, which recommended, in its report published in 1972, that a new Official Information Act was needed.

As a result, although successive governments did nothing, there was increasing concern both inside and outside parliament. Private Members tabled Bills and the All Party Committee on Freedom of Information built up support. Outside groups like the Outer Circle Policy Unit – which helped Clement Freud, MP produce one of the more successful Private Members' Bills – also stimulated the public argument over reform. The British section of the International Commission of Jurists, *Justice*, produced studies and draft legislation. The Labour government responded through its White Paper in 1978 which proposed, among other things, criminal sanctions for unauthorized disclosures of official information and – wrongly – made no proposal for a legally enforceable right to know. The White Paper was welcomed by nobody; it was shelved while further consultations took place and Ministers began to look seriously at the possibility of adapting Clement Freud's Bill, and they studied experience in other countries. Although a Green Paper was published in April 1979 which allowed for a statutory code of conduct, this died with the Labour government. The Conservative government attempted to introduce a retrograde Bill which included most of the civil service proposals which had been rejected a few months before by Labour Ministers. The Protection of Official Information Bill was then dropped in the face of all-party hostility in the wake of the publication of Andrew Boyle's book *Climate of Treason* and the Prime Minister's disclosure that Anthony Blunt had been a Russian spy. It suddenly became clear that if the Bill had been an Act the book might never have been published.

It is unfortunate that Ministers are even more secretive than are civil servants and hostile to parliament, even when over greater freedom of information a majority of MPs of all parties support radical change. Now that public opinion and most outside influential groups, including lawyers and consumers, also strongly favour change perhaps there will be one but there is no case for any government supporting any partial reform. It would be better to

wait and allow the existing Official Secrets Act to languish unused
on the statute book. It has almost reached the stage now when no
Attorney General will risk bringing any prosecution under the
infamous catch-all Section II.

The seriousness of the present situation in relation to official
secrecy is well illustrated in a recent Fabian Tract.[12] The author cites
some random examples of official suppression of information taken
from press reports in December 1979: an official report with full
details of the damage juggernauts cause to our roads was suppres-
sed by the Department of Transport; eminent academics told the
Social Science Research Council that the right decisions about
energy might not be taken in the future without public access
legislation in Britain; the full details of how children are affected by
lead pollution, and smokers by the carbon monoxide content of
cigarettes, were kept secret by the Department of Health; calls for
the rules governing rights to welfare benefit to be published were
again ignored; only public health specialists received, in the *Com-
municable Disease Report*, warnings and information about epidemics
of infectious disease and food contamination.

The opposition to reforms comes almost exclusively from those
who will be most inconvenienced by them, senior politicians and
civil servants. Opposition is often couched in terms of expense, with
frightening figures being produced as to the cost and numbers of
civil servants needed to administer the new freedom, reminiscent of
the Whitehall-inspired campaign against any serious consideration
of local income tax. 'The cost of the United States FOIA in 1977
according to the official, Congressional study was a little under $26
million, about £13 million. This is a substantial sum but needs to be
seen in the perspective of other government spending, for example,
expenditure in 1978 of $35 million for the maintenance of Defence
Department golf courses and, more pointedly, $1.5 billion for US
government public relations exercises.'[13] The assumption is that
once some information is released, demands will eventually be
made for all information to be released. Yet, expense and inconvenience have always been a necessary accompaniment of democracy,
and it is not sufficient to argue that documents will have to be sorted
and classified, and arrangements will have to be made for the
public's requests for information to be processed. Even if government decision-making could be only marginally improved in Britain,
if the momentum towards corporatism could be checked by greater
public examination of the working of government, then the limited
cost would soon be recovered by more acceptable, accountable and

better decision-making. Abroad, a number of countries have taken steps to create a statutory right of access to government information. In Sweden such a right has existed for over 200 years and proposed new laws are discussed by appointed commissions composed of people from a wide spectrum of backgrounds. Swedish Members of Parliament have before them the Commissions' reports, in addition to the reports of their own committee and the comments of Ministry officials, when they come to vote on the legislation. The actual interpretation and execution of Swedish law is in practice handled by independent administrative boards, and it is to strengthen the effectiveness and accountability of such bodies that the very wide provisions for disclosure of information have been devised. In Norway and Denmark, where the system is different from the Swedish one, there have been laws providing for statutory access to public information since 1970. In both countries Ministers and officials are accountable both to parliament and to the courts. In the United States, the Freedom of Information laws, which again give the citizen's statutory right to access to official documents, have been justified as being fully in accordance with the principles of the Constitution, as a device to help implement the principle that people are sovereign. France passed in 1978 a 'Law on Freedom of Access to Administrative Documents' while in the Netherlands the same year saw a 'Law on the Access to Official Information'. Internationally, among leading democratic nations, Britain is almost alone, together with the Federal Republic of Germany, in having made no formal provisions for access by the citizen to official information.

Obviously, clear guidelines will be necessary to safeguard security and other sensitive material, including information supplied to government in commercial confidence and papers relating to personnel matters or law enforcement. Yet the demands for freer information have come from such a variety of sources, and given the reception in parliament both to various Private Members Bills and to the Protection of Official Information Bill they seem to have such strong support from the House of Commons that some reform now looks inevitable. But we are unlikely given current political attitudes to move from a system of Cabinet government characterized by secrecy, a doctrine of Cabinet collective responsibility and of anonymity and protection from public controversy of civil servants to a Swedish-type system in a single step. The Labour government in 1979 – mainly because of divisions of opinion within its own ranks – put forward only tentatively the *Justice* proposal – for a general right of access to government files, in the form not of a legal right but of a code of practice to be monitored by the Ombudsman (Parliamentary Commissioner for Administration). There would be no retrospective application, and there would be no access to or involvement of the courts. But the Ombudsman would supervise the system and be able to order compliance with the Code of Conduct, and Members of Parliament would be able to exercise vigilance over the whole procedure.

The relatively cautious *Justice* proposal could, however, provide a satisfactory system if the Code of Conduct were part of an acceptance of a legislative right to know and it were put into a Regulation which would have to be subject to an affirmative vote each year. The involvement of the Parliamentary Commissioner for Administration would be buttressed by the Parliamentary Select Committee which oversees the Commissioner and which would report to the House on the working of the code. The House of Commons would have an annual debate and an opportunity to vote if the government did not progressively amend the Code in the light of experience and the comments of the Commissioner and the Select Committee.

Set up by the Labour government under the Parliamentary Commissioner Act 1967, the office of the 'Ombudsman' is designed to assist citizens who are victims of mistakes or maladministration by government departments. The Ombudsman works on complaints passed on by Members of Parliament, though when receiving a complaint direct from a member of the public the Commissioner usually passes it to the person's MP to see if the MP is prepared to ask formally for it to be investigated. In 1979, 758 complaints were received, of which 27 per cent were accepted for investigation. Usually complaints which are not accepted for investigation lay outside the scope of the Parliamentary Commissioner's powers or, rather than alleging maladministration, simply expressed disagreement with decisions reached by government departments in the exercise of discretion under, for example, planning legislation. Despite the relatively little use made of the Commissioner – only one complaint per 53,000 electors was made in 1979 – the Ombudsman has provided some extra safeguard for citizens in their dealings with the modern state bureaucracy. Its terms of reference are, however, still too narrow and access should not be restricted to use only via MPs. In the case of one small but significant group – pensioners wrongly coded for income tax purposes – the Ombudsman has scored an important victory. Provided the office is given the necessary resources to do the job properly, the Ombudsman could be a flexible but authoritative way of monitoring a Code of Conduct on

Official Information. Commissioners have won the confidence of politicians and officials, while their powers and the thoroughness of their investigations – together with their constitutional link with parliament – have helped to ensure that officialdom feels the power of democratic accountability at much lower levels of administration than was ever possible before.

Privacy is another major concern which cuts across the debate about open government. So much information on individuals is now possessed by state and para-state bodies that there is apprehension about the uses to which such information might be put; and everyone is concerned that any such information is both accurate and relevant. As the state becomes more pervasive and more centralized, so such concerns become more and more critical to the relationship between the citizen and the modern state. The Committee on Data Protection, set up by the Labour government in 1976 under the chairmanship of Sir Norman Lindop, looked with great thoroughness both into the question of who is to enjoy access to data and into how the privacy of the individual could be protected. An increasing amount of data is now held, much of it on computers, about people's lives and personal characteristics. Nineteen pages of Appendix 6 to the Report are taken up with a list of 'computer tasks' containing information about identifiable individuals held under the authority of different legislation. The legislation permitting government departments and agencies to collect such information ranges from such obvious examples as the Social Security (Pension) Act 1975 and the Census Act 1920 to the Horticulture (Special Payments) Act 1974 and the Welfare Food Order 1977. A total of fifteen different Acts of Parliament allow various categories of officials, including judges, access, in certain circumstances, to an individual's bank account.

The concept of privacy is a peculiarly difficult one to grasp. In countries like France and Germany a different emphasis – that of 'data protection' – is placed on the concept. The Committee did put forward, as a possible definition for legal purposes, the idea that: '"Privacy" means, in relation to any data subject, his interests to determine for himself what data relating to him should be known to what other persons, and upon what terms as to the use which those persons may make of those data.'[14] Not only are people worried about who holds what information about them, and particularly about how accurate it is, there is increasing concern that different computers holding records collected for different purposes might be linked up so that, for example, information given to employers in confidence for personnel record purposes might find its way into police hands or simply into the hands of other employees. In addition, lack of clear guidelines about the public's entitlement to know what is held on file about them leads, rightly and understandably, to fears that for example a prosecution, but not the subsequent acquittal, or a petition for bankruptcy but not its subsequent dismissal with costs, might find itself on official records. The Committee's recommendations would, if implemented, go a long way to reassure people. They proposed, in their report published in 1978, a Data Protection Authority to implement seven basic principles: the Authority would make rules for data users, maintain a register of all personal data users, investigate complaints and enforce compliance with the rules. A code of practice would govern the uses to which data could be put and conditions governing its disclosure. Most importantly – since fears are directed more at the prospect of an Orwellian '1984' situation developing among state agencies than in the private sector – the Committee proposed that the Data Protection Authority should not be subject to or answerable to a Minister, but rather that its members should be appointed by the Crown and subject to direct parliamentary scrutiny only, with the possibility that a Parliamentary Select Committee might supplement that function. In addition, it proposed to make the jurisdiction of the 'Ombudsman' apply to the DPA, with members of the public being able to take their complaints direct to the Commissioner while the decision of the Authority would be accountable to the courts. There is an overwhelming case for implementing these recommendations.

In one of his most perceptive essays, Henry Fairlie, one of the best post-war political journalists to work within the British parliamentary system, summarized for the politician four tasks: 'To try to reconcile the multiplicity of conflicting interests and wills which exist in any free society . . . To maintain public interest in political issues, for without such interest free government is meaningless . . . To act as a catalyst on public opinion. Eventually, and especially at moments of crisis, he may, as Bagehot demanded of him, "express the mind of the English people," but the mind is rarely clear enough to be expressed at all . . . To be the link between informed and public opinion. The two are very different.'[15] The way the Minister interacts with parliament and parliament with the Minister will determine whether or not parliamentary democracy can be revived in Britain. The role and place of Select Committees within the parliamentary system will probably be the decisive factor. That is not to argue that those Committees will of themselves resolve all the problems, or that there is any one single parliamentary, administrative or political initiative or device capable of reviving or restoring the power and influence of parliament. Select Committees do, however, have the potential to provide the varied stimulus which is needed in many areas of parliamentary government.

It is interesting to analyse the opposing forces in the argument about the introduction and extension of the powers of Select Committees. It gives some insight into what the Select Committees might contribute to parliament. The most powerful opposition comes from politicians themselves. Some politicians who have served, or who expect to serve, in government oppose them because they see them as challenging the power of the Executive: they present an obstacle to the power of the Minister to decide. Those politicians who suffer from 'manifestoism' and who believe in the supremacy of the 'mandate' or who regard decisions of party conferences as sacred, fear the power of Select Committees to erode the party basis of parliamentary decision-making, and dislike the inherently all-party nature of Select Committee recommendations. Politicians who prefer to operate on the basis of the 'grand strategy' and who are not interested in detail but delight in polemic and debate sense that Select Committees will divert attention away from the floor of the House and reduce the clash and conflict of adversary and opposition politics.

The opposition of civil servants is more diffuse. Administrators like a clear-cut, tidy, decision-making procedure: some see parliament in general and Select Committees in particular as interfering with the decision-making procedure, bringing into it delays, uncertainty and irrationality. Some see Select Committees as ill-informed and their recommendations as irresponsible, something to be suffered as the price for democracy, but whose growth should be resisted and their power curtailed. Some of the opposition comes from the House of Commons clerks themselves, who do not like the prospect of seeing their own position eroded by the introduction of specialized staff from outside the Commons.

Despite this powerful opposition – but in part because it is an opposition made up of so many different and at times contradictory strands – movement towards Select Committees has over the past fifteen years been the most successful area of parliamentary reform. Gradually they are acquiring professional specialist advisers, proper back-up facilities and are developing a political identity with an ability to arouse newspaper and public interest. They cannot hope to prosper and to acquire more powers unless they build up backbench opinion which will support them. The fundamental question is, however, yet to be resolved: will they be able to harness for themselve the voting power of parliament? Unless they are able to make this breakthrough all the academic studies and discussions about the role of Select Committees will simply be left to gather dust. It is harder to envisage, but not impossible, for parliament to do this under the two-party system.

The Home Affairs Select Committee, which looked into the reform of the 'sus' laws in 1980, made it clear that, if the government did not come forward with its own Bill to abolish 'sus' the Committee would itself produce a Bill: presumably by making use of the ten-minute rule procedure, where it could obtain overwhelming support for parliamentary time to legislate. Alternatively, it could be taken up under the procedure for Private Members' Bills.

Another vital way of harnessing the vote will come when a Select Committee challenges the government over an item of expenditure. A very sensitive mechanism is available within the existing parliamentary procedure for the control of the Executive. It has lapsed to such an extent that government has come to assume that it has the right to win on all expenditure decisions. The power of the Whips has over the decades been mobilized to guarantee the government's expenditure programme to the point of farce. The Public Accounts Committee is the most prestigious of all the Select Committees. It should be able to pick up a particular expenditure project, where it has been able to prove a scandalous cost escalation, and then reach an all-party agreement that the project should be cancelled; and it should then challenge the government either to cancel or to face a debate and vote on the cancellation. Otherwise, no matter how good the Committee's analysis, its findings will be ignored by Ministers and civil servants. The vote is the teeth of democracy in parliament. Take away the ability to put issues to the vote and there is no power.

Select Committees are already providing a far better forum for reconciling conflicting arguments and creating and catalysing public interest than the debates on the floor of the House of Commons. They have done so in complex fields such as computer technology, nuclear power policy and race relations. To the surprise of many people they have been able to investigate the highly-charged political area of the independent British nuclear deterrent, and more recently were able to conclude that the Soviet invasion of Afghanistan was defensive rather than offensive in nature. In such cases as the Musicians' Union dispute with the BBC over the planned closure of orchestras they have shown themselves able to move sensitively into complex fields such as industrial relations. The extension of Select Committee investigations into other sensitive areas is worth consideration: they could gradually replace bodies such as Royal Commissions, Special Commissions and departmental committees of inquiry. There are good grounds, for example, for scrutinizing all important appointments stemming from ministerial patronage – permanent secretaries in the civil service, chairmen of nationalized industries, state-run boards, authorities and councils, and the appointment of political ambassadors. The very thought of such a development will appal many traditionalists: it would, however, tilt the balance of power between parliament and the Executive back a crucial few degrees in favour of parliament. I would have liked the opportunity to go to a Select Committee to justify my appointment of Peter Jay to Washington as Ambassador.

Many of the changes advocated to revive parliamentary democracy will in themselves be of only marginal value but the cumulative effect could be considerable. It is never a good argument to criticize change because it will operate only at the margin. In a sophisticated democracy change involving a massive swing away from historic patterns and trends is very rarely the right course; changes at the margins represent important reforms if they are part of a well-thought-out series of interlocking marginal changes. The only reservation is that parliamentarians must ensure that, as they rebuild their power and influence, they do not replace bureaucratic inertia by political inertia. They must avoid creating a climate of opinion in which, for the sake of easy publicity, every mistake by the Executive is elevated to the status of a major crisis. In that case a system of government might grow up in which politicians would not be prepared to defend the need to allow for error. They would castigate civil servants for every mistake and would themselves elevate caution to being the only political virtue.

New ideas can come only from a readiness to experiment. Almost by definition, some experiments must occasionally fail. The greatest politicians have been those who have shown the ability to demonstrate that party interest never militates against national interest and that principles are not devalued by expediency. Parliamentary democracy can be the vehicle for reviving our nation, injecting hope and optimism, replacing dogma and doctrine with a practical yet imaginative future – a bolder leadership, something with which many people can identify and hold to in times of prosperity or recession, peace or war.

On this as on other issues the labelling of Left and Right within the political debate completely breaks down. Some so-called 'Left wing' politicians can be found rejecting a legislative right to freedom of information, wider use of Select Committees and even political advisers, some so-called 'Right wing' politicians are among the most active in championing all or some of these reforms. As is so often the case, when an issue is analysed division breaks down conventional labels and can be traced more to the divide between centralists and decentralists. The centralists, advocating or accepting corporatism in various guises, tend to want little or no change, fear the detailed scrutiny of Select Committees, resist giving to Committees the power to put their reports to the vote, and cling to keeping every issue a polarized political debate. If it is to check the Executive, parliament must not be afraid to seize back some power from the party machines. Until parliament wins back the power of the vote conceded over many decades to the Party Whip, and uses it on occasion as a body crossing the Party divide, then parliamentary democracy will continue to be unable to assert its own independence, and the present mix of corporatism, with an occasional lurch in the direction of Party dogma, will predominate.

Sentimentalists who relish the polarized debate on the floor of the House, little realizing how ritualistic and unattractive it is even to political activists, will fight any such changes. The average person, whose reaction to the sound broadcasting of parliament has on occasion been very critical, will realize that there are occasions when the floor of the House should become the theatre for the nation, a forum for real debate, the centre of genuine democratic challenge and conflict. But to expect it to fulfil this role day in and day out, to fear the creation of Select Committees, to regret the wish of MPs to specialize, is to advocate a pattern of parliamentary opposition for its own sake that engenders confrontation and in its own way diminishes politics in the eyes of the public. Politicians so ready to reform everyone else have been strangely reluctant to grapple with the reform of their own institutions. It is a majority of politicians who cling to the status quo and appear unable to adapt to a modern age, and who give the predominantly false impression that they like nothing more than to exchange insults across the floor of the House of Commons – and yet who go into smoking rooms to chat and even drink together after the actual confrontation is over.

Parliament which has so many strengths, so many unwritten practices and traditions, should never be underestimated, yet, for the generation who responded to John Osborne's play, *The*

Entertainer, it can sometimes seem like a succession of continuous performances by Archie Rice in the theatre on the end of the pier – ignoring the fact that the audience has disappeared, bored and disenchanted, to read their newspapers in the sun or take the excitement from the local cinema, bingo hall or televsion screen. For a younger generation it can seem reminiscent of the singer's lament, 'bring on the clowns'. It is time for parliamentarians to reassert their role as the practitioners of the art of democratic free government.

9

CONSTITUTIONAL REFORM

The present system of government in Britain is essentially Victorian in origin, though the power of the Executive in relation to parliament has increased. The system itself has remained surprisingly intact and a series of attempts at reform over the last fifteen years have all stumbled against a stubborn reluctance to contemplate fundamental change. The trend towards corporatism has been reinforced and the amount of democratic participation in the country at large has been unhealthily reduced. The result is stagnation and inertia instead of progress.

Scottish and Welsh devolution, regional government in England, proportional representation, the House of Lords, the European Assembly and membership of the European Community, and Northern Ireland, all pose genuine problems for our system of government yet the debate over these issues has never set in motion a fundamental reappraisal of the system or of the theory of British government. As in so many areas of British public life successive governments have responded to political pressures and public criticism by tactical decisions, the establishment of a Royal Commission, or Committee of Enquiry or the assumption in a Manifesto of commitments that owe more to transient moods and political prejudices than to considered or careful research and thought.

The recent history of failure over constitutional change is not just a sad saga of incompetence, prejudice and inefficiency, though all these have played a part; it is that in the absence of a theory of the state and a comprehensive view of its role and its philosophical relationship to society politicians have been buffeted by every transient pressure and have proposed piecemeal ad hoc changes which lacked both coherence and conviction.

It is interesting to note – in terms of how the cycle of constitutional change has moved over the last fifteen years – that it was reform of the House of Lords that started the process of constitutional change when a radical politician, Richard Crossman, was appointed leader of the House of Commons. After detailed discussions between the political parties, with representatives from the House of Lords fully involved, the government published its proposals for reform in a White Paper.[1] It was in some ways a model of how to proceed. Since the issue was so central to parliament and politics it was rightly judged that it was best to consider the issue among parliamentarians and not set up an outside enquiry. Even though the government's majority was large it was wisely decided to seek all-party agreement: the proposals eventually presented were broadly acceptable to the then Opposition. The error was in not realizing the widespread resistance among Labour MPs to any extension of Prime Ministerial patronage. The dialogue was confined to government and opposition spokesmen. There was no attempt to take formal evidence, no systematic consultation with other MPs. So when the Parliament (No. 2) Bill, which was framed to give legislative effect to the White Paper, was presented it ran into substantial opposition from backbenchers on both sides though for different reasons. Eventually, in April 1969, after the Bill had ground on and had taken up more and more time on the floor of the House, severely curtailing other government business, the Bill was withdrawn. Many people were involved in the opposition to the proposals but it was noteworthy for the strange tactical alliance forged between two then backbench MPs, Michael Foot, who wanted total abolition, and Enoch Powell who wanted to retain the hereditary principle. This alliance was to re-emerge over opposition to the 1972 European Communities Act and to provide the background to much of the support that the Ulster Unionists gave the minority Labour government until the censure motion April 1979. Both were united in their strong views about the sovereignty of parliament, the pre-eminence of the debate on the floor of the House of Commons and their romantic views of the role of backbenchers in the chamber of the House of Commons.

This combination of cross-party views and the considerable reluctance to guillotine a constitutional Bill meant that the status quo triumphed and the first major attempt at constitutional change ended in stalemate on the floor of the House of Commons. There had been 285 votes for and 135 against the Second Reading on a two-line Whip. Only 25 Labour MPs voted against and on a free vote 58 Conservatives supported the measure. Yet the Bill needed more than this; it needed an enthusiast as Leader of the House to drive the reform through. Richard Crossman had by then become Secretary of State for Health and Social Security. Writing in his diary at the time, he regretted he was no longer Leader of the House. 'I could have continued the experiment in radio broadcasting of proceedings leading up to the televising of Parliament. I could have kept going the specialist committees and the drive to get the House controlling the executive and pressing for more private business.'[2]

Personalities matter in parliament and reforms depend on a radical spirit rarely found amongst senior politicians, who are only too content to increase the power of the Executive. The demise of the Bill was a triumph for parliament, as some backbenchers claimed, but it also revealed the innate conservatism which bedevils British politics. It revealed an attitude among some backbenchers which was to haunt constitutional reform throughout the 1970s. The sovereignty of parliament became an absolute for these people. Any change posed a threat, none more so than the Treaty of Rome, which led them to oppose implacably any change in the sovereignty of Britain and particularly of parliament in relation to Britain's membership of the Community. The reforms of the Lords that were proposed in 1968 included the elimination of the hereditary principle so as to prevent any one party having a permanent majority and to allow in normal circumstances the government of the day to have a reasonable working majority. It restricted the power of the Lords to delay legislation to six months and abolished the power to withhold consent to subordinate legislation, giving only the right to ask for reconsideration. It involved a two-tier membership with a new category of 'non voting' members entitled only to speak. Existing hereditary members would continue to sit in one or other category but in future succession to a hereditary peerage would no longer carry the right to a seat in the House. The number of Bishops was to fall from 26 to 16 but the judicial functions of the Lords were to be retained.

The Labour government thought that a system of single-chamber government would not only be contrary to the practice of every other parliamentary democracy which has to legislate for a large population, but also that the case for two-chamber government in Britain had been strengthened since the end of the Second World War by the growth in the volume and complexity of legislation, the increase of the executive's activity and power, and its use of subordinate legislation. Moreover, abolition of the second chamber would subject the House of Commons to severe strain and paradoxically would result in less procedural flexibility and speed because of the need to guard against the overhasty passage of legislation.

The six-month delay period was to run across sessions of parliament, so avoiding the need for legislation to be reintroduced, and this was justified on the grounds that without it the House of Lords would be little more than a debating chamber – though the mechanism would be rarely used since the government would normally have a majority. It was described as a power of delay sufficient to cause the Commons and the government of the day to think seriously before proceeding with a proposal.

The failure of the legislation meant that over the next ten years there was little public discussion of the position of the House of Lords except that within the Labour Party the NEC established a working party and issued a statement, 'The Machinery of Government and the House of Lords', which was debated and approved by Annual Conference in 1977. It recommended a Manifesto commitment for the next election that a Labour government would abolish the House of Lords. To preserve the constitutional safeguard against an extension of the life of the House of Commons beyond five years, it proposed that any extension should be subject to approval by a Referendum or, in time of war, by a two-thirds majority of the House of Commons. There was considerable feeling within the Labour Party about the Lords in 1977 because of their wrecking action, relying on hereditary peers to obstruct the Aircraft and Shipbuilding Industries Bill, the Dockwork Regulation Bill, the Rent (Agriculture) Bill and the Education Bill. The Labour Party study claimed that the House of Lords had not been especially valuable as a revising chamber and quoted research demonstrating that the mass of amendments were 'tidying up' amendments. The NEC felt that if there was to be a second chamber it would have to be an elected second chamber and it was feared that it could then have a legitimate right to challenge the elected House of Commons and would develop such powers. The NEC statement admitted that a case had been advanced which set out the advantages of some, if not all, members of the proposed devolved assemblies having a base in a second chamber at Westminster, but they argued against this as they argued against the suggestion that directly elected members of the European Parliament should be members of a second chamber.

In retrospect it can now be seen as unfortunate that Jim Callaghan as Prime Minister did not oppose the 1977 proposals either on the NEC or at Conference. It was wrongly assumed they were acceptable and it was – not unreasonably – resented when at the Clause V meeting between the NEC and the Cabinet in April 1979 he argued strongly against a commitment to abolish the Lords in the 1979 Election Manifesto. There were sound arguments against such a commitment – and Jim Callaghan was not alone in his opposition.

After the election defeat this issue became the symbol of the argument that the Manifesto should in future be written by the NEC, a proposition which was lost at the 1980 Conference. It can hardly be argued that the absence of a commitment to abolish the Lords as a second chamber lost any votes and few remember that a commitment to abolish all the Lords' delaying powers was in the Manifesto. After Tony Benn's speech at the 1980 Conference, promising to abolish the Lords and to create a thousand peers to prevent the legislation being blocked, the existence or form of the second chamber has once again become an issue. Labour MPs are divided, and the Conservative government may remove some of the more absurd features of present procedure in order to be able to mount a more considered defence of the second chamber. The case for abolition of hereditary peers commands widespread support but there is little public enthusiasm for a single chamber parliament and it is not hard to see how images of the Orwellian 1984 will be deployed against the case for abolition.

There is a strong case for retaining a bicameral parliament as part of a coherent pattern of comprehensive constitutional change, and as part of a reassessment of the course to chart after the collapse of devolution in 1979. Devolution failed not on the floor of the House of Commons but through the referenda in Scotland and Wales, which were imposed on a reluctant government by backbench MPs. To analyse the roots of this failure it is necessary to go back to the political purpose which underlay the establishment in 1969 of the Royal Commission on the Constitution under the chairmanship of Lord Kilbrandon. It reported in 1973 only after the two-tier reform of local government had been pushed through parliament and the case for combining reform of central and local government had been lost. The Commission was quite clear about why it had been appointed: 'We have no doubt that the main intention behind our appointment was that we should investigate the case for transferring or developing responsibility for the exercise of government functions from Parliament and the central government to new institutions of government in the various countries and regions of the United Kingdom.'[3]

The Commission having rightly though narrowly interpreted its terms of reference soon found that during the course of its enquiry it came under pressure to report on different pressing areas of concern. With the Scottish Nationalist Party becoming a serious electoral rival to the Labour Party in Scotland, Scottish and Welsh nationalism was the urgent issue for the Labour government. Later the Commission came under pressure to pronounce quickly on English regionalism before firm decisions were made on the structure of local government. These decisions became politically necessary once it became clear that the Local Government Commission's Report proposing unitary authorities would not be implemented by the new Conservative government, for while the unitary single-tier structure called for a regional structure, retaining the counties made a regional tier arguably less important. Then Northern Ireland went to the top of the agenda for the Commission as violence in Belfast increased. Then the effects of membership of the European Community and its particular effect on the Channel Islands and the Isle of Man became an important area on which to focus. The Commission considered the position of the Lords in relation to the regions but concluded, 'In our view it would be neither practicable nor desirable for a change in the structure of Parliament to give effect to a regional policy to take the form of a change in the House of Lords. Reform of the House of Lords raises considerations extraneous to the question of regional government, and recent history shows these considerations would prevent any change in the near future; if a regional structure for Parliament were thought advantageous, therefore, it would be inadvisable to link it with the House of Lords.'[4] Given that the report was being written in the aftermath of the collapse of the proposed reform of the House of Lords the conclusion may have been an accurate political judgement, but that such an important constitutional concept could be so lightly dismissed is not easily justified and revealed the unimaginative approach adopted by the majority.

The dissenting minority report was more perceptive in its advocacy of devolution and in highlighting some of the weaknesses in the majority recommendations when it said, 'We cannot believe it is right or acceptable that the Westminster Parliament should be precluded from legislating for Scotland and Wales in a wide range of subjects (including education, housing and health) while at the same time about 100 Scottish and Welsh MPs at Westminster would have a full share of legislating in these same matters for England alone.'[5] It was this problem that was to bedevil the various legislative attempts made by the minority Labour government, and when it was debated on the floor of the House of Commons it helped to undermine the credibility of the proposals for devolution in the country as a whole. The criticism became known as the 'West Lothian question' after the Labour MP for West Lothian, Tam Dalyell, who persistently raised this question and fought devolution predominantly on it. Tam Dalyell and others considered it wrong that he, as a Scottish member for West Lothian, should be entitled to influence decisions affecting England without English members having a similar right to influence Scottish legislation. In this question many of the fundamental issues underlying devolution were encapsulated: sovereignty, separatism, over-representation, under-representation. It posed in simple terms an obvious inconsistency in the proposals, something which many felt to be a fatal flaw. It was the argument which was also used effectively by some English MPs who, though they opposed devolution for different reasons, could all combine to exploit this single issue. English MPs resented the fact that Scotland was already receiving more money per head from central government than any English region, and the fact that Scotland was over-represented to the extent of some fourteen MPs. These factors contributed to the concern particularly of the Northern group of Labour MPs, about devolution. In the crucial revolt on the guillotine motion on 22 February 1977, which effectively killed the devolution legislation in that session, the Northern group, which accounted for only 9 per cent of all Labour MPs, provided for 18 per cent of the Labour votes against 25 per cent of the Labour abstainers. There were, too, Northern members in the government who privately held considerable reservations about the legislation. What was significant was that the Northern Labour MPs, the most loyal and steady group in the Parliamentary Labour Party, actively demonstrated their concern, which became crucial when taken with the hostility of most Conservative MPs. Eventually the devolution legislation reintroduced in 1978 was enacted but only after the referendum amendment, moved by George Cunningham, a London-based Labour MP though a Scot by origin, was forced on the government by Labour backbenchers supported by the Conservatives. The amendment ensured that before the Scotland Act 1978 and Wales Act 1978 could be implemented there had to be a referendum in Scotland and Wales and an affirmative vote of at least 40 per cent of those entitled to vote, not simply a majority of those who actually voted. The referenda, as in the case of referendum over membership of the European Community, were advisory to parliament, but if less than 40 per cent voted, an order for the repeal of the relevant Acts had to be laid before parliament.

On 1 March 1979 the referendum was held. In Wales the proposals were decisively rejected; fewer than one in eight Welsh voters turned out to support the Scotland Act, nearly 40 per cent of the voters stayed away and the margin of the 'yes' vote was 3 per cent. It was described in the *Guardian* as 'a grudging thin and meaningless consent', a significant and fair judgement from a newspaper that for all the flaws saw the Scotland Act as 'a potentially liberating force in British politics'. The referendum result meant that it was judged impossible to force through the Scotland Act. This led to the Labour government being defeated by the Scottish Nationalist Party vote on a motion of confidence while the memories of the winter of discontent were still fresh, and to the calling of the 1979 General Election with the by then almost inevitable return of a Conservative government.

There are two fundamental decisions which the country, and not just its politicians must now face. Will the issue of devolution go away? Should devolution be implemented without resolving the 'West Lothian question'? All the evidence indicates that the rise of the Scottish Nationalist Party is not a temporary phenomenon in British politics. Its rise from 1955 can be carefully traced.[6] It has waxed and waned, but each time it gathers momentum again, usually on the tide of disillusionment with the UK economy. Each time the resurgence starts, however, it does so at a higher level of support. This ratchet effect is very likely to restart some time in the 1980s. Scotland feels that it is a nation, and it is a nation, and this is the justification for treating Scotland differently from the English regions. In Westminster, characteristically, the majority feeling is that devolution is dead, yet I believe that if the issue is ignored throughout the 1980s, it will ultimately come back and challenge the unity of the United Kingdom. The 'West Lothian question' has, however, now been shown to be of importance. The record of failing to grapple with the dilemmas it raises is clear: the attempt to introduce constitutional change in the absence of some measure of cross-party support has ended in ignominious failure. It is time to learn from the past and choose a different path towards the same objective.

The key lies in re-examining the arguments in the Memorandum of Dissent to the Kilbrandon Report which took a wider and more radical view of the constitution. The minority defined four essential objectives: '(a) to reduce the present excessive burden on the institutions of central government; (b) to increase the influence on decision making of the elected representatives of the people; (c) to provide the people generally with more scope for sharing in, and influencing, government decision making at all levels; (d) to provide adequate means for the redress of individual grievances. In our view all the evidence makes it clear that it is just as important to achieve these objectives for the people in the different regions of England as for the people in Scotland and Wales.'

This is a correct judgement – though the people of Northern Ireland should also be considered, but separately, and in the context of Ireland as a whole. The essence of the minority report was to set up seven democratically elected assemblies and governments for Scotland, Wales and five English regions. The proposals were seen as reinforcing the political unity of the UK while adapting UK institutions to membership of the European Community. The minority members of the commission felt that there was very little hope for real devolution of any independent legislative power to the different nations and regions of the United Kingdom. They saw their objectives as being 'substantially to reduce the burdens on central government so that Whitehall and Westminster have the time to promote and watch over British interests in Brussels – but to do it without any significant devolution of legislative autonomy.' This was a reasonable objective but their specific proposals did not arouse much public or political support. A synthesis is required which bridges the major political obstacles to constitutional reform that can now be more clearly identified than was possible when the Kilbrandon Commission reported in 1973.

The simplest, and neatest way of resolving the 'West Lothian question' is to accept that the Westminster parliament must retain the ultimate rights over all legislation in the UK in order to satisfy the political wish to ensure the overall unity of the Kingdom. It is surprising if that is accepted, that more attention has not been given to the concept of retaining a two chamber parliament, with the membership of the Second Chamber drawn from the several countries, nations and regions of the United Kingdom. The members of the Second Chamber would be elected for Scotland, Wales and the English regions, and Assemblies in the nations and regions would operate as extensions of the Second Chamber, and under the powers of the Second Chamber. The Second Chamber or Westminster Assembly as it could be called would act as a revising Chamber only, as at present for English and Welsh legislation, but having all the powers of investigation and scrutiny at present vested in the House of Lords, which would be used in the Welsh and English regional Assemblies. The Second Chamber, in recognition of the distinctive nature of Scotland's separate legislative history, would have the primary legislative responsibility for Scotland. This responsibility would be exercised through the Scottish members of the Second Chamber who would also be members of the Scottish Assembly. The

First Chamber, the House of Commons, would for Scottish legislation act as a reserve chamber, holding its existing powers but exercising them only as reserve powers, in the way the House of Lords broadly operates today in relation to the House of Commons. The term Lord and House of Lords would be abandoned for it has a connotation of privilege which can never be eradicated. The Second Chamber would be different from the present House of Lords. It would revise House of Commons legislation as at present except for Scotland; but as a Westminster Assembly it would also reflect that aspect of the nation which is a combination of nations and of English regions. Most of the special legislative provision and practice of the House of Lords would be retained and the judicial functions of the Lords would stay unchanged. There are already separate legislative powers for Scotland which are treated differently by the House of Commons through the mechanism of the Scottish Grand Committee; but, as part of a genuine legislative devolution, primary responsibility for legislation would pass to the Scottish Assembly drawing its powers from being part of the Second Chamber. In sequence, Scottish legislation would take its formal First Reading in the Second Chamber. The Second Reading and Committee stage of all Scottish Bills would be taken in the Assembly in Scotland, and probably the Third Reading. Scottish Bills would come to the House of Commons, as sometimes happens now on non-controversial Bills, after the legislation had gone through all its stages under the procedures of the Second Chamber.

The executive powers devolved to the Scottish Assembly and legislative powers as part of a Second Chamber would follow broadly the pattern of the Scotland Act 1978. It would probably be judged necessary for a Secretary of State for Scotland to be appointed to serve in the Cabinet, as was envisaged in the Scotland Act, even though the Westminster government would have transferred executive responsibility for a range of public services, and industrial powers to the devolved Assembly. It would be preferable for members of all the assemblies to be elected by proportional representation for otherwise one political party could achieve in some of them an unhealthy degree of dominance.

There is in any arrangement for devolution the potential for damaging conflict. The Scottish Nationalists could control the Scottish Assembly and might try to introduce 'creeping separatism' but the safeguard in these arrangements is that the House of Commons retains the power to reject any separatist legislation from the Assembly. Conflict is particularly dangerous with any form of legislative devolution, and the question arises what degree of freedom is sensible to minimise the possibility of conflict. Over Northern Ireland for many years the Stormont Parliament was not checked by the limited fall-back powers Westminster possessed and this contributed to the build-up of discrimination in Northern Ireland but the dominant party was not separatist but unionist. It was the fear of separatism and the feeling that the judicial powers of review and the fall-back powers of the Secretary of State for Scotland were inadequate, which helped to ensure that support for the Assembly was so grudging in the Scottish referendum. The argument used against this fear of irresponsibility was that the Assembly would behave responsibly and not enact legislation which would be deeply offensive to the Westminster parliament and damage the unity of the United Kingdom. This was a powerful argument, but it failed to convince. What is being advocated here is a change of roles whereby it is the House of Commons which would have to act responsibly and show restraint and not challenge the right of the Assembly to legislate differently from the views of the House of Commons, using the power to veto only where there were over-riding reasons of national importance. This is asking a lot of any political party with a majority but the operation of reserve powers is deliberately left to understanding and practice rather than being built into the legislation. If the House of Commons is prepared to grant legislative devolution to Scotland it knows this means it cannot at the same time repeatedly flout the political judgement of an elected Assembly; only over separatism or on the rare occasion when it has a good case on merit and is probably backed by a broad section of Scottish opinion will it consider exercising its blocking power.

The extent to which a Welsh Assembly had any legislative autonomy along the lines of the Wales Act must now depend on the evolution of opinion in Wales. In the light of the 1979 referendum result it would probably be wisest to leave such a development open rather than to test the issue soon through a referendum, and let the Welsh people see the working out of all the new arrangements first in relation to the Scottish Assembly.

In the English regions there would be no likelihood of introducing any legislative devolution and the English and Welsh members attending the Second Chamber as and when they wished would tend to specialize, as do at present most members of the House of Lords, in carrying out the revising and scrutiny role for legislation covering the United Kingdom or for England and Wales. The Second

Chamber would have no more than the six-month power of legislative delay envisaged in the Parliamentary (No. 1) Bill and they would have no power to withhold consent to subordinate legislation.

UK members of the European Assembly would be members of the Second Chamber with full rights though they would only attend when matters of specific interest to them were being discussed. It has always been in the best interests of the European Community and the UK that there should be a serious attempt to reduce the gap between the MEP and the MP, and the case for dual membership, were it physically possible, has been a strong one. Those in the House of Commons most suspicious of European federalism should see that the most effective way of combating federal tendencies within the Community is to encourage linkage between Westminster and European MPs. All the voting members of the Second Chamber would be elected and there would be no hereditary members. There is a need for a smaller section of non-voting members being appointed on much the same lines as today to carry much of the routine work of the Second Chamber. Such a proposition might be attacked as a continuation of patronage, but this could be reduced, as in the case of the Bishops, by stipulating that the holders of certain important posts in public life would for the period they hold office be automatic members. Such posts might include, for example, the Chairman, President or General Secretaries of the CBI and TUC, the Association of County Councils, the British Medical Association, the Royal College of Nurses, the Law Society, the Institute of Mechanical Engineers – active politicians and past members of the House of Commons to provide parliamentary experience. Too large an element of appointed members would be a mistake, but there is a need to enrich the experience of the debating function of a Second Chamber by having a non-voting sector which would explicitly cover specialised interests in the country. There is a value in having some former members of the House of Commons serving in a non-voting capacity in a Second Chamber to carry out the revising role which recent research indicates has been of greater value than has been previously assumed.

The role of the Welsh Assembly and the Assemblies in the English regions would follow that envisaged in the dissenting minority report. They would not, however, take over control of the executive responsibility for the outposts of central government operating in their area. Nor would the Welsh Office, as long as there was no legislative devolution, be placed under the control of the Welsh

Assembly. Control would stay with the Secretary of State for Wales and so would the Departmental Regional Offices stay under the control of the Departmental Secretary of State or Minister. But it would be necessary to establish for every English region a junior Minister with responsibility for co-ordinating Whitehall's policy for the region and answerable for the Departments to the regional Assembly. The Assemblies' executive functions would not be another tier of bureaucracy, but would replace the existing Health and Water Authorities. An Assembly would also take over the consumer responsibilities from the present regional Consultative Councils for the Gas and Electricity Boards. The Scottish and regional Assemblies would have a revenue-raising capacity to conduct their operations. In part this would be a continuation of the water rate system but an additional source of revenue such as taking a part of the revenue from local income tax, a regional petrol tax or regional VAT should clearly be introduced. The Assemblies would have a scrutinizing and strategic role for the development of their regions, backed up by all the powers of the Second Chamber to examine Ministers, civil servants, and outside witnesses and to call for papers. The members would operate as an Assembly within the region and as members of the Second Chamber in Westminster. It may be that at a later stage it would be found desirable, as envisaged by the minority report, for the Assemblies to take control of and responsibility for virtually all the outposts of central government. This would mean, effectively, the adoption of a federal structure of government for the UK, perhaps a logical development, but much would depend on the extent to which a regional identity developed under the envisaged changes. The evolutionary potential is there, as a German Foundation report contrasting North Rhine Westphalia and North West England demonstrated.

There will be great argument over the definition of the regional boundaries but there would be no intention at this early stage of changing either the boundaries or the functions of local government; though this would not exclude the more limited organic changes in the functions of some of the major cities envisaged by the last Labour government. The boundaries must coincide with existing local government boundaries. There are serious criticisms of the local government reorganization of 1974 but to institute another upheaval at a time when local government is still absorbing the present reorganization would be a folly, incurring considerable extra costs and further disrupting services. There is a strong case for more than the five regions envisaged by the minority report: there are at present eight standard regions in England and ten regions may be needed to reflect sensible boundaries. The far South-West needs to be a region separate from Bristol and the Southern part of England needs to be a region separate from the Greater London Council. The boundaries should be established in the light of two fundamental principles to increase regional identity and avoid change for its own sake. While not crossing existing local government boundaries, they should aim to minimize the disruption involved in amalgamating the boundaries of the existing executive authorities covering the Health, Water, Gas and Electricity boundaries and they should take into account the standard regions and existing police boundaries. It is amazing that no government has yet rationalized all the regional boundaries. Such a reform would in itself produce economies and reinforce regional and national identification which are admittedly much stronger in the peripheral regions of England than in the centre.

It is impossible to consider comprehensive constitutional reform without assessing the system of voting operating within the United Kingdom. Historians may highlight the way in which the problem of Northern Ireland has precipitated electoral changes which have already started to spread across the United Kingdom. The introduction of referenda started with a border poll for Northern Ireland formally announced on 24 March 1972.

It was again Northern Ireland which broke through the traditional attachment to the 'first past the post' voting system and introduced the single transferable vote in 1973 to ensure that there would be Catholic representation in the Northern Ireland Assembly. The principle of a different voting system having been conceded in one part of the United Kingdom, the long-standing movement for electoral reform was handed a powerful lever to argue for proportional representation in all parts of the United Kingdom. It was given a further impetus by the need to legislate for elections to the European Assembly. In this case the retention of the traditional voting system meant that for the very large European constituencies, the effect of a fairly small swing of opinion to any one of the major parties meant a distorted electoral result, predictably with no Liberal representation and many more unfairnesses than in a general election with a large number of constituencies being involved. It was the manifest unfairness of retaining the 'first past the post' system which led a majority in the Labour Cabinet in 1977 to conclude that a system of proportional representation through a regional list was the preferable system for elections to the European

Assembly. This view was formed before the decision was taken to enter into negotiations over the Liberal-Labour agreement and was one of the reasons why it was possible for the principal negotiators on behalf of the government, James Callaghan and Michael Foot, to promise that the proposal for a regional list would be put to a vote in the House of Commons. It was, however, against the interests of the Liberal Party that their negotiators did not insist that the continuation of the agreement was dependent on a successful outcome of that vote. Such a firm declaration would have ensured that the government kept to the principle of collective responsibility and that all who wished to remain Ministers would have then voted both for the principle of the European assembly inherent in a genuine acceptance of the 1975 referendum result and for the regional list system, since this reflected the Cabinet majority. It may or may not have influenced a sufficient number of backbench Labour MPs to support the legislation. It was an opportunity which may only recur to take a decisive step towards electoral reform for the United Kingdom if the Social Democrats and Liberals win the next election.

Whatever the merits of electoral reform, and it is impossible to argue that the 'first past the post' system is the fairest system, reform may not come on its merits. It may come because it is forced on the Labour or Conservative parties as the price they have to concede for remaining in government at a time when the balance of votes is held by Social Democrat and Liberal MPs prepared to oppose the government and threaten another election. The debate about electoral reform lacks reality because the public sense that it is not an argument about merits but about power. The two major parties, Conservative and Labour, fear electoral reform. Since 1945 both of these parties have had an equal share of government and they would prefer a system of alternating power. The Social Democratic Party now challenges that monopoly.

The first past the post system is producing an indefensible basis for forming a government with the power of absolute decision. In 1951 a Labour government could poll 40 per cent of the electorate and receive more votes in number than the Conservatives and still lose the election. They could poll a mere 28 per cent of the electorate in October 1974, however, and remain in government until May 1979, when the Conservatives won a big majority, but still only with the support of 33 per cent of the electorate. The Liberal Party has by any standards of fairness been appallingly treated. That in February 1974 they should have polled 6 million votes, 19 per cent of the electorate, and yet won only fourteen of the seats provides fuel for justified criticism of the system. But the system can claim in its defence that its power of adaptation is considerable, that it did ensure that from February 1974 to May 1979, when for most of that period the Labour government was in a minority, it had to listen more than it would ever normally have done to the views of the minority parties and that, although the Labour government formed no formal coalition, it reflected minority party views. Though attention was focused on the Liberal-Labour arrangement or pact, there were numerous deals and arrangements made between the Labour government and the Scottish Nationalist Party, the Welsh Nationalist Party, the Ulster Unionists and the Social Democratic and Labour Party. The Ulster Unionists demanded the acceptance of more Westminister MPs for Northern Ireland. The Scottish Nationalists, despite divisions within the Parliamentary Labour Party, demanded priority for devolution. There were the obvious manifestations but there were many other understandings and accommodations.

The basic argument remains that the justification for the present voting system is that it produces a coalition within parties and that both Conservative and Labour are normally forced by the very electoral system to remain broad-based political movements reflecting a wide spectrum of views, and that a coalition within a party allows, because of its better discipline, for more decisive government than a coalition formed across the parties. Yet the post-war history of Britain, particularly since Suez in 1956, demonstrates convincingly that the record of government in Britain is no better and in many cases a lot worse than the record of continental European governments where coalitions across the parties are more frequent, as are changes of government in Belgium, Holland and even Italy. The record of German governments from the 1950s onwards and of French governments since General de Gaulle, both with different systems, is clearly better than that in Britain. Anyhow the 1940–5 coalition was one of the best governments Britain has ever had. There was a form of coalition by tacit inter-party agreement between 1910 and 1915 and from 1977 to 1979. Britain has had single party government with total control this century for only forty-eight of the years up to 1980.

When the arguments and the mass of books and pamphlets on the subject have all been weighed, the question of electoral reform will be resolved by the pressure of power politics, not by merit or by constitutional theory about coalitions or the two-party system. The Labour Party having narrowed its electoral appeal and ceased to be a broad-based coalition, a new left of centre Social Democratic Party has been formed. If the Social Democrats win the next election they are pledged to introduce proportional representation. Failing outright victory Social Democrat and Liberal MPs and other minor parties after an election, are very likely to hold the balance. They could all insist that they would not vote for a Queen's Speech which did not contain a referendum to be held within three months on a specific 'yes' or 'no' vote to a specific electoral system which they would put forward. The two major parties would be forced to choose and either one or other might accept, or the Queen might have to ask the Social Democrats and Liberals to form a government and if it failed to command a majority agree to another election. If at the election the result again gave the minority parties the balancing power to insist on a referendum even if the two major parties refused to put such a commitment in the Queen's speech, the Queen would again have to ask the Social Democrats and Liberals to form the government and it is hard to see how the referendum proposition could be refused by parliament. If, as would be likely, judging by repeated opinion polls, a referendum resulted in support for the specific system of proportional representation proposed, then it is hard to see how parliament could refuse to pass the legislation. The chances of such a sequence of events occurring are hard to assess. It nearly happened in February 1974 and became slightly more likely in 1977. It is possible that it may occur in 1984. But if the Social Democrats win outright then electoral reform will come about as a result of logical argument and persuasion. It could arise from fear where a government, sensing electoral defeat because of a world economic recession and factors outside its control, while still holding a parliamentary majority, introduced electoral reform as the only way of protecting the country from the danger of an extremist government from either the Right or the Left. But even this would presuppose a readiness of the Prime Minister and other key figures to admit the possibility of electoral defeat, which is an unlikely admission since the more extreme the Opposition the more they would hope that they would win.

The case for proportional representation for the Scottish, Welsh and regional Assemblies is that in order to win public acceptance these Assemblies must reflect national and regional views without becoming the vehicle for separatism or being controlled 100 per cent by one party – which could easily happen under the present electoral system. Some people argue that the Treaty of Rome will itself force electoral reform in Britain in the context of the 1985 European Assembly elections. There is no clear justification for this belief, since the Community, having once accepted that the British parliament should choose its own system, would be likely to accept that this would happen again. Any British government ought to recognize that the distorted result from the 1980 election damaged the United Kingdom's reputation in Europe, and at home damaged for Labour voters the very concept of European Community. It is, however, very probable that the argument that introducing proportional representation for European elections would make it more likely that it would eventually be introduced for Westminister elections would again persuade most MPs to vote for the continuation of the 'first past the post' system.

The exact system of proportional representation is not as important as the decision to adopt proportional representation. It is essential that a specific system is agreed between the Social Democratic Party and the Liberal Party before the next election. Some favour the Single Transferable Vote; I have previously favoured the system that has operated successfully in the Federal Republic of Germany which allows predominantly for constituency MPs, but with a supplementary list system. No party receiving less than 5 per cent of the vote is eligible for representation and this stops a mass of small parties developing. There is also a provision in the constitution that a government can only be voted out as a result of a no confidence motion if there is a linked confidence motion in a new parliamentary leader who would take over and form the new government.

The constitutional changes discussed in this chapter are far-reaching. Yet they build on and synthesize existing patterns in the constitution and in the present structure of government. They take account of much of the debate on the constitution over the last fifteen years and they combine both decentralization and devolution. Social Democrats will need to champion and argue for these radical reforms, since they will offend many vested interests in Whitehall and elsewhere, but they represent a new radical way forward for extending democracy while retaining at every stage the unity of the United Kingdom.

10

LOCAL GOVERNMENT

In 1851, sixteen years before the first major move towards universal suffrage, most of our present problems and tensions between local and central government were perceptively forecast: 'It is by independence of thought and conduct to be only acquired by the habit of being continually called on to express an opinion upon, and to take an active part in, the management of the affairs of their own district, that men can alone ever be really fit to elect representatives to Parliament or the local Council, or to form sound and respectworthy opinions on the conduct of such representatives . . . Free institutions do not, then, exist and national independence can never be ensured nor individual independence and forethought ever characterize a people unless true local self-government is fully and freely exercised in every district throughout the land.'[1]

The issue of popular identification with decision-making processes is as vital today as it was over a hundred years ago. However, the truth is that the average citizen's involvement is still largely restricted to periodic elections, and the habitually low turnout at local government elections is an indicator of a fairly general apathy. There is a widespread belief that local government is not 'local' but an arm of central government, that councillors lose touch with their locality when elected and that local government officials have a 'civil service' mentality. Many of the criticisms made in Chapter 8 about Whitehall can be applied as strongly to the Town Hall. It is ordinary people's sense of alienation from the process of decision-making that breeds this harsh scepticism. But how to over-come it and how to involve people in the decisions that affect their lives is an extremely difficult problem. As Professor Donnison, who served for years as the Chairman of the Supplementary Benefits Commission, has written: 'The electorate is likely to remain sceptical about public services and their professional staff. The governments will have to take more seriously the capacity of ordinary people to do things for themselves. . . We need not just more nursery schools, but more mothers running their own playgroups with more support and training from the state.'[2] It is this faith in the latent ability of people to help themselves and to help each other, given adequate support, that is so often lacking among experts and professionals, planners and managers, and administrators and politicians. Their scepticism is not without foundation, but if the assumption that people are not able to help themselves is allowed to go unchallenged, democracy itself is threatened.

It is this scepticism which has motivated much of the current criticism of local government, has allowed central government to erode local government's autonomy and has underpinned the movement towards centralization. Of course, the need to involve people in the decisions that affect their lives is widely acknowledged and a great deal of lip service is paid to it. But despite that the opportunity to participate in decision-making at a local level is still denied to most people in Britain, and attempts to generate interest and action at local neighbourhood or community level often meet with suspicion and open hostility from those whose function it should be to generate just this interest.

The quality of people's lives, whether in town or country, must concern Social Democrats, and while attention has been focused on the problems of city life, many rural areas face both similar and particular problems. For example, the depopulation of parts of North Devon, inadequate or non-existent public transport, unpredictable seasonal employment and low wages all contribute to the same sense of isolation and alienation that people living in cities have.

It is all too apparent that many people feel they have no say in any changes in their neighbourhood; that their wishes and needs are not recognized by a remote and impersonal council bureaucracy; and that their elected representatives are not available to listen to grievances. That is not to denigrate the dedicated work of many councillors: many of them are well aware of the justified criticism of their role and function.

The definition and identification of a community can never fit within an exact, precise and rigid formula. The pattern of social, cultural and economic life, the local centres for education, shopping, meeting and worship, transport facilities and means of communication – all these have their influence.[3] One sociologist has defined community boundaries – 'as far as you can push a pram' – and this serves at least to remind administrators, with their car and mileage allowances, that the people they serve have a different focus. The reasons why people feel alienated from their neighbourhood or community are complex but the results are all too apparent: vandalism, violence and crime increase, and the very fabric of life becomes threatened. The development and fostering of a 'sense of community' must be the task of both National and local governments.

As the 1977 White Paper of the Inner City pointed out, 'too little attention has been paid to the economic wellbeing and to the community life of the Inner City areas and the physical fabric in some parts is badly neglected or decayed.'[4] The same White Paper not only identified the need for resources to be channelled to areas in need but recognized that 'involving local people is both a necessary means to the regeneration of the inner areas and an end in its own right. Public authorities need to draw on the ideas of local residents, to discover their priorities and enable them to play a practical part in reviving their areas. Self-help is important and so is community effort.'[5] Unfortunately there has been constant hostility and suspicion from many officials and elected representatives at all levels of government both nationally and locally when people actually do try to involve themselves.

The White Paper went on: 'There is scope for the development of new methods such as area management or neighbourhood planning – in which both members and officers establish closer links with the people they serve and seek to provide the local authority's services in a way more closely attuned to the requirements of the area.'[6] It is one thing to recognize the need for participation but another to suggest how it should be effected; the idea was mooted for new procedures that would enable the community to articulate its needs. 'In some places elected Neighbourhood Councils . . . may have a role in representing the communities' views and in mobilizing voluntary effort.'[7] This statement recognized that the tiers of local government set up in the 1972 Local Government Act had failed to identify and respond to the needs of people living in Inner City Areas and that alternative structures might be set up to cater for particular local communities. This idea was based on the finding of the Inner Areas Studies undertaken by the government which called for greater sensitivity to the needs of the local people by public authorities, for the involvement of local communities, for closer integration of services, for better use of existing resources, for positive discrimination in favour of run-down areas and for changes in organizations, in attitudes and in policies.

Three separate organizations at present speak for neighbourhoods in England: the National Association of Local Councils (NALC) –

representing some 8,000 parish councils in rural areas – small towns, and some larger urban areas. These bodies all have statutory status. Besides these there are the National Federation of Community Associations (NFCA) representing 500 voluntary community associations in all types of communities, and the Association for Neighbourhood Councils (ANC) representing the smaller number of nonstatutory, democratically elected, neighbourhood councils and others who wish to secure statutory status for directly elected neighbourhood councils in England. The ANC believe that the present separation of these organizations, all with closely related, though not identical, aims and interests, is damaging to the cause of neighbourhood democracy and voluntary activity. They believe that neighbourhoods need a single representative voice to speak to each other, to central and local government, and to the general public, and that this could be achieved by bringing the three organizations much closer together, sharing facilities, cutting out duplication, and unnecessary misunderstandings. They do not expect such a body to become, like the ANC, a pressure group for extending statutory status, comparable to that of a parish council, to neighbourhoods in English towns and cities. The case for one group to speak for neighbourhoods in England is very strong and if it allowed those members who wish to press for statutory status to do so without committing those who disagree, it is hard to see any objection. Statutory status means direct democratic election, a right to limited precept on local authority rates, and accountability to local people through the electoral process. I favour it, but like the ANC I see it as a democratic right, an opportunity to be taken only by those neighbourhoods who positively want it. I see no merit in imposing a universal pattern, or forcing a different structure on communities who are happy with their own voluntary organization. There is not yet probably sufficient agreement for any government to legislate. If it is to come about it will need a groundswell of support from the local people.

The issue that transcends arguments about statutory status for neighbourhood councils is the need to ensure that local government itself survives as a truly democratic force. Challenges to the autonomy, freedom and independence of local government are nothing new, but the present Conservative government is mounting the most sustained attack on its fundamental nature that it has ever experienced.

In contrast to the situation in the 1980s, at the start of the century local government was at the height of its power and influence. There

had been a rapid expansion between 1870 and 1900 when local
government expenditure rose relatively much faster than that of
central government. By 1902 it was providing housing, sanitary
services, police, road repairs and education, and some authorities
were running train and bus services, providing water, gas, electricity, libraries, public entertainments, and owned docks and other
municipal enterprises. Public health extended to municipal hospitals
and covered maternity, child welfare and the mentally handicapped.
Local government was even given responsibility for the unemployed
until the Unemployment Assistance Board was formed in 1934.
After the Boer War, during the years from 1904–14 with the
exception of 1912–13, local government actually spent more than
central government; today central government spends nearly twice
as much.

It is only looking back that one can see the true extent of the shift
from local to central government to statutory duties, responsibilities
and resources in terms of employment and finance. Analysis of the
comparative spending figures reveals some interesting trends.[8] As
one would expect, central government spending leapt during both
World Wars and was accompanied by large deficits, only to be
followed by considerable falls in expenditure. Local government
expenditure increased much more steadily and it always met its
expenditure from its current income. Grant income from central
government was 12 per cent in 1913–14, 27.4 per cent by 1939–40,
and 36.9 per cent in 1974–5, when it jumped because of a major
policy switch, to 39.8 per cent of total income in 1975–6. The extent
of this particular switch is further emphasized if capital expenditure
is excluded, revealing that in 1966–7 rates made up 33.8 per cent of
income, grants 37.1 per cent and other sources 29.1 per cent but by
1976–7 rates contributed only 23.8 per cent of total incomes, grants
had risen to 49.6 per cent and other sources provided 26.6 per cent.
It is clear that the dramatic shift whereby central government
became virtually the paymaster of local government is a relatively
recent trend, starting in 1967 and increasing significantly in 1975.
Central government grants, which at the start of the century when
local government had its greatest powers, were a negligible source
of finance, have now become the dominant source, at the same time
as the powers of local government have declined.

These facts and the extent of the growth of the centralized state in
Britain need to be stressed for a post-war generation that has
forgotten the days of the powerful and often enlightened municipal
authorities, a generation which tends to forget the great cultural

traditions of cities like Manchester, the strengths of provincial England, and which accepts the dominance of London and Whitehall – as if that were the only possible form of government for Britain. The time is overdue for a reassertion of a different balance where local government recovers some of its former powers and influence and where a more variegated pattern of government matches the rich cultural distinctions between Devon and Derbyshire, Leeds and Bristol. It may be that the public mood is starting to sense that the sickening hostility displayed daily for a decade in the national press towards local government owes more to the centralized nature of that press than to any objective assessment of the weaknesses and strengths of local government. In April 1980 a Gallup poll at a time when the Conservative government was campaigning against local government spending showed that three people wanted better local services even if it meant higher rates for every two who wanted lower rates even if it meant worse services. What was even more surprising was that when asked if councils had enough independence from central government only 17 per cent said 'too much', 32 per cent said 'about right' and a healthy 34 per cent 'too little'.[9]

Some people argue that a shift of functions from local government to national government is inevitable in an increasingly complex industrialized society which is predominantly urban. Larger-scale institutions, it is said, are required to deal with long-range planning and nation-wide industrial strategies. The arguments are exaggerated, though there is a limited regional function distinct from local government. The regional offices of national government administer and co-ordinate regional strategies. Parliament has been responsible for placing a statutory duty on government departments to carry out or supervise functions which were previously the responsibility of local government, and then by leaving the exact means of administration often to be worked out by the Department concerned, has strengthened Whitehall. Civil servants have decided that while they are in control of much of the finance, responsibility cannot be delegated to local government for detailed policy-making and administration. So central government, because of increasing financial involvement, has increased its own powers and sought to curtail those of local government. Ministerial control of departmental decisions in the English regions is slight, in comparision to Wales and Scotland, as is parliamentary scrutiny. Regional Assemblies would have a scrutinizing function that the House of Commons is unlikely to be able to fill, but this function does not reduce the role of local government. The form of Regional Assemblies suggested in Chapter 9 does not affect local government but increases the accountability of the appointed water and health authorities and scrutinizes the civil service.

An overwhelming case can be made in favour of restoring the strength of local government: 'Local government in England can and does help to secure an active democracy; increase the knowledge, competence and independence of the people; provide personally and locally responsive services; make possible the apt distribution of powers and duties; preserve central and local accountability and support yet more local sharing in decision and administration. It does so through its local legitimacy and independence of the centre. Each local authority has a professional administration responsible to members who are elected and thus accountable. In short, local government is a critically important constitutional and democratic institution.'[10]

What is needed is a rethink of political attitudes towards centralization and decentralization. In 1971 the Conservative government's White Paper stated that: 'A rigorous local democracy means that authorities must be given real functions – with powers of decision and the ability to take action without being subjected to excessive regulation by central government through financial or other controls . . . above all else, a genuine local democracy implies that decisions should be taken – and should be seen to be taken – as locally as possible.'[11] Some people may therefore have been encouraged to hope that the 1979 Conservative government would, as part of its general attack on bureaucracy, start to challenge central government's interference with local government; and indeed, in the early months of the present administration much publicity was given to the abolition and relaxation of a wide range of petty and largely unnecessary central government regulations and controls. However, the 1980 Local Government Planning and Land Act introduced a block grant system which has the avowed intent of preventing a local authority from spending more than central government thinks it should. This legislation represents the single most centralizing measure ever passed by a British parliament, with consequences that are hard to exaggerate. Yet there was no public outcry. A few newspaper editorials made reference to it but there was no sense of shock. Parliament debated the Act under a guillotine and despite a considerable undercurrent of discontent from Conservative local councillors and a revolt by a few Conservative MPs, including a former Secretary of State for the Environment, there was no perception that what was being enacted was a constitutional outrage.

The sad fact is that legislation reflected the Whitehall consensus for which successive Labour governments were as responsible as the 1979 Conservative government. Though during the passage of the Bill through parliament the Labour Opposition made most of the correct criticisms, they were unable to mobilize public concern about the fundamental constitutional nature of the measure, not just because they were constantly reminded of the actions and decisions of the previous Labour government but because the public sensed the ambivalence within the Labour Party itself on the issue of the priority to be given to local government. This ambivalence is too obvious to hide behind a barrage of political criticism and it needs now to be thought through; it is basically the same ambivalence that haunted the debate over devolution, but it also goes much deeper and reflects the historic divide between the centralist and the decentralist philosophy.

It is impossible to move towards a more decentralized society without challenging the trend towards central government control of local government. For local autonomy to be a reality local authorities must have a degree of freedom to determine the range and standard of their services and to choose to increase or decrease the level of expenditure which they devote to those services. This principle may appear so obvious as hardly to need stating but it is now threatened by the power that the government has under the 1980 Act to reduce support to local authorities which overspend in the financial years from 1980–1. The government can now, at the routine yearly inflation adjustment known as the Increase Order, reduce retrospectively the level of grant that the local authority anticipated it would receive.

At no stage in the argument has central government been able to show that in order to ensure the proper running of the economy the Treasury needs to be able to exert this degree of precise control on the quantum of local government expenditure. The national economy contains so many variables and the margin of error is so wide in expenditure forecasts that absolute precision of forward estimating is impossible. Local government expenditure is, in contrast to so many other expenditures, self-financing, so the problem is not one of deficit accumulation but relates solely to overall levels of expenditure. The evidence is that, far from being out of control, local government expenditure has been held by a combination of pressures and constraints very close to the levels asked for by successive governments.[12] The 1978 government expenditure forecasts had local government spending falling by 13.6 per cent in 1980–1 compared to 1974–5, whereas it had central government spending rising by 7.7 per cent over the same period. The consequences of having a few authorities overspending are very marginal to the management of the national economy.

Local government becomes a public issue once a year in early April when the rates bill arrives and for a few weeks there are angry denunciations of waste and bureaucracy as the rating system becomes the butt of many people's anger. Very rarely does any central government resist the temptation to distance itself from this public mood. It has often encouraged the criticism and sometimes responded in the heat of the moment by indicating that it would reform the rating system. Instead of a mutual respect between central and local government there has been growing antagonism. In 1966 the then Minister of Housing and Local Government, Richard Crossman, was determined to have a serious examination of local government and two Royal Commissions were established, for England under the chairmanship of Lord Redcliffe-Maud and for Scotland under Lord Wheatley.[13] Astonishingly neither of the Commissions was asked to examine local government finance. The Redcliffe-Maud proposals for unitary authorities came too late in the lifetime of the Labour government to be implemented, though they were accepted in principle. The new Conservative government in 1970 cavalierly abandoned the Commission's major recommendations and legislated for a two-tier structure of local government under the Local Government Acts of 1972 and 1973. Under the Water Act 1973 local authorities in England and Wales also lost their responsibility for water, sewerage and sewage disposal. The 1974 reorganization itself triggered a major political controversy over local government, with allegations of 'Empire building' due to the substantial rates increases and the overlapping of responsibilities of the two tiers. There were many complaints of extravagance, particularly over the new system of councillor attendance allowances and lavish buildings contracted by the old authorities. The general rate revaluation of 1973 also meant that some people whose property had been reassessed had to face rate demands several hundred per cent higher than before. The average increase in rate demands sent by local authorities to domestic ratepayers in England and Wales was a little under 30 per cent but this average figure concealed increases from over 160 per cent to decreases of 9 per cent. Coming at a time of high and increasing inflation all these factors combined to unleash a general outcry in the spring of 1974 to which the newly elected Labour government had to respond. On 27 June the Secretary of State for the Environment announced the appointment of a Committee of Enquiry under Frank Layfield, QC, 'to review the whole system of local government finance in England, Scotland and Wales and to make recommendations.' The Committee was asked to work quickly and the report was published in May 1976.[14]

The Layfield Committee, however, came up with embarrassingly radical proposals. They argued that the level of government grant determines the amount of local autonomy and that over the last twenty years autonomy had been eroded as the grant had steadily risen to the then level of 60 per cent. They felt that autonomy had also been reduced by Whitehall setting national targets in the key services of education, police, fire, social services and roads, services which in 1975–6 accounted for over 80 per cent of total spending. The results, they argued, were confusion over who was responsible for rate increases, a lack of financial control because the increase of grants had encouraged local authorities to provide higher levels of services which the government would pay for, and an uncontrolled increase in spending and rates. The most important findings were that local autonomy would be increased if local authorities were given some financial independence and that government grants should be reduced to 50 per cent of spending, that rates should be at two thirds of their present level, and that a local income tax should be introduced at 11p in the pound.

A note of reservation by Professor Day argued that the majority report was wrong to reject a 'halfway house' solution by which the government should set minimum standards in services and pay for them entirely, and that there should be a clear division of responsibilities between local and central government. He argued that unless this was done, the creation of financial institutions which give greater formal powers to authorities to raise revenue from sources such as a LIT would be unlikely to achieve any greater degree of effective local autonomy than the political will of the government would be prepared to tolerate'.[15] The majority report rejected this view because it felt that minimum standards could not be easily defined and costed. Professor Day denied this, saying that the difficulties were exaggerated and that such costing systems had already been worked out for the NHS which, though provided nationally, has significantly different costs in different parts of the country. The analogy with the NHS is somewhat unfair in that health authorities have no independent source of finance. The

Layfield Report majority argued, however, that the introduction of national minima 'would impair the ability of local authorities to consider the best balance of provision within their areas as a whole and would introduce distortions in the allocation of resources'.[16] Also, 'If as seems possible, the cost of meeting minimum standards were to account for a large proportion of local government expenditure, a division of financial responsibility on this basis would tend to place the major share of responsibility with the government'.[17]

The Committee estimated that LIT would cost about £100 million per annum and the Inland Revenue would need to employ about 12,000 more staff. The tax would be levied by the metropolitan districts, non-metropolitan counties and by the Scottish regions, all of which would retain rating. Rating would be the sole tax for metropolitan counties and for non-metropolitan and Scottish districts, and all authorities would have grants. Rating, they argued – to many people's surprise – should be retained because it was felt that it is a visible and efficient tax, cheap to administer and difficult to avoid. However, since it does not take account of ability to pay and neglects the earning non-householder, it was recommended that it be supplemented by LIT and that a number of rating reforms be initiated. Rates, it was felt, should be based on the capital value of a property rather than on the rental value, that regular and frequent revaluations should be undertaken and that rates should be paid by instalments, as is the case in Scotland.

The Committee considered that a LIT was a 'serious candidate as a new source of local finance' as it alone offered a substantial yield and contributed to the accountability of local government. A number of possible schemes were considered. Scheme A was based on local assessment and collection whereby the Inland Revenue would provide local authorities with the necessary information to assess the tax. This scheme had very high administrative costs. Scheme B was on the lines operating in a number of other countries whereby the LIT is based on an end-year assessment for both local and national taxes. This was ruled out due to the Inland Revenue's policy of minimizing the number of taxpayers requiring an end-year assessment. Scheme C was based on self-assessment and was rejected as the costs were put at £200–250 million (1975 prices), representing 50,000 staff. The Committee came down in favour of a LIT within the present administrative framework. However, the estimated cost of £100 million annually and the 12,000 extra staff thought to be needed offered a marvellous target for local government's numerous Whitehall critics and was used unscrupulously by the centralists within the government to defeat the scheme. Referring to Scheme C some analysts have criticized Layfield on the grounds that, 'No satisfactory explanation was provided of how this remarkable high figure was derived. Not only does the £200–250 million estimate for self-assessed LIT wildly exceed the estimated costs of an officially administered version, but it is in the same league as the £249.8 million that it cost to administer all Inland Revenue duties in 1974–5'.[18]

The Inland Revenue have ruled out self-assessment since they argue that it would be costly to examine a proportion of returns to check for fraud and that there would be no incentive for taxpayers to render prompt returns. To which it may be replied that 'neither of these operations incurs such staggering costs abroad . . . there is no reason why taxpayers cannot be provided with an incentive to file prompt returns that have been completed accurately by a specified date. The Committee did not recommend self-assessment for income tax, local or otherwise.'[19] A number of countries levy a LIT, normally at a single rate. In Finland the rate varies between 13 and 18.5 per cent, Norway 18.5–22 per cent, Italy 8.9–14.7 per cent. Sweden is a good example of local and national taxes being almost totally integrated, with low administrative costs.

Much now depends on the detailed design of the forth-coming computerization of the PAYE system. The danger is that its design will be decided with little public debate and with the centralist civil servants closing political options under the guise of technical decisions. Only in Scotland is PAYE at present fully computerized. A pilot scheme is being carried out at six offices in the Midlands and a report has been completed on the implications for a national network. The evidence of the Chairman of the Inland Revenue, Sir William Pile, to the Public Accounts Committee is suspiciously vague on the degree of flexibility that will be built into the computer system. By 1985 computers, he thought, would be able to handle self-assessment but, 'We could not switch to an expenditure tax and use that same system. We could not, I think, introduce a LIT because there could be too many rate bands for employers to operate'.[20] In addition the kind of self-assessment that could be handled would have to be different from the American system and a very different system would be needed if a comprehensive LIT with multiple rates were adopted. Others argue that if we switched to self-assessment a LIT could be easily introduced. It is vital that this area is opened up to public debate, and examined in depth by a Parliamentary Select Committee before any irrevocable decisions are made.

The 1977 Labour government Green Paper was a most disappointing and negative response to the case for radical reform. It reflected every conceivable Whitehall prejudice and was deeply centralist in outlook. It rejected LIT for the following reasons: '. . . the Government do not accept that local accountability depends on the proportion of revenue raised locally; or that any clear advantages would flow from the introduction of LIT. The freedom of local authorities to vary the LIT rate would have to be closely constrained so that it did not unduly complicate central government's economic and financial management and there would need to be some equalization of the proceeds of the tax between richer and poorer areas. Partly for these reasons, it seems highly questionable whether the great majority of electors could be made aware of the LIT element in their normal PAYE deductions so as to achieve the Committee's objective of securing an effective local discipline on local authority expenditure decisions. The Government are not convinced, therefore, that the case for the introduction of LIT has been made.'[21]

This response neglects the fact that there are 15 million domestic ratepayers and 24 million income tax payers, and therefore 9 million people who are already contributing to the finance of local government without many of them realizing the full extent to which they are doing so. Layfield recommended that LIT be integrated into the national tax system and that notices of coding by the Inland Revenue should indicate to each taxpayer the local taxing authority. This would not be necessary under self-assessment, since the employer would calculate how much tax to withhold and then would add on a percentage to take account of LIT. Under a system of self-assessment a LIT would require far fewer additional staff than the 12,000 estimated by the Inland Revenue, since a local tax like the provincial tax in Canada would necessitate only the use of different withholding tables and the addition of one or two lines to the tax return. Against this must be set Sir William Pile's evidence to the PAC that a LIT with multiple rates would require a new computer system.[22] It is unclear whether the same objections would apply to a self-assessed LIT since he did not discuss this kind of tax, though he did say that self-assessed PAYE could be undertaken by the computer system if certain conditions were met.[23]

The Green Paper also rejected the localist approach recommended by Layfield because it 'would involve a surrender by central government of a large part of their present influence over local services'. It argued that since Layfield was set up the financial climate had changed so much that the need to control expenditure had become dominant, and, moreover, that LIT would involve large differences in the taxes paid in different parts of the country. Instead the Labour government proposed for consideration and discussion with local authorities a unitary grant by which ratepayers would pay roughly the same rate poundage for a similar level of services regardless of where they live. This would have the result that 'ratepayers would be in a position to ask, if the rate poundage were above the standard rate poundage, whether their local authority was less efficient or was providing services to a higher level than other authorities'.[24] Yet Layfield did recognize the real concern of national governments to control the level of spending as part of the overall management of the economy and recommended that LIT, if introduced, should be accompanied by a local spending regulator whereby the government could take from authorities a rising proportion of the revenue they were raising if the overall increase exceeded a certain level that had been set nationally. As a disincentive to excessive expenditure the amount of spending which could be financed by successive increases in local taxation would be progressively less. But Layfield was concerned that: 'the powers [of central governments] should be expressly designed to meet the government's concern with economic management and should involve no wider intervention in local government affairs than is needed for that purpose.'[25] This was a sensible recommendation but one which has been ignored by successive governments since.

Layfield considered that the local tax regulator did not undermine the accountability of local government to the electorate and, further, was capable of being 'made sufficiently powerful and flexible to provide the government with the control it needs'.[26] A second control was also suggested, by which the national government could specify the proportion of capital expenditure to be borne out of revenue rather than from borrowing. It was noted that this control has been adopted in Denmark and that, 'It could be used selectively, with different rates of revenue contribution by region, type of authority or purpose. It could be applied or varied at comparatively short notice.'[27] The amount of borrowing could also be influenced by interest rates and by regulating the terms of access of the Public Works Loan Board. A better relationship between central and local government, in which each party attempts to keep the other informed of its requirements, would also help to secure better management of the economy: 'If local authorities are to be in a position to take account of the government's policy on national requirements they need to be given a better appreciation of that policy than they have had in the past; and the government in formulating those requirements needs better information as to their implications for local authorities.'[28]

The Green Paper did not discuss this point; in fact, generally it did not bother to rebut the arguments of Layfield but simply stated that the government wished to retain control over expenditure. It was not only the Treasury who rejected Layfield's case for LIT. The 'protectionist' school of Cambridge economists also alleged that the 'fatal confusion' in Layfield was that it presumes 'local autonomy to derive uniquely from its power to raise local taxes, thereby ignoring the autonomy from a grant that is not hypothecated'.[29] They argued that grants should be distributed on the basis of norms of standardized expenditure set for each authority and did not accept that this would undermine local responsibility since the local authority would be deciding the distribution of the grant unfettered by central government. It is a very limited view of responsibility which believes it right to separate decisions over the size of expenditure and its financing from its distribution, and not surprisingly identifies the 'protectionist' economists with a centralist philiosophy. 'The Cambridge economists interpret responsibility narrowly and fail to take into account the political implications of the financial arrangements they advocate. Both central government and local authorities are elected; they have political bases and behave politically. They will seek political advantage for themselves from a grant system. When grant is high local authorities will try to place responsibility on the centre, claiming that local problems cannot be tackled because grant is inadequate. When it is so dependent on a large grant, that is also unstable, a local authority is transformed from a body that takes its own decisions in response to local pressures to become itself a pressure group on the centre urging more grant. It seeks to make out that it is a special case with distinctive features that the existing grant settlement has not taken account of. In turn the centre will respond with inspection to check up if the special case is justified and if the need to spend is present. So the departments are pulled into the detailed affairs of local authorities by a high level of grant.'[30]

The Labour government had set up the Layfield Committee as an act of political expediency to defuse a potentially serious political row: it soon discovered, however, as evidence from the various Departments began to be given to the Committee, that there was certainly no predisposition in Whitehall to favour any proposal for fundamental reform. It was the Department of the Environment in its evidence to Layfield that first introduced at a bureaucratic level the concept of the unitary grant which later became the foundation of the 1980 Act, and there has been much misunderstanding about its parentage and about who at various times supported it. The unitary grant was discussed by Layfield as the most appropriate form of grant, should government want to assume the major responsibility for local government expenditure and determine the spending patterns of individual authorities. However, since Layfield rejected this centralist model, the unitary grant was also examined in the context of the localist solution as a device for redistributing government grant while also giving local authorities responsibility for raising more of their own finance by means of LIT and rates. The Green Paper concealed the departmental origin of the unitary grant proposal, giving the impression that it came from elsewhere, and did not reveal the detailed discussion of its implications and consequences in Layfield. 'Disingenuousness could scarely go further . . . The Green Paper stands as a classic case of a threat to democratic institutions created by carelessness, muddle and poverty of thought.'[31]

Admittedly the Green Paper was not, like a White Paper, firm government policy, but that is a poor excuse. The foundation was laid for the 1980 Act by a Whitehall consensus which certainly covered the Department of the Environment and Treasury officials who had initiated the unitary grant, at least for five years, from 1975 and through the periods of responsibility of three Secretaries of State for the Environment, Anthony Crosland, Peter Shore and Michael Heseltine. It underlines how important it is to ensure that collective ministerial approval is given to Departmental evidence to Commissions of Enquiry and how unwise it was for the few of us in the Cabinet who were in favour of Layfield's 'localist' option to let a Green Paper float a dangerous concept like the unitary grant under the pretext that the government was not committed.

The 1979 government actually made the political decision to legislate to introduce the block grant, which is the same as the unitary grant, though they have attached to it some particularly obnoxious sanctions against overspending. But the 1980 Act – hard though it may be for socialists to admit – was merely the most offensive aspect of a trend that had continued unchecked during the period of a Labour government. The intent was clear: to shift decision-making to the Department of Education and the Department of the Environment. The essential decision that must now be taken, if local government is not to lose its autonomy, is quickly to find and agree an alternative source of finance and to accept as an essential first step the Layfield recommendation that government grant should not be above 50 per cent of local authority spending.

In the early years at least of any switch to a new source of local finance the Layfield judgement that rates should be maintained is probably correct, though since the Conservative government has delayed the revaluation that was due the anomalies will increase and the potential take decrease. It is hard to see a Conservative government abandoning the derating of agricultural land and building which was introduced in 1929, but as Layfield indicated there are strong arguments for opening up this additional source of finance for local authorities. The 1979 Conservative government is pledged to abolish rates at some future date and this, along with the general public dislike of them, makes it unlikely that the rating system can ever recover wide national acceptance. The case for its retention is, however, stronger than is ever acknowledged by the general public and any new tax would soon make rates more acceptable in retrospect.

There are a number of alternatives less well-known and less documented than LIT. It might be feasible to incorporate rates, which are a property tax, with a new wealth tax. The property element of a wealth tax would go to provide local authority finance, but that portion levied on investments and objects of value could go to the Treasury. Local sales tax, though criticized by Layfield, is another possibility, particularly if it could be levied at a regional level and then distributed to local authorities on a per capita basis. Similarly, an additional specific regional petrol tax is an option which would have the advantage of taking some account of shifts of population such as summer tourism, which put additional costs on local authorities but is more attractive as a source of finance for national and regional assemblies. It is probably wiser to accept the introduction of an additional source of revenue initially as a supplement to rather than a substitute for rates. Then as the rates are frozen the revenue coming from the new tax could be built up, and only when the teething problems that surround the introduction of any new tax are over would the rating system be abandoned. Rate income is too large and too certain a source of revenue for it to be prudent to risk abolition without knowing the exact impact of a new tax.

Once a local authority has a buoyant source of finance the whole debate about local finance changes. Provided some mechanism such as the regulator proposed by Layfield is introduced to discourage local authorities from using their revenue raising powers without regard to their cumulative macro-economic effect, all that is needed is to find an acceptable mechanism for distributing the grant. Since the 'resources' and 'needs' elements have now been abandoned and the block grant put in its place, there have been strong arguments for moving towards a total simplification of the grant system and for introducing a simpler distribution based more on population.[32] One advantage claimed for the block grant is that the assessed needs expenditure per head and the standard rate poundage will be openly declared. But local authorities fear that this will lead to pressure for uniformity and loss of autonomy and argue that even if some deprived authorities were to lose some grant revenue, it is better to have a known grant which is not controlled by Whitehall. They fear that under the block grant system 'local government will become a pressure group rather than a government, arguing its case at national level together with other pressure groups.'[33]

Though the case for simplification is emotionally very attractive, particularly while fears of central government interference have yet to be tested by experience, it needs to be considered with caution. It is potentially dangerous to abandon any way of channelling central government money into areas of highest need, because social needs may be highest in areas that are depopulating and have a low income, and have little chance of raising much local revenue from rates or from any additional source. A redistributive formula, if it could be openly negotiated, is compatible with local autonomy provided it is accompanied by greater freedom for local authorities to raise their own finance. Failure to recognize this has been the basic mistake behind all the discussion of the unitary/block grant. The flaw in the previous system was the automatic increase in central government's grant when a particular local authority decided to increase its spending. This meant that the Rate Support Grant was not a fixed sum and if local spending increased as a result of local decisions during the year it did affect the government's expenditure forecasts and did require supplementary estimates. If local government has the freedom to raise its own finance, then how central government fixes its grant is predominantly its affair. If the central government grant is reduced in size then the local authorities' flexibility in raising revenue makes any readjustment more tolerable. They can offset central government decisions over redistribution and need in their grant by a local decision to raise extra revenue. Central government could act on its responsibility to try to ensure overall national standards and to stimulate spending in specific areas as a result of national policy, but local government would retain the right to challenge the priorities of central government from its own financial resources.

Central government must protect the education service from the growth in the private sector. Legislation to ban charging fees for private education touches on major issues of human rights (see Chapter 11). In 1978–9 local authorities spent £45–50 million supporting pupils at independent schools. Central government paid a further £37 million in boarding school allowances to public servants, mainly in the armed forces but also in the diplomatic service. It is legitimate and right to phase out this financial support for the private sector and to make tax changes as a disincentive to the growth in private education. But this will need to be accompanied by an increase in the quality and number of boarding places available in local authority schools for non-handicapped pupils, which in 1978 in England and Wales numbered only 8,900. Improving local authority schools remains the best way of curbing the growth in private education and offsetting their social divisiveness.

A redefinition of responsibility between central and local government and the greater financial independence of local government is the only way to revive local democracy and reverse the stultifying embrace of Whitehall.

A major reason for the failure of the 1970s reorganization of local government and the NHS has been that the reformers – whether civil servants, Ministers or MPs – have refused to confront the real dilemma: decentralization or continued centralization. In the NHS the issue of local control has been fudged at every decision point and the result has been an uneasy and often unworkable compromise between a civil service run Department of Health and Social Security and health administrators running, in effect, three other layers at the Regional, Area and District level with members of the medical profession as individual decision-makers holding most of the power.[34]

The Royal Commission on the National Health Service, established by the Labour government in 1975, had the opportunity to challenge the centralized structure of the NHS but failed to grapple with this issue. Some argue that 'the job of a Royal Commission is consensus engineering'.[35] While that may be the correct approach for a Royal Commission in constructing its recommendations, it should not apply to its analysis of the issues under its scrutiny. Past Commissions of enquiry have sometimes produced very fundamental critiques. In 1842 the Chadwick Commission's 'Report on an Inquiry into the Sanitary Conditions of the Labouring Population of Great Britain' challenged the then current belief that disease was all the fault of the undisciplined and unclean labouring class and that all that was required was greater discipline and individual responsibility. It argued instead that disease was transmitted among the labouring classes by environmental pollution resulting from overcrowding, lack of drainage and inadequate water supply. This led to the Private Act of Parliament introduced by Liverpool in 1846 for the appointment of the first Medical Officer of Health, the Public Health Act of 1848 and, later, the great Public Health Act of 1875. This set the climate for preventive medicine, making staggering improvements in health care which far outweigh the significance of drug treatments; it is now in the 1980s that we should again look to preventive medicine for major improvements in health care.

The Royal Commission on the NHS in its report[36] dismissed the gloom and the doomsters and rejected the naive belief that responsibility for health issues could be taken away from parliament or that a revival of health insurance offered a credible method of financing the service. It is to the Commission's credit that it was, in its own words, content to eschew 'blinding revelation' and that it made a series of detailed but evolutionary recommendations for adaptation supporting the altruistic philosophy which inspired the creation of the NHS. Yet its analysis of the way in which the longer term structure of the NHS might develop was disappointingly unimaginative.

On 5 October 1945 in his first memorandum to the Cabinet, Aneurin Bevan wrote, 'We have got to achieve as nearly as possible a uniform standard of service for all'.[37] He rejected a local government system of care because he felt it would make the achievement of such uniformity impossible, arguing that 'there will tend to be a better service in the richer areas, a worse service in the poorer areas'. Even in 1945 this argument did not convince all his colleagues. The Home Secretary, Herbert Morrison, argued for continued local control of the public health system. In 1937 the aggregate finance of the 1,100 voluntary hospitals was in the red, with government grants preventing collapse. In 1946, of the 480,000 beds in the system, four out of five were in municipal hospitals.

The argument over centralized or local control has continued ever since, and now goes much wider than the single question of whether the NHS should be under local government control. The Royal Commission did not perceive that arguments on this issue go to the roots of the financing of the NHS, its control and the whole orientation of health care in its widest sense, community, environmental and preventive. It never considered separately elected health authorities or objectively reviewed the arguments for and against central control. It was wise to reject immediate fundamental changes, but it could have charted a course for the future within which the structural adaptations of the early 1980s to the Areas and the Districts could be set in context. As the Commission's own research points out, 'the irony is that despite [Aneurin] Bevan's argument for a national service in 1945 central government has been more successful in eliminating the grosser variations in the distribution of resources in some local authority services than in health.' Education was cited, by the Royal Commission as the best example, where central government allocation has, by using clear national criteria, been able to keep variations within very tight limits. The Commission quoted for example in its evidence that the coefficient of variations between pupil/teacher ratios for 104 local authorities was 7.6, whereas the population/general practitioner ratios from 98 Family Practitioner Committee areas showed a coefficient of variation of 10.5. Such evidence as there is shows that a national service is not a necessary, let alone a sufficient, condition for achieving a 'uniform standard of service'.[38] This is very important since many socialists justify centralization on the grounds that it promotes equality.

It is worrying that, after over thirty years of the National Health Service, the provision of health care, however it is measured whether in terms of expenditure, bed allocations or manpower distribution, still shows dramatic variations between health districts, and among health areas and regional health authorities. The inequality of provision has its roots in the fact that instead of concentrating on essentials, priorities and policies, Ministers and parliament have connived at the myth that they control the whole service, becoming bogged down in detail while effective control has passed to the central bureaucracy. The failure for the first fifteen years of the NHS to do anything other than to hand out money on the historic allocation pattern to the English regions would never have been tolerated by the English regional health authorities if they had owed their position not to government patronage, but to the people of their region by election. In marked contrast, Scotland, with its own Secretary of State, has been able to extract a 24 per cent advantage over England in health resources, and Wales has been brought from well behind to a position where they have now a slight advantage over England. Nor would the relationship between hospital and community have been ignored for so long if the voice of the local areas had not been so weak in relation to the region and to the Department. The dominant share of hospital health resources given to London was not just historic but part of the Whitehall-London bias that is another characteristic of centralized government. Central government listens to the teaching hospitals and to the Royal Colleges, and Westminster-based politicians to the London doctors they consult and know.

An example of the centralist tendencies within the NHS was its resistance to the implementation of the Resource Allocation Working Party (RAWP) recommendations which were aimed at correcting geographical inequalities. The London-based health service unions supported the London teaching hospitals and refused to face the logic of the facts of London's preferential resource allocation. Attempts to redress sectoral and class inequalities have met the same resistance from the powerful Royal Colleges where the interests of the surgeons and the general physicians predominate. There are admittedly imperfections, statistical crudities and physical problems associated with the allocation of resources and it is very difficult to define need criteria objectively[39] but the fact that problems of allocation have been given such low priority in the first thirty years of the NHS reflects its continued insulation from provincial and local pressure.

It is, of course, insufficient to allocate resources on the basis only of hospital need. In inner city areas and in particular in London, where there is over-provision of hospital services, there is under-provision of community services and a need for a more refined allocation system for personal social service needs. The introduction of joint financing in 1975, with NHS money being available for joint projects with social services, was an attempt to help the integrated development of community care.

The disadvantage of central allocation to the health regions is that they are appointed bodies more influenced by professional and hospital pressures than by democratic community priorities and they can very easily distort their allocation by the way in which they make allocations to their own Areas and Districts. In London, where there is over-provision of acute services in the centre but poor provision at the periphery and where in between the community health services are of uneven quality, it has never proved possible to redistribute hospital resources for the benefit of London's relatively poor community services. A sensible re-examination of London sub-regional allocations has been completed, but the proposals of London University to close and merge teaching facilities and post-graduate hospitals have met predictable resistance. The institutional resistance is so strong that rational argument rarely determines the correct distribution of resources. Democratic and media pressure could have a more important influence and until Nottingham, Leicester, Sheffield and Plymouth openly challenge the dominance of London in the decision-making process within the NHS, they will continue to be deprived. The NHS must reinforce local control and establish sufficiently sensitive criteria for central allocations, whether of money or of manpower, to be made direct to district health authorities and not through the regions.

The regions argue that there are dangers in encouraging local health authorities to think in terms of self sufficiency, that they will develop overlapping facilities and opt for prestigious projects. Local duplication has been a theoretical danger for the Education Service as well, whether for Polytechnics, Colleges of Technology or Teacher Training establishments; but in marked contrast to the Department of Health and Social Security, the Department of Education and Science has accepted local-national partnership, concentrating on the development of the school inspectorate and on research and development. In Scotland the Health Authorities Revenue Equalization (SHARE) allocates across a population of 5.2 million people to fifteen Health Boards of very different size, with a spread of population from the Islands (68,000) and Borders (100,000) to Lothian (756,000) and Greater Glasgow with 1,059,000. It is clear from Scottish experience,[40] with complex patient crossflows, regional and sub-regional specialities and leading hospitals, that it is feasible, as well as desirable, to allocate direct to the new local health authorities below regional level.

The Royal Commission recommended the removal of an administrative tier and the government decided in 1980 to form new health authorities from existing single district areas, either by merging existing districts or by dividing areas. The flexible approach, as recommended by the Commission, with no single criterion predominating, was the right solution, and it could have minimized the damage to effective collaboration between the previously matching boundaries of the area health authorities and local government social services departments. But the government's approach has been to allow the regions to play down the importance of retaining conterminous boundaries with Social Services. Unfortunately some of the new authorities will be too small to have proper services for mental illness or mental handicap and, where the social services are not conterminous, there will be problems over joint funding and joint planning. With only four local councillors out of sixteen on the new authorities, the influence of local government will be deliberately reduced.

The Health Service has been limping back from the despair which followed the 1974 reorganization and it needed to be cajoled gently into a more efficient and effective organization. The creation of so many new district health authorities is very unlikely to produce the £30 million saving in administrative costs and manpower claimed by the government in 1980. The government would have made more economies if it had made fewer authorities.

A study by health administrators estimated that creating 180 district health authorities with an average of only 2,051 beds, in comparison to 90 with an average of 4,200 beds, will substantially increase management staff costs and add an extra overall cost of over £30 million. It is probable that the best trade-off between cost-efficiency and community identification would have set a figure of around 120 new authorities. By creating some 200 the government will make it easier for the regions to retain their managerial stranglehold, so that the apparent effect of decentralization will be illusory.

Apart from questions of organization, the danger of the changes being introduced in the 1980s by the Conservative government is that they are tending to reject the philosophy of the wider definition of health implicit in the 1974 reorganizations. The hospital is again becoming the focus of health decisions and priorities, with doctors dominating the discussion. Important though it is to improve the administration of the hospital, there is no case for reverting to a hospital-orientated health service, for forgetting the fundamental value of integrating fully the range of community services for patients and families and for failing to establish a far higher priority for preventive care.

Once the new authorities are established, the question will have to be answered to what extent they are to be given real freedom to manage. Should they in addition to a central financial allocation have the right to raise local finance? Health has – unlike Education – never had a local constituency for higher spending; the hybrid democracy continued in the new health authorities and in the regional authorities still has no power to raise money, other than through local lotteries. They are the creatures of government control, lacking the power of independent action that comes only from some measure of financial independence. No health authority is capable of setting the pace or of experimenting against the Departmental trend. There will continue to be an endless moan from health authorities about the inadequacy of their resources or a resigned acceptance of the government's financial decisions.

It is the undemocratic structure which has proved to be both inefficient and ineffective. There are many hard-working, informed people appointed to health authorities who, for many years, have given their time and energy without financial reward to the National Health Service. Their authority, however, stems from the central government who appointed them; they are often remote from and unknown to the locality they serve, and they have been more influenced by professional and hospital pressures than by demo-cratic community priorities. The local authority nominees, while injecting some element of local accountability, accept a considerable curtailment of their normal democratic freedom and feel inhibited and restricted. It is a sad fact that the Health Service is represented by amorphous and undemocratic authorities, Quangos which should be abolished and replaced by democratically elected bodies. The Royal Commission seemed to hold out the vague possibility of change if some form of regional government was introduced. Meanwhile it wanted regional health authorities to continue but argued that they should be made directly accountable to parliament instead of, as at present, to the Department through the Permanent Secretary. The Commission explored the local government option, but not the localist approach.

The Royal Commission was given evidence from Sweden pointing to the value of redirecting control from the centre to the local area[41] which, had it been imaginatively projected and built on, could have come like a breath of fresh air into the Report and, at a later stage, into the NHS. The Swedish Country Health Authority, or *Landsting*, is elected every three years by proportional representation; the *Kommun* is their equivalent of our local authorities. A *Landsting* raises a local health tax as a percentage of taxable income or of income left after deduction of tax-free allowances. The percentage in 1975 varied from 9 to 11 in the 24 different *Landstingen* and averaged 10.21 per cent. To take an example, the Malmönus *Landsting* serves a popula-tion of 480,000. It has an Assembly of 109 elected members which meets several times a year, and whose most important meeting is in October, when the budget and local tax rate are decided. In 1975 it spent £257 million and the tax rate was for 10 per cent of taxable income. Between assembly meetings the administration is run by an Executive Committee consisting of fifteen members. Senior medical and administrative staff attend the meetings.

In Britain it would be neither necessary nor desirable to adopt the

Swedish pattern wholesale and if elections to the health authorities were made by proportional representation and if health service representation on the authority was maintained, the fear that authorities would be endlessly dominated by one party would diminish. Involving over a hundred elected people in general policy, though not in management, is an interesting concept. In some ways this wider involvement is provided for already in the NHS by Community Health Councils (CHCs). The CHCs have been a success and it is helpful that, after initial doubts, the government has decided they should continue. Their members are representative of the locality and help to bridge the gap between executive authorities and the voluntary groups and the wider community they serve. The government would be very unwise to curtail CHCs' activities either by financial restriction or directive.

In Sweden, the government provides 21 per cent of the total income and makes equalization grants to the poorer counties where the taxable income per head is lower, so that the available money per head is roughly the same. Central government retains authority over the allocation of doctors and other strategic decisions. In Britain, central government, having been for over thirty years the sole financier, would have to continue for some time as the major source of finance. The amount that might be raised for health locally would need to take account of the financial burden put on LIT for local government finance. It would be necessary for central government to determine that proportion of NHS expenditure which could be accepted as being locally determined by the health authority and this would have to be compatible with overall national economic management.

It will be argued by some that, rather than having separate health authorities, health should be put under local government. Apart from the ferocious resistance such a move would meet from the doctors, there is a case for separation on merit. Health authorities would attract candidates for election different from those standing for local government, and if the election dates were the same for both, turnout would not be a problem. The new health authorities account for a major amount both of local expenditure and of local employment, and, unlike local authorities, they have now established the principle of industrial democracy, having as full members representatives of some who work within the service. The authorities have benefited from the value of the professional and scientific involvement of these representatives. They should, however, be elected by the people they represent as the Labour government proposed when I was Minister of Health, and not be selected as they are now. The professions and the Health Service trade unions are solely responsible for not taking up that specific offer of industrial democracy, which demonstrates the all too familiar resistance to the implementation, where more than one union is involved.

Once the members of new health authorities were elected it would be right to look very carefully at the results in Northern Ireland of the 1973 decision to integrate health and personal social services. This is again an area where the Royal Commission's analysis was disappointing. It commented that 'the demographic change which will be the greatest single influence on the shape of the NHS for the rest of this century, is the growing number of old people and particularly those over 70. This will increase the need for long-term care. In addition, demand for services for the mentally ill and the mentally handicapped are likely to grow'[42] – but its conclusion was against a merger under the present system. Yet an integrated, localist approach would produce a structure far better able to cope with this demographic challenge than the present one, which has done little to translate into practice all the rhetoric about community care. If integration were made part of a major shift towards democratic control of the NHS, it would be far more acceptable to the social services which, under the present centralized system, rightly fear that they would be dominated by the medical profession.

From 1974 to 1979 the Labour government tried very hard to redirect resources into the 'Cinderella' areas of mental illness and mental handicap, geriatrics and disablement. Even the previous government had, with Sir Keith Joseph as Secretary of State, demonstrated its concern with the publication of the White Paper on the Mentally Handicapped which had been started under the previous Labour government. In 1976 the National Development Group for the Mentally Handicapped was set up under Peter Mitler and the White Paper on Mental Illness was published. Within the health and social services spending areas, the joint financing of community projects was introduced, and other changes were made whereby the Hospital Advisory Service became a Health Advisory Service to work with the Social Work Service, and with a remit to draw the health and social services together. But despite all this activity, the Royal Commission, three or four years later, could find little evidence of any real shift in priorities towards the disadvantaged specialities. The resistance to change is strong, particularly from consultants in the acute illness sector protecting their specialities, and from trade unions unwilling to see any closures among the acute general hospitals, which they see primarily as employers of their members. The mass media, too, are geared to the dramatic surgical health story and show only sporadic interest in the chronic specialities.

A decentralized, democratic NHS would at last mean that the case for community care would be put openly to local people, and more local people would have to face up to solving their problems locally and argue about priorities. The evidence is now clear that an unelected centralist authority is incapable of facing these issues. The process of electing people to the health authority means that the rate payer and tax payer will be involved in arguments about what they should contribute financially. Similarly, the greater the discussion locally about co-ordination between health and social services, between hospital, hostel and home, the more likely we are to see genuine community care and sensible planning.

The localist approach will still necessitate central government involvement in inspecting and upholding minimum standards. As a major financier, central government will still have the right to demand that its priorities are followed and will still have a responsibility for allocating resources on the basis of need. The Regional Assemblies advocated in Chapter 9 on the Constitution could take any residual strategic responsibilities of the present appointed regional health authorities and plan regional and sub-regional facilities. This would mean a much reduced function for central government, which could then concentrate on its real tasks: the overall strategic planning of the NHS and financial and manpower distribution, which would include the protection of Cinderella areas like mental illness and handicap.

The argument for giving elected district health authorities the power to raise finance is important. So long as the new authorities are wholly centrally financed, the feeling that their money is in some way a bonus from afar will continue to reduce the discipline of prudent housekeeping. The DHSS will always, at times of national financial stringency, reduce brutally their allocation without regard to local circumstances. The regions, insulated from local commitment and concerns, taking decisions from a distance, will cancel local schemes at great cost and great inconvenience. This cycle of financial irresponsibility is endemic to the present system. Putting a larger proportion of the burden of financial responsibility for local health services on local health authorities and through local democratic management on to local people means that they are more likely to pursue steadier capital investment programmes and to plan more realistic forward revenue spending. The separate capital and revenue allocation system should also be abolished, increasing the scope for flexible planning. The introduction of LIT for health and local government services will not allow vastly greater overall expenditure levels. There will be the same resources to tax locally as is done centrally, but the relationship between taxation and local services will become much clearer. The partnership between local and central NHS would continue but, just as it is vital to shift the balance towards greater local financial responsibility for local government, so it is vital to accompany the administrative reforms of the past decade in the NHS with the radical innovation of giving the new health authorities access to an independent source of finance.

A decentralized health service will mean that government and parliament will be unable to continue woefully to neglect their responsibilities to promote the health of the nation. One example of this neglect is the confinement of the NHS to being just a sickness service. Another is the craven attitude of successive governments to those two powerful commercial interests, the tobacco industry and the alcoholic drink industry. The evidence of the increasing harm that the widespread promotion and use of these two products does to the health of the nation is now incontrovertible. The difficulty is that the government lacks the statutory reserve powers without which negotiations with industry are bound to result in inadequate measures. In 1975, after a considerable internal fight within the bureaucracy and among Ministers, the Labour government made the decision in principle to legislate by a short one-clause Bill to put tobacco products within the scope of the Medicine Act. There is a strong case for doing the same with alcohol. It is not enough just to blame resistance from the Department of Industry, the sponsoring Department for the tobacco industry, or from the Treasury, fearing a fall in revenue. The real problem is a lack of Ministerial resolve, fearing to follow the advice of Health Ministers and listening instead to the vested interests of the newspaper and advertising industries, couched in the humbug of supposedly protecting the freedom of the individual. The advantage of using the Medicine Act is that it would put these products firmly into a medical background, allow the government to be guided by specialist medical advice, introduce a range of statutory processes covering advertising, sales and the ingredients of cigarettes and alcohol and provide an elaborate appeals machinery for the industries which has been proved to be fair by the pharmaceutical industry. Once government has the

Medicine Act behind it, the whole balance of power in its relations with the two industries will be transformed.

The attitude of governments to preventive health resources over the past few decades needs to be compared with the situation that would have arisen if central government in the last century had refused to lay down statutory public standards but had relied instead on persuasion and education and had said that it was up to individuals to boil their own water supply. If one compares, for example, the amount of ministerial time and effort, parliamentary legislative time and scarce financial resources spent by the Labour government of 1974–6 on phasing out pay beds from NHS hospitals with the fact that they did not then find time to tackle smoking or seat-belt legislation, one must wonder about the real social priorities of the Labour Party. It is even more revealing that legislative reluctance has often been rationalized by saying that what is involved is an interference with people's freedom; yet so were the measures taken to prevent typhoid and tuberculosis.

Yet legislation and screening are not enough. There is also a need for a positive programme of intervention to promote better health, and early childhood has been identified by the Working Group on Inequalities in Health as the period of life at which intervention could most hopefully weaken the continuing correlation between health and class. This means shifting resources towards ante-natal, post-natal and child-health services. An interesting example of what can be done has been analysed by Dr Marsh, a general practitioner in Stockton on Tees.[43] It means improving the quality and coverage of general practice and community nursing in those areas where the health statistics show above average mortality or morbidity rates. It means also, as the Royal Commission recommended, integrating the Family Practitioner Committees with other services, as is already done in Scotland and in Northern Ireland. It means concentrating on providing better day care for children under five and bringing together education, social services and voluntary agencies. In order to do this central government needs to have better statistics but also the means for monitoring progress and conducting special studies in selected areas, seeking out the best method of reaching agreed objectives, particularly if extra finance is to be provided from central government to locally autonomous health and local authorities.

The Department of Health and Social Security already has a potential independent assessment body in the Social Work Service, but it has not developed anything comparable to the authority and independence that the Department of Education and Science's

School Inspectorate enjoys in its relationship with local education authorities. Nor has the Health Advisory Service developed the necessary bite to insist that its recommendations should be seriously considered, though it has done useful work in trying to improve standards in the areas of mental illness, mental handicap and geriatrics. An essential accompaniment to a more decentralized structure for the NHS must be an enhanced role for central government as the advocate of improved standards of care, and along with that the fostering of an 'auditing' mentality at every level within the health and social services. Doctors must take more into account that they make economic decisions as they prescribe for patients, order diagnostic tests, admit patients to hospitals and determine their length of stay. As variations in treatment, results and costs which stem from individual doctors' decisions show a pattern impossible to justify, the scrutiny of clinical work by fellow doctors is starting to win acceptance. So is the fact that medical care has to be rationed by the public and by politicians, and this too is helping to shift attitudes within the medical profession. As long as doctors were able to invoke politicians' rhetoric about a comprehensive service as an excuse for not making choices, the debate about the NHS concentrated solely on the quantity of money and of services. Now it is focusing more on priorities, choice and standards of care. This debate needs to be pushed down to the district level and the community confronted with specific local choices.

The scale of provision for home helps, meals on wheels, disablement aids and specially adapted housing for the disabled determines whether disabled people can stay and cope at home or have to be kept within the NHS. Yet decisions on these matters are often made in terms of budgetary restraints wholly divorced from NHS needs or resources; and, similarly, NHS decisions which affect community services are often taken wholly apart from the financial situation and forward plans of the local authority. It is very easy for each to shuffle the responsibility off on to the other. There are, however, new and interesting developments. The hospice movement is a new approach to caring for the terminally ill and it is now developing a service for people who wish to die at home, giving them specialized care in the home rather than taking them away from the environment they know. With imagination and a structure for overcoming the institutional and administrative barriers, community care can transform the lives of the disabled and the elderly.

Without a really radical shift in the pattern of care, there is little chance that society will be able, either physically or financially, to care for its ageing population. It will require new techniques and new attitudes: the scale of adaptation needed has so far barely been perceived. That the government in 1980 could assert that integration between hospitals and community services 'has been substantially achieved' reflects an unreal complacency.

Another role of central government must be to protect the NHS. A small private health sector does not seriously damage the health service but if that sector grows the distortion it can introduce in terms of the rational allocation of skilled people and specialized facilities can harm the NHS. It is legitimate and right to phase private medicine out from within the NHS and for government to take financial and other measures actively to discourage the growth of the private health sector. In 1980 3,366,000 people were estimated to be covered by private health insurance, and if the 1980 growth rate were to continue it would be 10 million by 1985. Legislating to ban private health is an issue of human rights discussed in Chapter 11. The result of the last Labour government's attempt to phase out pay beds in NHS hospitals was a substantial increase in the waiting lists for NHS patients, caused by industrial action and a growth in private health insurance. There are lessons to be learned from this, one of which was the Labour government's inability to grasp the fact that without a financial inducement for hospital consultants to opt for a full-time commitment to the NHS there was insufficient inducement for them to acquiesce in a policy which threatened many with reduced earnings. Improving the quality as well as the quantity of provision of the NHS is the best way of curbing the growth of the private sector.

As Britain has become more and more centralized, so the authority of those in power becomes ever more distant, and the policies they pursue are likely to become more confrontational. We are already seeing in Britain a tendency for police methods to change and for centralist pressures to begin to take effect within the institution of the police itself. We need a rational debate about the role of authority in democracy and the issues affecting law and order, but a new and dangerous polarization seems to be developing between, on the one hand, those on the extreme Right who argue that simply strengthening the forces of law and order will cure the complex problems of crime, alienation and public disorder which infect our society, and, on the extreme Left, those who argue that alienation and repression come essentially from an authoritarian and unaccountable police force.

Social Democrats must not be afraid to be seen to champion a proper role for the police in modern society. To allow the present police to be depicted by its critics as an evil reactionary force on the side of conformism and the status quo is to abdicate responsibility. It also lends credence to a point of view that, generally speaking, is not supported by the facts. Any human society has to face up to the need to restrain the lawless and ensure that the law is observed. The history of the police in this country means that we start off with a long tradition of democratic, community policing on which to build. What we need now is to revive and identify that tradition in order to apply it to life today.

The public has been highly critical of the introduction of the panda-car and of the disappearance of the neighbourhood 'bobby', and in many areas the policeman is now back on the beat, proving not only a deterrent against crime but providing a friendly and accessible symbol of authority to the population as a whole. Not surprisingly, some neighbourhood police have themselves been critical of the approach to the community of outside mechanized squads lacking the close relationship which they themselves have built up on the beat. The Chief Constable of Devon and Cornwall, Mr Alderson, commented on the drift in the last fifteen years 'from what was primarily a foot-patrolling preventive force into a mobile reactionary force' and noted that there has been a 'gradual alienation of the police from the public which alters not only the nature of policing but the police officers themselves'. Recognizing the growth of criticism which he felt to be unfair, he recommended that 'the police response ought to be to make it clear that they represented no particular class and to get close enough to the public for ordinary people to be able to put attacks into perspective and realize that such criticism did not tally with the police officers they knew.' This is wise advice. While some people criticize the police for playing any part in social activity designed to prevent crime, the evidence is that this social contact increases the social awareness of the police. This is particularly important at a time when the police have not been immune from the trends towards bureaucratization and centralization that are evident in other areas of our national life.

There is concern about the accountability of the police and the replacement of the old Watch Committees in the cities and boroughs and the Standing Joint Committees in the counties – which often exercised a considerable degree of political control over the local force – the new Police Authorities are larger and some people feel ineffective in making the police force democratically accountable. In the past twenty years since the Royal Commission on the Police the number of separate police forces in England and Wales has declined from around 150 to 43. Increasing use of the National Computer – it dealt with 33 million transactions in 1978 compared with 18.5 million in 1977 – also means more centralization, as does the nationally co-ordinated training system, which gives the police a stronger sense of professionalism.

What society has to do is to choose between freedom and freedom from crime[44] and to establish the style and level of policing necessary to protect the public from crime while not making the individual vulnerable to arbitrary police behaviour. Social Democrats know that, while the use of force is distasteful to some in almost any circumstances, there are many more, the majority, who wish to be protected from crime and thuggery. In general it is not Conservative voters who are most vulnerable to many forms of crime – hooliganism at football matches or vandalism on council estates, being mugged in darkened streets, coming home from the bus-stop or the station. Those who make up the Conservative Party's 'natural' suburban constituency and who are most vociferous over crime are more likely to take cars from home to work or entertainment and to live in areas with a lower crime rate. Yet regardless of position in society or the Party they support, all voters have the right to protection from these evils and the law must operate to protect everyone, whether they come from the immigrant community or are 'disgusted Tunbridge Wells'.

A welcome feature of the way Britain has handled police matters is the absence of a national police force. Although some small democratic countries, including Denmark, Finland, and Norway, have successful national police forces, such a development should be firmly resisted for Britain. The 1962 Royal Commission on the Police stated that the creation of a national force would not be 'constitutionally objectionable or politically dangerous' but it would, at a time when more and more of the levers of power have been passing to the centre, be a major and serious step in the move towards a centralized state. It would make for less identification and accountability to the community but, above all, it would give central government – through its politicians and civil servants – direct or indirect control of a vital institution. The diffusion of authority is one of the most important structural safeguards against the abuse of authority, which is much easier under a centralized structure.

The Royal Commission made a serious attempt to grapple with the central/local dilemma, and it pointed to the two often conflicting objectives of accountability and efficiency. The 1964 Police Act envisaged police forces under the direction and control of the chief constable being 'adequate and efficient' in terms of resources; while the police authority had powers to deal with general questions of policing policy though not with personnel or other matters which were under the chief constable's authority. Central government, in the form of the Home Office's financial and general control, working with the Inspectorate-General of Constabulary, acquired a much greater role in establishing priorities and standards than ever before. The Royal Commission concluded that the chief constable should 'be subject to more effective supervision than the present arrangements appear to recognize' and this view was accepted by the then Home Secretary. But the working of the Act has tended to exclude the police authorities from discussing policing policy and their right to acquire information has been restricted. Chief constables have tended to claim that 'operational' matters are their sole concern but this terminology is not used in the Police Act, which gives the police authority responsibility for providing 'an adequate and efficient police force in their area'. It is time that police authorities challenged the limitations that have been placed by practice, not statute, on their powers. It is time a police authority challenged – if necessary in the courts – the limited interpretation of its powers and if these are then found to be as limited as some say, the case for further legislation will be much more convincing. There is a case for a police authority which feels that a Special Patrol Group should not be established in their police force insisting that this is a decision for them, not for the chief constable.

A police authority is made up of two-thirds local councillors and one-third local magistrates. As in many aspects of local government, police forces have become so large and extensive geographically that the Devon and Cornwall Police Authority, for example, finds it difficult to comprehend the scale of the operations. People who live in Penzance and serve on the Police Authority may not have the same interest in the police of Barnstaple as they would in the police of St Ives. The matter of size together with the growing professionalism of the police has tended to make it difficult for police authorities to retain a grip on their functions in overseeing the efficient use of resources and they come to rely on the judgement of the chief constable and Her Majesty's Inspector of Constabulary. There should be no further police mergers and in some cases there is scope for splitting the large forces up into smaller units.

Many local councillors have expressed strong views about the working of the new system and this is not just nostalgia, for the present system poses some real problems of democratic accountability. In London it is possible to claim that the present arrangements make local involvement and accountability almost impossible, and in some other areas, even though elected local representatives and magistrates sit together on the police authority, there is often the feeling that much of what happens in local policing is in fact controlled from Whitehall or is at least the result of co-ordination between the forces. Many police authorities meet relatively infrequently, some as little as once every four months. Chief Constables who have a good and informal relationship with their authority members will say that they learn from them a great deal about the local area and how it is governed. Conversely, the involvement of local elected leaders in the problems of policing is good both for the leaders and for their Parties. But they must feel that they have real responsibility or good councillors will not serve on police authorities, preferring to spend their time in areas where their decision-making capacity is stretched and they feel responsible and involved.

In maintaining the balance to ensure freedom and security the task of the Social Democrat is to share and legitimize authority. In legitimizing authority politicians must be zealous in the defence of liberty and be prepared to challenge authority and to rub against the grain of public opinion in order to protect minority rights.

PART FOUR

THE
FUTURE

11

NEGOTIATE AND SURVIVE

Foreign policy cannot be developed by taking into account only national priorities and policies. It must develop out of negotiations with other nations, it has to reflect in part their views and their perceptions. The European Community becomes less and less a purely foreign policy issue; it is central to our national economic life. The North South development debate similarly crosses economic and trading frontiers and in consequence the political issues concerning them have been covered within many of the preceding chapters. The search for peace is, however, a key issue of foreign policy and has to be dealt with separately. Those who seek peace may differ on methods and means, but we have a common end and must try to agree on facts, and narrow our differences wherever possible so that our common purpose is not overshadowed.

Protest aimed at peace is not worthless; but it will not of itself be sufficient. Governments will have to be convinced, decisions will have to be taken as a result of bargains struck between nations, compromises forged between Heads of government. The depressing development would be of a mutual contempt: the protesters of the politicians and the politicians of the protesters.

Yet while fear of nuclear war is again creating in some people a growing mood of protest, in others it is prompting support for the government's increased military spending programmes. There is as yet no sign that it is providing the stimulus to negotiate, to replace the polarized emotions of protection and protest with a concerted demand that all governments negotiate genuine, not cosmetic, arms control agreements which really will lessen the risk of nuclear war. Fear having been aroused by the government, there is little to be gained by trying to play down the horror. A new debate over nuclear strategy was coming anyway. Afghanistan and Poland have affected détente and coincided with European anxieties about US leadership; and concern over the hard-line stance amongst some in the US who seem ready to contemplate limited nuclear war.

The NATO decision to allow the US to start making plans to deploy its cruise missiles in 1983 if there has been no previous arms control agreement, and to retain the UK deterrent, was bound to stimulate an argument over whether Britain was likely to become more of a Soviet target than we were already. We have, in fact, always been a target and there is a tendency to forget that the US have operated from UK bases with nuclear weapons since the early 1950s, using B29 bombers, then B47s, F45s and today F111s as well as submarines from Holy Loch.

The European Nuclear Disarmament movement's view that it is credible for East and West in Europe to act now as if a 'united, neutral and pacific Europe already exists', is absurd when Europe is neither united, neutral nor pacific. It is very hard to believe that the peoples of Eastern Europe are going to have a determining influence on the policy of the Warsaw Pact, when one considers the struggle for freedom in 1981 in Poland. Loosening up the political rigidities of Eastern Europe is a much to be desired objective. The emergence of Helsinki monitoring groups, despite the consequences for individuals, is a triumph for the free spirit. But to argue from this that such people will be able over the next few years to bring about significant nuclear disarmament in Eastern Europe by directly influencing their governments is not only to indulge in a pipe-dream but to misread the military philosophy of the Soviet Union. The Soviet leaders will negotiate with other governments, as the SALT dialogue has shown, but they are as concerned about balance as the United States and very fearful of any dramatic or bold steps. While I share most of the protesters' concerns about the risks and dangers of nuclear war and of using terms such as 'limited' or 'theatre' nuclear war, I believe along with, I suspect, millions of other people, that to embark on a course of unilateral disarmament, neutralism or disengagement from NATO and to act as if the Warsaw Pact's military strength did not pose a threat to our independence is profoundly dangerous. In essence it would risk repeating in the 1980s all the mistakes of the 1930s.

The key issue is not protection versus protest; the question is whether protest can be the springboard for political action; the trigger for negotiation and agreement. As the late Admiral of the Fleet, Earl Mountbatten of Burma, said on the occasion of the award of the Louise Weiss Foundation Prize to the Stockholm International Peace Research Institute at Strasbourg on 11 May 1979: 'To begin with we are most likely to preserve the peace if there is a military balance of strength between East and West. There real need is for both sides to replace the attempts to maintain a balance through ever-increasing and ever more costly nuclear armaments by a balance based on mutual restraint. Better still, by a reduction of nuclear armaments I believe it should be possible to achieve greater security at a lower level of military confrontation. As a military man who has given half a century of active service I say in all sincerity that the nuclear arms race has no military purpose. Wars cannot be fought with nuclear illusions which they have generated. There are powerful voices around the world who still give credence to the old Roman precept – if you desire peace, prepare for war. This is absolute nuclear nonsense and I repeat – it is a disastrous misconception to believe that by increasing the total uncertainty one increases one's own certainty.'

It is important to start bringing to disarmament and the whole argument about the feasibility and the desirability of a nuclear-free Europe in particular, let alone to unilateral disarmament, a greater intellectual astringency on terminology and definition, and more honesty in quoting from eminent people's speeches, than has been obvious so far on the part of all the participants. Lord Zuckerman and the late Lord Mountbatten are often quoted in a way which suggests they have said that Britain should unilaterally abandon all nuclear weapons. This is not, and has never been, the case. Both played a prominent part in negotiating and following through to deployment the original Polaris Agreement. Lord Zuckerman advised me on nuclear matters from 1977 to 1979 when I was Foreign Secretary. I share many of his anxieties about nuclear strategy. He warns of the three dangers; the first being that if we go on talking about the use of nuclear weapons as though this was a real option in world politics, then they will be used. The second danger being 'a technological trend which aims at obliterating the critical difference between nuclear weapons on the one hand and so-called conventional weapons on the other'. Lord Zuckerman then argues the central case against the protectionists contemplating limited nuclear war. 'We persuade ourselves that nuclear weapons can be made small and precise, and not as harmful as an equally precise conventional weapon with more destructive power. In my view this trend undoubtedly lowers the nuclear threshold, at least partly because it encourages people to believe that nuclear weapons (for example, so-called neutron bombs used ostensibly to hold up a massive tank incursion) can be real weapons of choice. This leads into the third danger I see – the growing belief that nuclear weapons could be used in what is now fashionably called a "theatre war". I do not believe any scenario exists which suggests that nuclear weapons could be used in field warfare between two nuclear states without escalation resulting.'[1]

It is insufficiently recognized that there are a number of politicians, scientists and military men in Britain and in many other countries who are not so starry-eyed as to believe in unilateral disarmament but who have for some years challenged the established consensus from inside and outside government. Some idea of the contrast in thinking can be seen by comparing the views of three former recent British Chiefs of the Defence Staff.

Field Marshal Lord Carver, who has publicly argued against a Trident system, said in an article in the *New Statesman* of 15 August 1980, 'We should take our share, as we do, of manning theatre nuclear weapon delivery systems, including those which use American warheads, so that the allies are seen to share the responsibility, the odium and the determination to use them if need be . . .' He warns one against believing that even if the Soviets could be persuaded to disband their tactical or theatre nuclear armoury and retain only a strategic force directed at the USA and China, one should think of conventional warfare as being a comparatively harmless affair. 'The Yom Kippur War of 1973 reminded us of the purely military effects of modern warfare. In a contest that lasted less than three weeks, with limited forces in a limited area, both sides lost about half of their tanks and a quarter of their aircraft. To provide sufficient material to last out a prolonged major conventional war demands immensely expensive industrial effort, and its use would bring about a devastation in the area of operations.'

Yet in sharp contrast to what Lord Carver says about NATO's tactical nuclear weapons strategy, Admiral Lord Hill-Norton, a former Chairman of the Military Committee of NATO who wants Britain to buy Trident, thinks it is idle to suppose for a second that we can fight a battlefield nuclear weapon. He said, in *The Times* of 18 August 1980: 'I believe with Hermann Kahn, that once you cross the nuclear threshold you have taken an irreversible step which is almost bound to lead to a strategic nuclear exchange, which in turn is almost bound to lead to the end of civilization . . . I will go to my grave being certain that if you let off a neutron bomb anywhere in Europe you have gone 90 per cent of the way to triggering a strategic nuclear exchange.' The real as opposed to the propagandist argument against the neutron bomb is that it does make it more likely that a battlefield nuclear exchange will be started.

Air Marshal Sir Neil Cameron in a lecture to the Royal Society of Arts on 30 April 1980 also criticized the concept of limited nuclear war when he said, 'that so-called battlefield nuclear weapons are not means of winning military victories. That is a conclusion to which NATO has inevitably come, through the work of its Nuclear Planning Group over a dozen years or more ago . . . The war-fighting school of nuclear theorists has lost the argument in the West. The role of nuclear weapons is to deter war – all war – not just nuclear war, between East and West.' A scepticism of tactical nuclear weapons is perhaps more prevalent amongst naval officers than army or air force officers, but apart from Lord Mountbatten and Lord Zuckerman there are a number of political leaders who have never believed that it was credible to expect a politician to authorize a battlefield nuclear exchange.

It is often alleged that the Soviets have a nuclear war-winning strategy and the views of the late Marshal Vasily Sokolovsky, who was their Chief of Staff in the 1950s, are quoted from his book *Military Strategy*. Also the fact that many Warsaw Pact exercises and planning are based on the first use of nuclear weapons is often cited. But the Soviet Union thinks the same about NATO exercises and plans. There are undoubtedly Soviet militarists and politicians who think limited nuclear war is a credible strategy and that the Soviets can win, and the same opinion exists in the United States. We should not ignore the fact that while there are, as I have indicated, people who challenge this view in the West, so there are important voices who also challenge that view in the Soviet Union. In a rare interview in the *New York Times* of 28 August 1980 Lt. General Mikhail Mishtein said, 'We believe that nuclear war will bring no advantage to anyone and may even lead to the end of civilization. And the end of civilization can hardly be called victory. Our doctrine regards nuclear weapons as something that must never be used. They are not an instrument for waging war in any rational sense. They are not weapons with which one can achieve foreign policy goals. But, of course, if we are forced to use them, in reply to their first use by an aggressor, we shall use them, with all their consequence, for the punishment of the aggressor.'

The reasons for Britain's and Europe's nuclear strategy goes back to the early 1950s, when the conventional defence forces of NATO were widely felt to be outnumbered 5–1 by the Warsaw Pact. Some even put it as high as 10–1. Even though NATO's conventional forces have been considerably improved since then, NATO still does not feel confident enough in its conventional forces to guarantee that it could repulse a Warsaw Pact conventional attack. For this reason NATO has refused to agree to a declaration subscribed to by China and proposed by the Soviet Union that they would never under any circumstances use nuclear weapons first if they were under attack. NATO has therefore made it clear to the Warsaw Pact that if it were overrun by conventional forces the Warsaw Pact could not assume that NATO would not retaliate with nuclear weapons. Gradually over the years the so-called doctrine of the flexible response has meant that NATO has acquired, as have too the Warsaw Pact, a whole range of battlefield nuclear weapons and weapon systems capable of striking behind the battlefield area. Various attempts at producing coherent nuclear guidelines have been made by NATO to guide the military field commanders and ensure political control and the same has been done by the Warsaw Pact. The result has been one of differing options but with considerable doubt about whether many of the options would ever be comtemplated. The best expert opinion concludes from the available evidence that the only consequences of moving from a conventional military exchange in Europe to a nuclear exchange might be a temporary lull but that this would be followed by an accentuation of previous trends, though at a much greater level of destruction. An American strategic thinker, W. McGeorge Bundy, with experience both inside and outside government has written, 'the confusion over strategy in NATO has been almost continuous, but in this respect constructive. NATO's incoherent mixture of deployments, conventional and nuclear, tactical and strategic, while it has served no serious war-fighting scenario, has none the less served the common peace. There is here a tantalizing paradox which applies also, in a different way, to the general strategic balance: war-fighting at the level of thermo-nuclear exchange has become unreal as an object of policy, but a real capacity for it, and the possibility that it could happen are real elements, vital elements even, in the calculus that keeps the peace.'[2]

It is hard to envisage war in Europe. Certainly, while NATO remains as strong as it is at present a major Warsaw Pact attack, with or without warning, against NATO is extremely unlikely. It is most likely to arise out of a miscalculation. For example, if there were strike action in East Germany, following a rising trend of militancy in Poland, it might lead to the deployment of Soviet troops. This might then be resisted by the East German strikers. Part of the East German army might join the strikers and the East Germans might appeal for West German help. The West German government might mobilize its forces but refuse to help, and would try to cool the situation. But armed West Germans might anyway cross the border to help. This would be resented by the Soviets. Despite warnings, the crossings continue. The Soviets might then retaliate into West Germany, and the conflict could escalate, despite both Germanies and both military pacts having no wish to engage in direct military conflict. The danger of an 'incoherent' NATO strategy is that not everyone is tough-minded in his analysis and that an option which might strike many politicians as fanciful could become, almost by default, the accepted wisdom for the military.

It is time openly to abandon the option of a limited battlefield exchange of nuclear weapons and to accept the logic of the studies and research which have all pointed to the fact that most of NATO's nuclear systems, particlarly the short range battlefield systems and systems where the range ensures they can never reach into the Soviets' own territory, can neither bring about military defeat nor pose to the Soviet Union an unacceptable risk. The arguments for NATO initiating a short range battlefield nuclear exchange are unreal. In the event of an all-out conventional attack the only sensible political nuclear response would be to authorize a demonstrative nuclear explosion in an unpopulated non-military area of the Soviet Union as a warning that the nuclear threshold was about to be crossed. A battlefield response would have less value as a warning and be almost certain in invoke a similar battlefield response by the Soviet Union. In the case of an accidental attack it would be folly to authorize a battlefield response; here the only option would be to respond conventionally, yielding what ground one had to in the hope that the attack would be countermanded and to use the already negotiated machinery for political dialogue and exchange in order to abort the action. Such agreements were first signed between the UK and the Soviet Union in 1977. In the most likely of any form of attack, one which steams from a miscalculation of a local incident, the main thrust of any response should be political, to defuse the political tension which had provoked the incident, and here a battlefield nuclear response would be folly.

The politicians must ensure at all times that there is no power for NATO's military commanders or Soviet military commanders to take a battlefield decision to release nuclear weapons – even if a sensitive military installation was overrun. Whereas the NATO guidelines are clear about the need for political authorization, the tradition of a field commander putting his blind eye to the telescope did not die with Admiral Lord Nelson. It is dangerous to allow the military commanders to believe that battlefield nuclear weapons might ever be politically authorized, and to allow them to plan and exercise on the possibility.

There would be great security advantages in negotiating away all of NATO's and the Warsaw Pact's short range battlefield weapons and putting this as a higher priority than some of the strategic arms limitation issues, important though they are. This would mean NATO abandoning Lance missiles, short range nuclear capable aircraft, nuclear artillery, atomic mines, Nike Hercules missiles. NATO has some 7,000 nuclear weapons, 5,000 of them situated in West Germany; at least 65–75 per cent of these could go without any loss in capability and incidentally release a considerable number of US armed personnel currently guarding the security of these systems. Though the French would probably not participate, the broad aim of such a negotiation would be to cover all nuclear systems with a range not covered in SALT II within an arms control agreement related to, if not part of, the SALT process. It would cover formally the US and British long range bomber aircraft and US and British strategic ballistic nuclear submarines, and informally, in the sense that they would be taken into account, the French force. The aim would be to stabilise at equivalent, preferably reduced, levels with the Soviet Union's SS-20, SS-4 and SS-5 missiles if they continued in service, Backfire and Blunder/Badger aircraft if they remained in service, Golf Class submarines and SSM3 cruise missile carrying submarines. Within this sort of arrangement it might be possible not to deploy cruise missiles and exclude battlefield nuclear weapon systems from a part of continental Europe. This would be a negotiated disengagement, but in order to convince the West Germans that this would not increase the risk of a conventional attack taking a slice of their territory, they might wish the withdrawal of battlefield weapons to be covered by land or air based cruise missiles outside the disengagement area and would not be content to rely on long range aircraft or intercontinental ballistic missiles. It is the West Germans above all, who need to feel confident in any change of strategy. They have as an act of policy shown no wish to acquire their own nuclear weapons but they are a crucial power in central Europe and have made a decisive contribution to détente. We must take account of the fact that they appear to believe that the capability of the Soviet Union to attack Western Europe with weapons like the SS-20, quite separate from their central strategic forces targeted on the United States, represents a new and destructive political threat to Europe. This is presumably why Chancellor

Schmidt raised the issue of a Eurostrategic balance in 1977. This is what has underlain their wish to upgrade the Pershing missile and for the US to deploy land based cruise missiles in Europe, and why they were, in particular, very concerned about any future limitation on cruise missiles in the SALT process. If some cruise missiles were based in West Germany near the French, Belgian, Dutch border, this might give the necessary reassurance while any SS-20s were still deployed by the Soviets. Cruise missiles would not need to be deployed in the battlefield area, though they could be targeted into the battlefield area.

Whether an area of nuclear disengagement, on both sides of the border between the two Germanies, could be negotiated as a nuclear-free zone is therefore predominantly an issue of West German confidence. It is not a new idea; it was a FDP representative in the West German Parliament, Dr Pfleider, who, in 1952, first put forward the idea of 'disengagement in Central Europe.' The idea re-surfaced a little later during the discussions of the so-called Bonin Plan, but only assumed international importance at the Berlin Conference of 1954, when Sir Anthony Eden came out with the idea of a Central European zone of arms limitation and control. Eden later submitted a variant of his proposals – an idea of a 'demilitarized zone between East and West' – at the Geneva Summit Conference of 1955, and at this meeting Marshal Bulganin, then premier of the Soviet Union, declared 'that the Soviet Government was of the opinion that their eventual objective should be to have no foreign troops remaining on the territories of the European states.'

An amended version was put to the Committee of 18 Nations in Geneva, on 28 March 1962. The proposal envisaged that the proposed zone would be open to any European state wishing to accede. Its purpose was 'to eliminate nuclear weapons and to reduce armed forces and conventional armaments within a limited area in which these measures could help to reduce tension and substantially to limit the danger of conflict.' Although the final version appeared to bear some resemblance to the British ideas, the Rapacki plan was rejected primarily because the United States and the then West German government were not keen, although later Helmut Schmidt said that it could with advantage have been explored more carefully.

The NATO governments never seriously worked out what the implications for military planning in the area would have been after carrying out such a plan. In those days the fear was that it would make West Germany vulnerable to attack, but now that the strategic ballistic missiles have become so accurate, this has become less of a problem. Now, even though there are still some command and control problems, a Polaris or Trident missile can be fired from hundreds of miles away from under the sea and be targeted in a tactical battlefield sense to land within yards of the chosen area. The US land based missiles fired from Nevada are even easier to target, so in theory the arguments against removing nuclear weapons from Europe are less strong as the difference between tactical and strategic weapons becomes blurred. Also, since Hugh Gaitskell's suggestion the policy of *Ostpolitik* has transformed relations between East and West Germany. The frontier question is now settled, they have established major economic and trading links and the Berlin situation appears reasonably stable. The Soviet Union have also seen that the West is not prepared to act militarily to exploit internal dissent within the Warsaw Pact and never contemplated action in 1956 over Hungary, in 1968 over Czechoslovakia or in 1980 over Poland. This accommodation was institutionalized in the Helsinki Final Act signed in 1965 and though détente has not stopped, nor could it, or should it, stop the ideological war, it has produced a measure of confidence in terms of crisis management and an accepted discipline in terms of solidifying the current map of Europe.

Against such a background the possibility of negotiating the abandonment of short range battlefield nuclear weapons and an area of disengagement is greater in the early 1980s than it was in the late 1950s but it will still require a massive shift in attitudes to arms control on both sides that may be impossible for President Reagan and his administration to contemplate.

If a limited nuclear-free zone could be negotiated, it might be possible at a next stage to extend it by giving up all airborne nuclear weapons systems and/or all land-based missiles other than those based in the US and in the USSR. To achieve sufficient confidence to allow such far-reaching agreements the United States, Britain, France and the Soviet Union would need to agree to negotiate arrangements to enhance the survivability of existing nuclear submarines carrying either ballistic or cruise missiles. It would need to cover a ban on active trailing of such submarines and the establishment of large areas within the Arctic Ocean – so as to be away from naval operational areas – where there would be a ban on all anti-submarine warfare techniques, and particularly on the placing of under-water hydrophones, which promises to be an area of expansion if it is unchecked by negotiations. Negotiations would enhance the value of existing French and British deterrent systems and those of the US and Soviet submarine missile fleets. It should make it possible to downgrade the current strategic debate over the so-called Eurostrategic balance and for all to accept the asymmetry inherent in the geography of Europe, whereby a limitation of land based missiles to Soviet and US territory will always favour the Soviets since they can target their SS-20s on Europe whereas there is no equivalent, if one excludes French land based missiles, even if US cruise missiles are deployed. For some time US strategic missiles have had a multiple targeting strategy on Soviet military installations, as well as on Soviet cities, quite independent of European based systems and though there has been a lot of comment on the new Presidential targeting directive 59, it is not wholly new. The anxiety this new targeting strategy arouses stems from its apparent linkage in some people's minds to the acceptability of limited nuclear war or a first strike potential. By highlighting the switch made some time ago to include military targets the new directive has lent credence to the view that a missile exchange could be limited to military targets, a mistaken and dangerous belief.

If such a series of phased agreements could be contemplated, guaranteeing the invulnerability of the US and Soviet submarine missile systems, then the US might feel able to delay and eventually cancel the vast expenditure necessary for the deployment of the MX missile, though it is hard to see the Soviet Union ever giving up its land based missile systems. The advantage of both sides relying primarily on an invulnerable submarine deterrent force is that they are clearly second strike systems and this could bring a greater degree of mutual confidence in the intentions of all sides to avoid a first strike strategy, which is missing at present between the US and the Soviet political leadership.

It is very necessary, given this undercurrent of scepticism in both NATO and the Warsaw Pact about limited nuclear war and different perception about what is the currently accepted strategy, that a discussion is started within NATO and the Warsaw Pact which seeks to challenge the militarists and tries to negotiate a newer, more acceptable means of deterrence. When Chancellor Schmidt met President Brezhnev in Moscow in July 1980 the Soviets declared their readiness to start negotiations on medium range nuclear weapons without either waiting for the ratification of the SALT II accord or requiring that NATO's modernization plans be rescinded. If progress is to be made before the completion of the SS-20s' deployment and before the modernized Pershing and cruise missiles are scheduled for deployment it is urgent to have discussions.

There is a strong case, which I advocated as Foreign Secretary, for Britain, France if she wished to, and West Germany and perhaps one other Warsaw Pact country to be involved as negotiating partners, not just to be consulted on these discussions. It is this case, for Britain to use the fact of its possession of nuclear weapons to join in such a new and wider forum for negotiations, that is the positive aspect of multilateral disarmament. It would be impossible to sustain such an argument if a Labour government in Britain had decided to abandon nuclear weapons, for neither the US nor the Soviet Union, already sceptical about widening the participation in SALT, would then see any case for the UK to be present. All the signs are that the US will not seek to involve Britain, and the present government appears to have no wish to be involved. It is deeply sceptical about disarmament negotiations and seems actively to want US cruise missiles in the UK rather than reluctantly accepting the need to deploy them if negotiations over the Soviet SS-20 missiles do not succeed. West Germany also may not want to be involved. But how long can Europe effectively opt out and allow critical negotiations for its security to be handled by a US President with no direct European involvement? The 1980s are different from the 1960s when the SALT process started, the leadership role of the US has been eroded and may never again carry the same automatic authority in Europe. We are moving from an era of consultation into an era of partnership. The task of President Reagan is to give leadership to the Alliance without destroying the relatively new concept of partnership. But the European countries will have to contribute as partners, particularly Germany, France, and the United Kingdom.

In discussion with President Brezhnev and Mr Gromyko I found them ready to consider carefully and sympathetically the case for British involvement and possibly that of other countries in any discussion on arms control that focused on Western European security. The Labour government gradually became convinced that there were advantages in involving Britain in future SALT discussion provided that West Germany wanted our involvement, and we would have preferred it if they too would participate in any discussions affecting nuclear weapons located in either the Soviet Union or Western Europe and targeted on each other's territory. We were not prepared to involve Britain as the only Western European country, unless this was positively welcomed by our European allies, nor would we have wished to be involved if either or both the United States or the Soviet Union were obviously unenthusiastic.

I am very wary of accepting the concept of a Euro-strategic balance as distinct from the overall East-West global strategic balance. It was Chancellor Schmidt who first raised the question of the so-called Euro-strategic balance in 1977 and it is West Germany which has argued strongly that the SS-20 should be discussed in SALT III. Once raised, the issue has to be grappled with in SALT, yet new intercontinental nuclear missiles have an incredible accuracy. This new-found accuracy challenges all strategic thinking since it questions the vulnerability of second-strike nuclear forces and emphasizes once again the superiority of the submarine platform for a second-strike strategy. It also makes it possible to target these weapon systems as part of a theatre strike strategy. The distinction between strategic weapons and theatre weapons has therefore become increasingly blurred and makes for considerable confusion in discussions over the so-called theatre balance or Euro-strategic balance.

The US Administration would not have faced a fraction of the Congressional problems with SALT II if Britain and West Germany had been full partners in the actual negotiations. Public statements of NATO support for SALT II are not the same thing as European participation, especially if accompanied by well publicized private doubts at various stages of the negotiations. A multilateral negotiation would also be less likely to polarize views inside the United States. There is no reason why a key non-nuclear weapon state like West Germany should not be involved in the negotiations, even if on some sensitive issues, for example on warhead technology, it excluded itself from the exchange of information. The Soviet Union could obviously oppose West Germany involvement or counter by insisting on the involvement of East Germany or another Warsaw Pact country, but instead she might see advantages from involving West Germany, as a way of making any agreement with the US stick and deal with substantive Soviet concerns. At present, fears of arousing suspicion about West Germany nuclear intentions, the reaction of her continental partners, perhaps in particular France, and sheer inertia, are all factors in the West German apparent reluctance to be involved.

If the Federal Republic refuses involvement, and if Britain's other European allies wish, Britain should welcome becoming a full negotiating partner in SALT III. It would be an extension of British involvement in the Comprehensive Test Ban (CTB) talks. The present British government has not hitherto wished to be involved, as much as anything else for fear that this would mean that Polaris or its replacement, the submarine-launched Trident, or cruise missiles would be on the table at such negotiations. The weakness of this argument is that Polaris, or the Trident missiles the present government have decided to purchase, will be on the table anyway, even if Britain is not present. Britain's mere presence or absence would not mean that the Soviet Union would allow the United States to exclude the British contribution from her overall numbers. Britain's presence would allow public opinion to take a far more balanced decision on the future of Britain's nuclear deterrent and set that decision in the context of European security and arms control negotiations. Britain would be free to go ahead purchasing new missiles if she so decided at any time she wished, for SALT has not prevented the US or Soviet governments from making weapon decisions during the negotiations.

Britain will carry little credibility in asking other non-nuclear weapon states to take arms control more seriously if she is not even prepared to participate in negotiations herself because of the fear of including her own nuclear weapons. Britain cannot easily justify, only on grounds of national deterrence and national military requirements, her continuation as a weapon state. Her possession or discontinuation of nuclear weapons has a very high political content. Ensuring West Germany stays non-nuclear and that France is not the only European nuclear weapon state are political, r ot military, objectives, as is ensuring that our public commitment to disarmament is to use our nuclear knowledge constructively in all arms control forums. Not being a super-power, Britain can with skill help to bridge gaps in understanding between the two super-powers and between the non-nuclear weapon states. Britain's dilemma is the cost of remaining a nuclear power. Afghanistan has revealed a worrying difference in perception about détente between Europe and America. While West Germany is the key country for closing the difference, Britain also can exert an influence, provided she does not just mirror US perceptions but remains sensitive to European concerns.

A wider membership of SALT III will take time to achieve. It may not be accepted initially and substantive negotiations over SALT III will take time. If it starts at least as a purely Soviet-American negotiation then consideration will need to be given to other forums for discussing Euro-strategic issues.

The Mutual Balanced Force Reduction talks have had, since 1975, a nuclear component through the West's Option III offer, but few would argue that this forum could or should be expanded in this way. It is better for the Mutual Balanced Force Reduction (MBFR) talks which have become hopelessly bureaucratized through many years of inertia and political neglect, to concentrate on making progress with the new Western proposals. This limited Phase I proposal follows closely a proposal which I, when Foreign Secretary, put to West Germany in early 1979. MBFR needs a political impetus and a commitment to meet at Foreign Minister level which NATO agreed in principle in Washington in 1978. Again West Germany has a key role which so far it has not fully exercised. Strategic arms negotiations are very complicated, deal with highly classified material and as I argued in *Survival*, the journal of the International Institute for Strategic Studies, in May 1980, there is a need to keep to a small group of nations. Indeed one of the strongest arguments against widening the membership of SALT will be the problems of multilateral negotiations. Yet there are powerful arguments against creating a new separate negotiation to cover Western European concerns. To do so will reinforce the concept of a Euro-strategic balance and could of itself contribute to the danger of separating US strategic policy from that of Europe. If it were decided to keep unchanged the existing forums of SALT, MBFR and CTB and Helsinki it would be worth considering whether any linkage could be established.

Discussion over the future structure of arms control, whether or not one widens SALT III, must face the desirability of French participation in some form. At long last France is taking a serious interest. France has taken her place at the enlarged Geneva disarmament talks and she proposed a European Disarmament Conference in 1978. This proposal for the 35 Helsinki countries plus Albania to discuss arms control, excluding nuclear weapons, across the breadth of Europe from the Atlantic to the Urals is starting to arouse more support. A radical and positive role for a European Conference would be if it could be scheduled for some years ahead, say 1983–4, and be the forum which would bring together and co-ordinate decisions taken in the framework of SALT, CTB, MBFR and Helsinki. Yet to carry any conviction or to have any hope of success such a Conference would need to be able to bridge the gaps between France and West Germany on the one hand, and increasingly Britian and the US on the other, before there could be progress with the Soviet Union.

To avoid creating a new structure it might be worth taking Berlin as the focus. Quadripartite machinery between the Soviet Union, America, Britain and France as the four occupying powers already exists. Also existing is the Bonn Group for co-ordinating views between France, Britain, West Germany and the United States. Not only do these meet at official level but also regularly at Foreign Minister level and, from time to time coinciding with Economic Summits, at Heads of Government level. At Guadeloupe the four Heads of Government were acknowledged to have discussed security issues. It is worth considering whether a grouping of five – the Soviet Union, the United States, West Germany, France and Britain – would be an acceptable steering group to act as a link between the existing arms control forums which affect European security. In this way highly secret nuclear weapon systems might be discussed and some coherence and political leadership be given to the present disparate and disappointing arms control negotiations. It raises sensitive issues and must not undermine the existing very successful Berlin machinery, which is of course designed for a different purpose. But one of the difficulties in international affairs is to introduce any new forum without so adding to numbers of countries involved that the forum cannot negotiate successfully or exchange highly classified information.

The whole area of arms control and disarmament needs a fresh impetus. The United States, Soviet Union and Western Europe are all now embarking on yet another twist to the already spiralling arms race. Poland should not be the excuse for abandoning arms control negotiations. It should rather be the stimulus to try once more to re-establish a genuine bargain in which both sides gain important objectives and in which both sides trade off gains by accepting restraints.

It would be possible, if such a degree of arms control could be negotiated, for the UK to reconsider the relevance of its own independent deterrent, though the existing Polaris covers Britain's needs for at least the next twelve to fifteen years. My position, which has never varied since I first became involved in nuclear deterrence, as Under Secretary for the Royal Navy in 1968, has been a strong commitment to negotiating nuclear arms control agreements. I opposed the purchase of Poseidon to replace Polaris in 1970, when I was on the Defence and Overseas Affairs Sub-Committee of the Expenditure Committee. I thought it was militarily unnecessary and something Britain could not afford to spend so much defence money on. Both in and out of government I opposed the Trident system as a Polaris replacement on similar grounds. It is impossible to purchase Trident without major reductions in what we might otherwise spend on the conventional defence forces. There is an argument that we can extend Polaris well past 1995 by cannibalizing A3 missiles and with a prudent programme of replacing equipment at the time of refits. Certainly Polaris hull life will now last much longer than was once feared. By 1990 there may have been a transformation of weapon technology, with important advances being made in laser technology. No one can predict the future, nor is it easy to predict the progress of arms control and disarmament over the next decades. If in 1990 there was still felt to be a need, for European political reasons – which have always been more important than military reasons – for Britain to retain its own deterrent, then we should consider purchasing cruise missiles to be fired from the existing torpedo tubes of our hunter-killer submarines. This would provide the UK with an ability to threaten a second strike, capable of inflicting unacceptable damage on a few Soviet cities in the unlikely event of a breakdown in NATO or, even more unlikely, of a uniquely threatening situation developing for the UK in a general East/West war. It would not be as sophisticated or as effective a system as Trident. Nor would it be sufficient for the US, whose strategic needs are very different, but it would be a lot cheaper and financially supportable for the UK. To argue the economic limitation is no more than a realistic judgement of what is the size of the UK defence budget we can afford, since it is already distorting other expenditure priorities. No decision, on this basis, would be needed over whether to replace Polaris for ten years, during which time the UK would contribute fully to NATO's deterrent as at present, and would also contribute constructively as a nuclear weapon state to discussions over détente and arms control in every possible forum. It would allow Britain to argue now for a five-year ban on nuclear tests in the Comprehensive Nuclear Test Ban discussions.

A nuclear test ban would for the first time demonstrate to the non-nuclear-weapons states that the countries with nuclear weapons were starting to take their commitment to stop vertical proliferation or sophistication of nuclear weapons seriously, and they would therefore carry more weight when they argue with other countries for the full implementation of the Non-Proliferation Treaty, NPT, and for other countries to help in the curbing of horizontal proliferation or the spreading of weapons to non-weapon states.

It is ten years since the NPT came into force, and there are now 115 signatories. India exploded its own nuclear device in 1974 and has refused to sign the NPT; it is watching Pakistan's nuclear development programme with care and meanwhile keeping open its

options on nuclear weapons. Pakistan shown every sign of continuing to develop a nuclear weapon capability, completely ignoring
US representations, and those of France and the UK, to desist. This
was happening even before the invasion of Afghanistan, which will
only serve to increase the Pakistan leaders' resolve. Israel undoubtedly has the capability to deploy nuclear weapons, which it
can fulfil at any moment. South Africa is on the brink of developing
a military capability. Were Brazil and Argentina to develop a nuclear
capability it would mean ignoring the Treaty of Tlatelolco which
seeks to make Latin America a nuclear-free zone. South Korea can
probably be restrained for a little longer by the US. Iraq's intentions
are unclear. The possible link between Israel and South Africa is a
very disturbing nuclear issue though the possession of nuclear
weapons will have little relevance for the sort of guerrilla warfare
and urban violence which faces South Africa. It is unlikely now that
any of these countries will be influenced to halt or slow down any
currently planned developments by a CTB agreement, but it could
make it easier for them to stop new developments or to delay
existing developments.

Britain has played an important part in the London-based Nuclear
Suppliers Club in trying to reduce the risk of proliferation, again
showing there is scope for a positive constructive use of Britain's
position as a nuclear weapon owning state. In this area Britain could
take a lead by completely opening up establishments like Windscale
for international inspection and trying to get all states with nuclear
weapons to accept that the size of their plutonium stockpile cannot
continue to be held secret if there is to be a genuinely open
international check on the plutonium cycle for all states, whether
they have nuclear weapons or not. Britain, which played a constructive role in the London summit of the Seven in 1977, should also try
to ensure that the decision to establish the International Nuclear
Fuel Cycle Evaluation Group is now followed by full implementation
of all the recommendations in the agreed report which was published early in 1980.

The protesters seem to wish to depict Britain as being uninterested
in and unimaginative over arms control and disarmament; in fact the
record is not a bad one, though it could well be improved. In the UN
Special Session in 1978 the British role was widely judged to have
been a leading one and the British delegation helped to construct the
formulation of the final document. The challenge now is to ensure
that substantive progress is made at the 1982 Second Special Session
to ensure progress in the second decade of disarmament. We need

to ask why some measures of disarmament have succeeded and others failed. How the future trend towards greater arms expenditure can be checked at the early stage of research and development. These are some of the objectives of an Independent Commission on Disarmament and Security Issues which has been set up under the Chairmanship of Olof Palme and of which I am a member. It hopes to stimulate progress on disarmament as hopefully the Brandt Commission will stimulate progress on development, and influence the UN Special Session in 1982.

The first Disarmament decade during the 1970s produced some very limited progress. It started with the entry in force of the Non-Proliferation Treaty, and the Treaty on the Prohibition of the Emplacement of Nuclear Weapons and other Weapons of Mass Destruction on the Sea-bed and the Ocean Floor in 1971. The only actual measure of disarmament was the Biological Weapons Convention of 1972. The Strategic Arms Limitation Agreement of 1972, the 1977 Convention Banning the Military Use of Environmental Modifications Techniques and the signature, though not the ratification, of the second Strategic Arms Limitation Treaty in 1979 were all worthwhile but progress was very disappointing. The arms race continued and easily outstripped the measures to control it, with too many agreements being cosmetic. Apart from the Antarctic there were no new regional arrangements such as the Treaty of Tlatelolco in Latin America and the Non-Proliferation Treaty review Conference of 1980 has been unable to produce a new momentum and build on the findings of the International Nuclear Fuel Cycle Evaluation Report. There is a chance, though a dwindling one, of agreement on the Comprehensive Test Ban negotiations. The French proposal for the establishment of an international satellite monitoring agency, having its own observation satellites, would allow the world community as a whole to participate in the effective verification of arms control agreements. Discussions in the revamped Committee on Disarmament now involve France and China and may be able to achieve more. The Committee has highlighted four major disarmament issues to be covered by working groups: security guarantees for non-nuclear weapon states against nuclear attack, a comprehensive programme of disarmament, the prohibition of radiological weapons and a complete ban on chemical weapons. The use of chemical weapons in wartime is prohibited by the Geneva Protocol of 1925 but it is full of drafting weakness and gives scope for varying interpretations which has allowed poison gases to continue to be made for retaliatory purposes and has given rise to dispute over riot control gases such as CS gas. Both the Soviet Union and the US have developed gases that can completely paralyse the human nervous system in a fraction of a second. The fact that the world is poised on the brink of an escalation in manufacture and deployment of these most horrifying weapons should be every bit as much a cause for concern as the build up of nuclear weapons. The growth of anti-satellite weapons and new forms of anti-missile weapons shows the danger we face of the arms race escalating into space.

Other issues for the 1980s are to seek to reverse the lack of progress on limiting sales of conventional arms. Third World countries with scarce resources who purchase arms, as is their sovereign right, are being sold sophisticated weapons by both East and West, with both of them paying too much attention to profit and ignoring the warning of the Brandt Commission when it drew attention to the fact that: 'While the prevention of nuclear war remains the first ambition of disarmament, "conventional" (non-nuclear) weapons account for 80 per cent of all arms spending. In fact all the wars since the Second World War have been fought with conventional weapons, and in the Third World, where they have killed more than ten million people. In some of these wars, such as in Korea and Indochina, the major powers were actively engaged; in others they have been in the background. Some of the most lethal wars have been fought with "small" arms. The Lebanese civil war, for instance, has caused more deaths than all four Arab-Israel wars. The war in Cambodia is an even more tragic example. The North's sales of conventional weapons to the South are increasing. These represent 70 per cent of all arms exports.'[3]

It is inconceivable that the developing countries will ever accept that the rich developed countries should withhold from them their sovereign right to purchase weapons for their own country. That is a recipe for neo-colonialism and has already been resented over the developed world's restrictions on nuclear power technology for developing countries. The developing world concentrates all its political pressure on the nuclear weapons held by the few nuclear weapon states, a vital issue, but not the only issue, or in terms of world development the most important issue. What is needed is an imaginative radical change in the UN over world security issues away from national dominance and towards a new world security order.

Until the sending of Russian troops into Afghanistan, and, a year before, the flying in of large Cuban forces into Ethiopia, there was a growing confidence about the chances of peace in the world. The threat of a war between the major powers appeared to be wildly improbable. It seemed that a mutual fear of nuclear destruction might have ushered in a new era. But we have now seen in the suspension of SALT II and the debate preceding it how a delicate negotiation, arrived at through painstaking effort, can be placed in jeopardy by internal political arguments which a United States President cannot always be certain of controlling, as well as by external events to which a President feels he has to respond.

It is not only political factors which can disturb this balance. Advances in science and technology, whether in the nuclear weapon field or in that of chemical and biological warfare, or the erosion of the Nuclear Non-Proliferation Treaty, could quickly alter significantly many of the political equations. In the case of non-proliferation the Treaty has given us limited respite, but many countries have not signed it and not all who have signed will remain signatories if circumstances do not soon change and if no progress is made towards other disarmament measures. Conflicts keep breaking out with conventional weapons and the last decade has brought danger and destruction in the Middle East, South East Asia and in parts of Africa. These are all reasons why we should not become complacent in the face of the failure to date of the United Nations to handle the problems of world security as we had once hoped, and of the UN Special Session of Disarmament to make significant progress. A new approach to security problems is urgently needed. One such radical new approach was contained in *The Reform of Power*, which though published in 1968 may yet prove to be prophetic of developments in the direction of a safer and more stable world order.

At the time of its publication the book received respectful if guarded reviews, with the expected criticisms of those detailed arguments which disturbed the reviewers' own prejudices. Leonard Beaton's pungent remarks about the defects of the UN and the unreality of the General and Complete Disarmament plans bandied about by the major powers ruffled many feathers. It has also been easy to argue about the difficulties surrounding some of his ideas, such as the proposal to assign national forces to a World Security Authority in much the same way as is done for NATO. But the specialized agencies of the UN such as the World Health Organization have been a success, in part because they are staffed by specialist experts, not by diplomats. There are obviously many difficulties over such a proposal in the present uneven world political climate. But none of these detailed criticisms diminishes the force of the basic concept. This is that while it is hopelessly unrealistic to suppose that the Sovereign State is going to disappear in the foreseeable future and that it must therefore be assumed that national security will remain a primary concern of all states, there is none the less a mutual international security interest which is not at present adequately expressed in the form of a functional international institution. As Beaton put it: 'there is a national security interest and a world security interest; both are proper objectives of national policy.'[4]

He therefore proposed the setting-up of a World Security Authority charged by the participating powers with the responsibility of developing and giving substance to their mutual security interests. Some of the obvious candidates for its concern are the strategic arms balance; the non-proliferation of nuclear weapons; the working out of convincing defence guarantees to non-nuclear powers under threat from a nuclear power; and the development of peace-keeping forces to avoid the involvement of major powers in local conflicts.

The precise machinery which would be needed to carry out these functions will require long, detailed debate and negotiation. It would need to be linked to the United Nations Security Council but in a way that would allow it to develop as an authoritative independent body, attracting a dedicated international staff composed of experts in the military, scientific and political field. It is essential that they should be capable of gaining the respect and confidence both of governments with differing ideologies and of world opinion.

In my view it would need to handle much of its work on a regional basis. I doubt whether Latin America or Africa can make a very valuable contribution to the discussion of European security problems – or for that matter that Europe can make much of a contribution to Africa's security problems and I have always opposed the idea of a European intervention force as a relic of colonial attitudes. The Authority should be designed to handle the supervisory elements in all arms control and disarmament agreements. It may well be that to begin with it would be allowed by member states only to handle a number of comparatively minor matters, but as it gained practical experience, as nations came to appreciate its value, and as they became acclimatized to this new way of looking at security problems, it could play an increasingly central role in international affairs.

There may be some scepticism as to whether it would be possible to gain world-wide support for the creation of such a body. Would the Soviet Union, for instance, find it unacceptable? I am not convinced that they could oppose it if it was endorsed by the UN Special Session in 1982. It demands no surrender of sovereignty unless such surrender is willingly accepted by the particular nation itself, as would be the case if international inspection were agreed to verify a disarmament measure. In the present Comprehensive Test Ban negotiations the Soviet Union, the United States and Britain have virtually agreed on the sitting of monitoring equipment on their own territory. The Soviet Union, faced by African support for a United Nations Transitional Assistance Group to go to Namibia for UN supervised elections, has not used its veto, nor did they do so over a similar proposal at one stage for Zimbabwe.

Then again the evidence of the SALT talks, the willingness of the USSR to participate in MBFR and the European Security talks, and the co-operation with the USA in working for a ceasefire in the Middle East, all lead to the conviction that most countries, and not least Communist countries, now see the advantage of approaching the subject of world security in a manner which is no longer expressed in simple adversary terms. As an early 1970s' report of the Committee of Nine to the North Atlantic Assembly put it in examining the problems of détente: 'European-American security policy during the next decade means in essence to pursue simultaneously two seemingly contradictory objectives: maintaining an adequate military balance and promoting a détente with an adversary who thereby also becomes a partner.' The partnership concept carries within it tensions inherent in its contradictory objectives, and détente does not mean friendship.

In a world which now possesses a destructive capacity which can turn our planet into a lifeless desert, we have by a mixture of good luck and good judgement so far achieved a rough balance of power which, despite recent events, still makes a major war unlikely. The whole human history and experience tells us, however, that such a period of balance is likely to be short-lived. There are dangerous signs now that could be the signal for an irreversible deterioration. We ought to seize this moment of pessimism and fear to create a world system which would attempt to ensure that the inevitable fluctuations in the power equation will be handled rationally and peacefully. The path Leonard Beaton proposed, with modifications, represents the best and possibly and only hope for achieving a warless world. As he says: 'The way forward is to create a central professional military organization to discover where the common security interest is and to administer it. Such an organization may eventually help to widen the area of concerted action but it should not depend for its creation on a pre-existing alliance relationship. A certain concert of the powers is needed, for example, to operate the International Civil Aviation Organization. Without such a concert, world aviation would be impossible. But this mutually valuable technical objective does not depend on dedication to perfect amity; nor has it required governments to concede ultimate control over their own air space. There was a common interest to be served; it required specialized technical skills; and the necessary organization was created in common to solve the common problems.

'Once such an organization had come into existence in the security field and governments knew its working and understood its character, its responsibilites would expand to the extent that governments identified common security interests. In any one period that might be very much or very little, depending on the skill with which the institutions were managed and on the political climate in the world. No doubt there would be periods when the system would do well to survive and continue to discharge its most pressing obligations. But as in federal states, there would be a natural tendency for power to accumulate at the point at which problems could most easily be solved. All the evidence is that on the great security issues this would be at the centre.

'A chess board is either black with white squares or white with black squares. In going from one to another, the board need not be changed at all. The powers similarly are now organized on a sovereign basis with international arrangements. They could go over to an international system with sovereign arrangements with no essential alteration in their present capacity to defend themselves and their allies. But they could create the technical and military context and perhaps the political conditions in which their common servants could achieve the common object of severely limiting or even abolishing war which may otherwise elude them.'[5]

The inertia in many areas of disarmament stems from the negotiators becoming firmly bureaucratic and institutionalized.[6] Progress depends on consensus – the military have an inbuilt caution expressed in the doctrine that 'everything must be balanced and simultaneous' – so movement is very slow. Step-by-step changes with a political impetus offer a much greater chance of progress, and the risks of this have to be offset against the risks of continuing as we do at present. The problem is that each country or group of countries is hesitant to make the first move. We are in danger of being inhibited by the wish to march in step towards disarmament and no one is prepared to be the first to break ranks. To achieve movement towards disarmament governments must be prepared at times to take the initiative as part of a coherent strategy to achieve momentum in all multilateral negotiating forums. It is the emphasis on large unilateral steps, divorced from the context of any multilateral negotiation, which is unrealistic.

Protest and Survive[7] was right to argue that 'deterrence is not a stationary state'; it must be buttressed by constant negotiations for peace, but they must be real negotiations based on bargains, not just on concessions. Deterrence, however, need not be a 'degenerative state'; certainly no more of a degenerative state than the spectre of unilateral disarmament would be – undertaken for the best of motives but achieving no response. Eventually this would lead to a vulnerable state where freedom is threatened and the choice is subjugation or war.

The task in the 1980s is to prevent an appalling conclusion similar to the failure of the 1930s. The need for peace should be a driving ambition for every politician. Its morality needs no elaboration. Yet sincere people differ over how peace can best be guaranteed. Pacifism is a belief, often carried with great conviction, but history warns against believing too easily in the good intentions of other nations, particularly those who have different political ideologies from our own. Sadly, to ensure peace we have to be prepared to defend ourselves and our country. The task for Social Democrats is to spend on defence only what is necessary and to strive constantly to reduce the levels of armament worldwide and to create a mood of greater confidence and trust between nations. In a nuclear age to protest is understandable, to protect is inevitable, but only if we negotiate will we survive.

12

THE ENABLING
STATE

The previous chapters have attempted to provide some of the detailed constitutional, financial and attitudinal changes that are necessary if Britain is to move towards a more decentralized structure of government. They have redefined Parliament's and central Government's role in a number of areas. They have, however, never sought to pretend that there is a simple, clear-cut dividing line between central and local decision-making, nor that the modern welfare state can somehow wish away all forms of central decision-making and direction. There is an inevitable ambivalance among Members of Parliament in particular as to their role. The temptation to seek greater involvement is strong, the urge to invoke legislation is hard to resist. There can be no rigid formula applicable for all occasions and in all areas of policy. Good government is an art, not a science: it requires judgement and balance and an understanding of how people behave. There is an important developing role for the state as an enabling rather than a controlling force. Government can achieve its objective more readily by creating a climate receptive to its aims than by imposing specific legislation. The scope for circumventing legislation in an open democracy is immense, as government concentrates on closing legislative loopholes, so the additional complexity opens up other loopholes and the bureaucracy grows. Simplification is often fairer in practice than it at first appears and the all pervasive 'nanny' state far less effective in practice in promoting equality. What is needed is an enabling state.

Any government that wants to construct a strategy for the reduction of inequalities must analyse the pressures which inhibit its freedom to redistribute wealth. It is in many ways a diversion to concentrate only on the pressure of the very wealthy or of top management. Those pressures do exist, and have influenced Labour governments as well as Conservative governments, but it is an illusion to pretend that they have been the dominant or even a very influential force. Labour governments have been more influenced by the resistance to paying tax among their own voters; Conservative governments influenced most by middle income taxpayers. The way through these often conflicting pressures can only lie in the democratic process of publishing the facts, arguing for the priorities which the facts support and constantly challenging vested interests wherever they are. It means ensuring that the debate about inequality does not centre only on income but also on access to services: and that the debate on the provision of basic services – those available to all as part of the social wage – is not just a question of simply looking at money quantities without also taking into account how that money is allocated and the quality of the services.

The quantity of services has become a vested interest in that it provides jobs, and with the public service unions naturally concerned about this aspect as well as wage rates, it is important that their pressure is counterbalanced by pressure over quality. If the quality of service falls then resistance to paying taxes and rates will rise among the very people for whom public services could provide a measure of real improvement in their overall standard of living. We must enable people to choose quality.

The only way of achieving a more equitable distribution of income in a democracy is to secure a greater awareness by the mass of the population of the facts about poverty, and by greater diffusion of wealth-holding. The cost for the social security system of an effective anti-poverty strategy will be very great and the taxes necessary to provide for such a social strategy will be very high. Unless more people can feel secure and satisfied by their present and future standard of living they will resist paying such tax levels. Additional incomes from a share in profits and the security afforded by an ownership of assets is still the prerogative of the few. What is needed is to widen the definition of standard of living from a comparison of income to a concept that embraces asset-holding, whether in terms of home ownership, secure rented accommodation, shares or savings, and sees security as the ability to benefit fully in our society from access to a good education service and health service – and to have confidence in the financial and care provision available in old age, sickness or disablement. It is this wider concept of the social wage, where the taxpayer sees his or her standard of living in broader terms than the after tax figure on the wage slip, that will cause the voter's resistance to paying tax to alleviate the poverty of others to be moderated. Nationalization is neither a necessary nor a sufficient condition for social change of this kind: reliance must be placed on changing people's attitudes, on promoting industrial democracy, and on industrial co-operatives, wider share ownership and, above all, wider home ownership.

There has been no greater determining factor in wealth creation in post-war Britain than home ownership. Radical reforms of housing were promised by the Housing Review initiated by Anthony Crosland in 1974 but hopes of reform were dashed by the disappointingly timid 1977 Housing Green Paper.[1] Housing policy is split inevitably between local government, whose task is to respond adequately to social changes and to anticipate and take account of the aspirations of council tenants, and central government, which is responsible for the tax and social security framework which affects the housing policy of every local authority. The Labour Party has been fairly criticized that a 'narrow preoccupation with the traditional issue of the level of council house rents blinded it to the growing impact of owner-occupation on the distribution of wealth – an issue now taken up by the political right.'[2]

The only radical way forward is to treat housing and tax reform as part of a comprehensive package designed to end the massive distortions and inequalities produced by government subsidization of owner-occupation and by the damaging shift of financial resources into house purchase and the trading up of house prices. Since the Second World War housing has come to represent by far the best investment and hedge against inflation, and as such it has seriously distorted the pattern of investment. From 1946 to 1978 retail prices increased 7 times, house prices $12\frac{1}{2}$ times and industrial shares only 5 times, with the share of personal wealth held in land and dwellings doubling from 1960 to 1974 and the proportion held in company shares falling by half.[3] Part of this shift can be explained by the replacement of personal shareholding by institutional shareholding and by the low profitability of industry, but it is an alarming fact, in terms of an industrial nation's priorities, that 90 per cent of net personal savings in Britain – compared with 60 per cent in the USA – flow into pension funds, life insurance and owner-occupied housing – all of which enjoy favourable tax treatment.[4] The disproportionate flow of funds into the building societies reduces the funds available to industry, forcing companies to borrow from the commercial banks, increasing interest rates and raising the money supply. Over-investment in owner-occupied housing, especially by the wealthy as a consequence of tax advantages, has helped to bid up the price of housing and as an indirect result has helped to reduce labour mobility, with this process being subsidized by government tax policies. In 1978 direct subsidies from central and local government to the housing revenue accounts of the local authorities totalled £1.6 billion, mortgage interest relief cost a further £1.1 billion and the relief on capital gains on owner-occupied houses cost £1.5 billion. The size of the total, £5½ billion, is hard to justify given the adverse macro-economic consequences of subsidies to housing. It should also be borne in mind that a reduction in the level of subsidy would allow either a substantial fall in income tax, with £1.0 billion being equivalent to a 2p reduction in the basic rate of income tax,[5] or it would allow necessary public expenditure priorities to be protected.

Reform of the tax treatment of housing should be guided by two aims: firstly, to reduce the amount of investment in housing as a whole by tax neutrality between housing and the rest of the economy; secondly, to achieve equal tax treatment for different kinds of housing in order to prevent distortions and cross-subsidization within the housing sector. The aim is not to reduce the level of provision of housing since it is clear that a large number of families are still inadequately housed. A reduction in government subsidies to owner-occupiers will allow a freeing of resources to provide housing for the inner cities and for those in greatest housing need, instead of the present wasteful subsidization of those social groups which already enjoy high incomes and a good standard of housing. Two methods of altering the tax treatment of housing have been suggested with these two aims in mind.[6] The re-introduction of tax on the imputed income derived from home ownership which as Schedule A was abandoned in 1963. This tax treated the ownership of a house as a form of consumption rather than as an investment; it would be administratively feasible to reintroduce if considered as part of the reforms of the rating system as recommended by the Layfield Committee.[7] The tax deductability of mortgage payments would be retained in order that a person with a mortgage equal in value to their house would have no tax to pay. The tax would have the consequence that all existing owners would suffer a tax loss and a capital loss although the effects of this could be eased by a phased introduction of the new tax, allowing house prices to adjust gradually. An alternative to the re-introduction of the tax would be to end or phase out mortgage interest relief either by maintaining the £25,000 ceiling in money terms and allowing it to fall in real terms or by restricting tax relief to the basic rate of tax.[8] The former would allow a gradual lowering of house prices, would be administratively simple and would lead to the ending of interest relief if inflation persisted. The second possibility would allow interest to be paid net of tax and would simplify the operation of tax relief and mortgage subsidies and would also be the means for a phasing out of interest relief.[9]

Both sets of reforms would increase the cost of housing to owner-occupiers and in order to prevent cross-subsidization within the housing market it would be necessary to alter the cost of housing to council tenants. This would not necessarily imply that the general level of council house rents would have to rise, as the return on local authority housing is already high relative to that obtaining in the owner-occupied sector;[10] but it would involve for some tenants sharp increases that would have to be phased in and even so would cause some distress. Any changes in the method of taxing housing would necessitate the introduction of a new social security benefit to take account of housing costs. A new social security benefit could be made administratively simpler if it was introduced in conjunction with national rent pooling for council properties, to offset certain of the differences among councils due to the age of buildings. A unified housing benefit, as advocated by the Supplementary Benefits Commission,[11] would improve incentives, reduce the poverty trap and would reduce the staff of supplementary benefits offices by 2,000 or more. This is the area of prime responsibility for government. It is primarily for local government to improve the position and rights of council tenants by giving more choice of dwelling, improving the rights of tenants in relation to the arbitrary powers of housing managers and by encouraging experiments in democratic control of decisions affecting the provision of housing.[12] Central government can create the basic legislative framework but its implementation is for local government. The case for helping first time house purchasers by preferential lending terms and tax treatment has been accepted in principle, but the schemes have always been overtaken by inflation and lending restriction particularly affecting local authorities. There is a need to improve access to credit for those young families with low incomes who are unable to obtain mortgages from the building societies. A possibility is to set up a public mortgage agency, linked to the expansion of local authority mortgage schemes.

These wider issues of housing and housing finance should concern every Social Democrat and form part of a strategy which welcomes the wish of many families to own their own house but seeks to treat fairly those who are council tenants or who prefer to live in private rented accommodation. Housing should be seen in the context of the whole economy. In the name of justice and in the pursuit of equality we have no alternative but to take radical steps to reform housing, and these steps are bound to offend large sections of the population which have benefited from past distortions.

It is necessary to study sociological evidence on the class structure and rates of social mobility in attempting to reduce poverty and inequality. The evidence shows that Britain is still far from being an 'open' society in which everyone has a roughly equal chance of attaining higher education and well-paid jobs, and that social mobility between the classes has not substantially increased over the last thirty years. The expansion of education since the Second World War has helped increase the chances of working-class children moving into higher social classes but in a truly mobile society the amount of upward mobility would be very much greater than it is at present.[13] There is far more scope for government enabling action if it concentrates on geographical inequality. Initially much of the statistical work concentrated on regional inequalities in the distribution of health and educational resources, and the worst regions were often also found to be those with older declining industries with the highest levels of persistent unemployment. More recently the focus of attention has concentrated on identifying smaller areas of geographical need and poverty. The evidence had been accumulating for some years, but it was not until the 1970s and specifically in 1977 that the severity of the problems in the inner cities were first tackled with a substantial, though still inadequate, allocation of resources.

The riots in the St Pauls district of Bristol in April 1980 and in Brixton in London in 1981 dramatized the problems again of the inner-city areas. All of Britain's major cities have their problem areas such as Handsworth in Birmingham, the Highfields district of Leicester, Moss Side in Manchester. They all share roughly the same characteristics, they are areas which knew their heyday at the turn of the century, and where the housing and other social structures are often old and dilapidated. What were large homes for Edwardian households have now often become overcrowded tenement buildings occupied by old inhabitants lacking the will or the means to move to the suburbs, together with immigrants such as the Irish, Asians and West Indians, and some who positively choose the inner city – including middle class people who, in some London inner-city areas, are returning the Victorian and Edwardian mansions to single-family occupation and are bringing in the phenomenon known as gentrification. But generally speaking inner-city areas are marked out by a number of pronounced demographic characteristics: the population is concentrated in the young and old age-groups, relatively few households are owner-occupied, families are larger, and more likely to consist of only one resident parent, than is the average for the country as a whole, and there is a distinct lack of skilled or qualified people.

Teachers often do not want to live in these areas and dislike the prospect of travelling long distances to get to school; and even if they do travel they are isolated from a community where they do not live. Doctors and social workers face the same problem. The inner-city areas have the highest percentage of lock-up surgeries; the family doctors often live outside the area and use deputizing medical services to cover at night and at weekends.

More importantly, these are areas of declining population and declining job opportunities for those who remain. Ever since the last war inner-city authorities, particularly in London, have made it part of their policy to reduce 'overcrowding' by encouraging people and employers to move out to new towns and expanding areas for London such as Peterborough, Harlow, or Crawley. As a result, many working class families who previously lived in crowded or otherwise inadequate accommodation in Inner London have been able to enjoy newer, more modern housing, a healthier environment and better schools, hospitals and recreational facilities. The demographic characteristics of the suburbs and new towns are almost the exact opposite of the inner-city pattern: families are smaller, a higher proportion of the population lives in family units, more are aged 20–40 than are very old or very young, very few are immigrants and many are owner-occupiers. Most importantly, there is relatively little unemployment.

In the inner-city areas, by contrast, there is high unemployment, heavily concentrated among school-leavers and, above all, among black school-leavers. This is the section of the population where post-war social policy has been least successful. There are two major issues to be faced: the whole process whereby deprived inner-city areas are formed; and the race relations' dimension. The polarization in society between the inner city and the suburbs is as dangerous as any of the divisions facing society. It is a division which mirrors the political polarization which has increased so much under the Prime Ministership of Mrs Thatcher. In the May 1979 election the Conservatives appealed to the values which some of the skilled workers and the upwardly mobile of the suburbs hold dear and did spectacularly well in outer-city affluent working class areas such as Basildon, Billericay and Dagenham. Conversely, Labour did particularly well in the inner-city areas, and there is some evidence to suggest that otherwise 'lukewarm' Labour voters were more likely to turn out actually to vote Labour if, other things being equal, they were members of minority ethnic groups rather than white. The 'haves' in contemporary Britain are those families whose parents are both working and who can afford to run one or two cars, take foreign holidays and buy the clothes, furniture and gadgets advertized on commercial television; the 'have-nots' are those for whom the products and life-style extolled by the commercial television are visible and desirable and yet out of reach. The deprived in the inner city like unemployed young blacks are not a revolutionary sub-proletariat but people who want access to the material benefits of our society and who want to gain society's esteem and respect. Existing social and racial tensions are being exacerbated by a government which tells the successful that their success is the product of their own 'initiative' and proceeds to reward them even further by cutting their taxes and releasing them from some of the burdens of financially supporting those less well-off than themselves while the overall tax burden increases.

Such a polarization could have devastating consequences for the future cohesion of British society. The electoral challenge for Social Democrats is not just to ease these tensions and reverse the polarization but, as a prior condition to being able to do so, to win the allegiance of those skilled workers who have been won over to the Conservative Party by their belief, which is certainly not without foundation, that Labour is the party which embraces, and wants to enlarge, an interfering and wasteful bureaucracy, and is committed to a taxation system which penalizes them for working overtime or for being skilled craftsmen. And further to demonstrate to unskilled workers that their interests have not been served by Labour Governments.

The practical and immediate task is the physical one of redeveloping the inner-city areas, restoring to them industrial life, and reversing their descent into the status of ghettos which house the unwanted and those on the margins of society. Money will of course be needed, but simply setting up undemocratic Inner City Development Corporations, as the Conservative government has done, will of itself solve nothing. These new Corporations may be able to cut through the stultifying bureaucracy that has allowed wasteland to proliferate, they may pioneer new projects designed to rejuvenate the housing in such areas and to attract employers back, but they will fail unless they can re-create what is all too rare now in the inner cities – genuine neighbourhoods where people of different classes and backgrounds can live harmoniously together – and this will require the co-operation of local people and the involvement of the local authorities who view the Corporations with suspicion. Inner-city areas have an attraction for some people, and with the very high cost of commuting caused by the ever increasing public transport fares, more and more suburban dwellers might be persuaded to return to the inner city. The inner city needs positive discrimination over resources and a commitment to refashioning a genuinely mixed community.

Yet central government must be very cautious about interfering with a local authority's freedom to develop its own policy. A council that wants to sell its stock of council houses, providing it is not adding to the homeless, should be allowed to do so even if central government feels the local authority is acting unwisely. Similarly a council that refuses to sell its stock of council houses should have the freedom to do so, even if central government thinks the council should sell. Central government should lay down tough criteria to phase out distorting financial subsidies, to prevent creating or adding to homelessness and should intervene if these criteria are not applied; for these are issues affecting national housing finance and overall social policy. But however well intentioned, detailed direction from Whitehall runs flatly against the essential democratic freedoms of successful local government.

Another area where Government can enable is in encouraging industrial co-operatives. If co-operatives are to expand, and if their ethos is to influence the general industrial climate, then they will have to benefit from positive discrimination. The faint hearts will argue that all sectors of the economy should be treated the same, but all governments have discriminated in the past between the private or public sectors and a Social Democratic government should be quite prepared to give legislative support for industrial co-operatives. The Co-operative Development Agency Act was helpful, and it is essential that the Co-operative Development Agency gets further finance, and that the Industrial Common Ownership Act funding be renewed. But marginal changes will not be enough. What is needed is a fiscal revolution, and introduction of a co-operative budget that takes as its central objective the promotion of industrial co-operatives and which is openly and unashamedly discriminatory. Such legislation will challenge the status quo and offend some of the vested interests that have grown used to a comfortable, almost bureaucratic, existence within the corporate state.

The main reason why the number of industrial co-operatives is still so small is the inability of most groups of workers with ideas to provide sufficient capital from their own resources. If we are to see the growth of co-operatives coming from new enterprises it will be necessary to ensure that potential co-operatives enjoy at least as good an access to capital as do other small firms. The report 'The Financing of Small Firms' set out the difficult position facing small firms in attempting to obtain risk capital: 'There are two main aspects of the banks' relationships with their actual or potential small firm customers to be considered, the availability of finance and the terms on which it is offered. The banks are often alleged to be too cautious about both. Their attitude towards risk, and ability to assess it, are said to make them unnecessarily restrictive in their lending policy, particularly towards new or rapidly expanding firms. In addition the terms on which they do make facilities available are sometimes criticized as being too severe. Rates of interest around 2 per cent higher than those charged to larger businesses appear to be fairly typical and the level of security demanded also tends to be high, with personal guarantees often being required.' The position facing co-operatives is often even worse than this in that banks usually prefer the conventional form of company organization and are sceptical of the democratic element of participation. In Mondragon, in the Basque region of Spain, this is not a problem as the Co-op bank loans workers their initial capital stake interest free for 24 months and acts as a source of finance for established co-operatives; and in the United States co-op banks make loans totalling around £7,000 million. The Co-operative Bank in Britain lends merely £25,000 to co-ops and does not have any provision for treating them more favourably than conventional organizations. There is a strong case for financial incentives to be made available to the Co-op Bank for a special Industrial Loan Fund to invest in co-operatives at a low rate of interest and for giving all banks special treatment for co-operative loans. It has also been suggested that co-operatives should be allowed to raise initial share capital from members if this was raised in the form of shares on which an unlimited return would be paid for a specified period. Non-voting shares, as exist in Canada and the USA, could also be issued to non-members to raise outside finance and such shares could be made tradeable in order to increase their attractiveness. This kind of share would also allow trade unions and their pension funds to invest in worthy ventures instead of in land or in conventional firms. The Industrial and Provident Societies Act could be changed to make it clear that membership of a co-operative is not the same thing as shareholding in a co-operative and voting rules could be adjusted accordingly. These forms of outside finance and non-working members are not supported by all groups within the co-operative movement, and while it is important that democratic control by members should not be undermined by an overwhelming source of outside finance the need for proper financing remains paramount.

In some countries, such as Britain and the USA, co-operative law allows the residual assets of a co-operative on winding up to be distributed to shareholders in proportion to shareholdings. In other countries, such as France and Italy, this is prohibited by law and the distribution has to be made in proportion to membership. If a co-operative has some outside shareholding and if a gap develops between share values and asset values, there is a danger in the UK at present of a premature dissolution since the shareholders will want to make a capital gain at the expense of people working in the co-operative. A study of the decline of nineteenth-century producer co-ops, has found that the proportion of share capital owned by workers fell from 25 per cent in 1948 to 18 per cent in 1968. This is likely to have reduced incentives for workers, since the increase in outside shareholding will, if taken too far, gradually turn a co-op into a conventional capitalist business. The UK law should be changed to ensure that distribution on dissolution follows the pattern of membership and not of shareholding. It would help co-operatives if investment in co-operatives was made deductible for personal tax purposes and this would be vital if the government were to lift the tax liability from employees when given the option to buy shares from their companies. The rate of corporation tax paid by co-operatives could be further reduced relative to the rate paid by other companies. There could also be tax concessions in relation to personal tax liability on interest on co-operative shares.

Changes in company law are also needed to facilitate the conversion of small businesses to co-operatives when the owner either retires or dies. As the law stands at present, there is very little incentive for the owner to hand over his business to his employees since the employees will be subject to capital gains tax and may therefore have to sell a part of the business, thus defeating the previous employer's whole object of ensuring that the business remains intact and under the control of his previous employees. Such a transfer of ownership should be encouraged by the removal of the liability to capital gains tax, as part of a wider package of reforms relieving the burden of tax from the distribution of the shares of business to co-operatives. To encourage such a transfer, it is also important, as previously stressed, to have easily available loan finance.

Existing legislation is currently being examined to see if greater help can be given to ease the problems of a large company wishing to split its operations. Recent research has shown that the 1970s' merger boom did not produce more efficient companies but created unwieldly empires and reduced profit ratios. Large companies now realize that smaller units are often more viable and there is no reason why when splitting parts of a large company there should not be conversion directly into co-operatives. The first publication of the Co-operative Development Agency was about converting a company into a co-operative and this is provided for both in the Industrial and Provident Societies Acts and in the Companies Acts; but it has been discouraged by capital gains tax and capital transfer tax liability at the time of conversion. This problem has been solved to some extent by provisions in the Finance Acts of 1976 and 1978 which provide for exemption from this tax liability if a permanent trust is formed for the benefit of employees. Conversions might be further encouraged if changes were made in company law so as to create a special class of 'co-operative company' with provision for statutory indivisible reserves and if tax arrangements were unashamedly discriminatory. Many of the shareholders in such companies might take the view that community of interest and tax considerations could result in their receiving a better return on their investment than they might otherwise do. Once a number had converted, considerably more might be encouraged to do so.

If the will existed, the government could stimulate the growth of new co-operatives and the number arising through transfers. Even without government stimulus there will be by 1984 something like 500 industrial co-operatives and if a Social Democratic government introduced a Co-operative Budget, this number could be quadrupled within the lifetime of the parliament. Expansion is not an end in itself; the pace should not damage the co-operative ideal and the integrity of the movement. No one knows what level of co-operative development would produce a macro effect on the whole economy but any expansion would produce a beneficial effect on attitudes within industry. There is no immediate likelihood of the solution favoured by Peter Jay of a single legislative switch to a workers' co-operative economy. The way forward over the next decade will be through the steady introduction of piecemeal changes[29] but the bolder approach may be not as futuristic as it at present appears if the movement towards co-operation gathers momentum and gains an aura of success, then a co-operative economy may not seem as improbable as at present.

The development of co-operatives is a move towards a decentralized society, and is a genuine third way in the polarized debate about workers and owners. What is needed is a political timetable that starts to lay the groundwork for profound changes of attitude over a period of decades, not just a five-year electoral period.

Government also has a responsibility to enable citizens to protect their individual rights. One simple, not perfect but nevertheless helpful, decision would be to utilize the international code of human rights in the European Human Rights Convention and the United Nations Covenant on Civil and Political Rights, in ways which extend the rights of British citizens. We ratified the International Covenant on Civil and Political Rights in May 1976 with reservations and derogations, but we have yet to ratify the Fourth Protocol of the European Convention. To ratify this Protocol would introduce a permanent guarantee for certain important rights fundamental to a democratic society over and above the transitory concerns of Ministers in the executive. A British government might well have to introduce two or three reservations and might have to consider making an additional derogation to take account of the 1976 Prevention of Terrorism Act. There are clear precedents for making such reservations and they would not need to be permanent. Ratification would advance the tally of rights protected within the UK from 17 to 21 and would complete our acceptance of the European system of enforceable rights.

The Convention should be actually incorporated into UK law and the effect would undoubtedly be to enhance individual rights by giving individuals access to the courts if they thought their rights had been infringed. In cases involving press freedom, prisoners' rights, or the tapping of telephones, it would be possible under the Convention for specific grievances to be given a proper hearing where this is at present not so.

Some people object to accepting international human rights provisions because they see that it could fetter the freedom of a British government to ban by law the private education of children or the practising of private medicine. The UN International Covenant on Economic Social and Cultural Rights, which was ratified by the Labour government in 1976, in Article 13(3) obliges the state parties 'to have respect for the liberty of parents and, when applicable, legal guardians, to choose for their children schools other than those established by the public authorities'. The European Convention on Human Rights in Article 2 of the first protocol obliges states to respect the rights of parents to ensure education and teaching in conformity with their own religious and philosophical convictions. In a judgement on the interpretation of this article it was seen as guaranteeing the freedom to establish private schools and as 'safeguarding the possibility of pluralism in education, which possibility is essential for the preservation of the "democratic society" as conceived by the Convention'. This adds a further complexity to the issue. Governments of the Left which have generally been the keenest to try to establish international codes of conduct for the protection of minorities and civil liberties, could find their own freedom to act as they might feel best limited by international criteria. Yet the same international criteria pose a very considerable restriction on the freedom of any Right-wing government wishing to introduce racialist legislation or to restrict minority rights. It is right, as I argued in Chapter 10, for government to withhold all financial support and encouragement from private educational or health provisions, and to separate private from central government sponsored activity. As Minister of Health I was deeply involved in the phasing out of pay beds in NHS hospitals and faced serious industrial action from hospital consultants. I have never charged nor ever will charge a patient; and my own children go to state schools. But I do not accept that it is legitimate or compatible with the values of a democratic society, in the 1980s, for a Social Democratic Government to ban the charging of fees for private education or private health without first having a sustained period in government of giving positive support to the public educational and health services and discriminating actively against private educational and health services. These services might then wither away to be of little significance, and the extremely disturbing choice avoided of whether the price of abandoning society's libertarian values was worth the social advantages. The onus of proof lies on those who wish to destroy a human right. The European Convention on Human Rights is a powerful external check on all governments who ratify it and not easily flouted.

Another controversy is whether or not the adoption of a Convention on human rights should be entrenched, as is the Bill of Rights in the United States. In this country this would mean that the Convention should prevail over existing legislation if a court should decide that an Act is in violation of it, while all legislation passed subsequent to the passing of the Convention should be interpreted in

line with it. This would challenge the present total freedom or sovereignty of parliament, yet it would be an important safeguard for
human rights in this country. There needs to be careful debate about
this issue. The important first step is to ratify the Convention and to
ensure that all individuals have remedies available if their rights
have been violated. At present, many millions of people whose
income is above the Legal Aid limit have no access to the law
because they cannot afford to meet its spiralling costs. This must be
remedied. Neighbourhood law centres, with young lawyers working for a salary and bringing low cost legal advice could ensure that
the law was the friend of the under-privileged and disenfranchized.
Nothing has been more depressing than the inability of successive
governments seriously to challenge the restrictive practices and
remoteness of the legal profession. There are arguments for having a
Minister of Justice answering for all aspects of law and order. But
whatever the merits of this, and it is bound to raise anxiety about
putting so much power into one person and one Department's
hands, there is a strong case for the Lord Chancellor and the
Department being answerable to the House of Commons and not
being tucked away in the House of Lords.

The enhancement of individual and minority rights would not
only counter present trends towards bureaucratization and centralization but could also increase the prestige, and therefore the
legitimacy and authority, of the whole process of law and order in
this country. This is not something to be feared. Social Democrats
have far more to gain from the entrenchment of the rule of law than
the Right, provided we are prepared to ensure that the full weight of
the law is put at the disposal of every citizen.

Government can and should provide a framework for the society
in which the citizen lives. It can encourage specific values in society
to develop, specific policies to be introduced but its power to enable
is more important than its power to control. It is in the enabling
power of government that the strength of social democracy lies.

NOTES

PREFACE

1. J. Mackintosh, D. Marquand, D. Owen, 'Change Gear', *Socialist Commentary*, September 1967.

2. Fabian Tract. No. 4, 1886. Quoted in C. Ward, 'Self-help Socialism', *New Society*, 20 April 1978.

1. SOCIAL DEMOCRATIC VALUES

1. F. A. Hayek, *The Constitution of Liberty*, Routledge & Kegan Paul, 1960.
2. R. Titmuss, *The Gift Relationship*, George Allen and Unwin, 1970.
3. J. Vaizey, *Whatever Happened to Equality?*, BBC Books, 1975.
4. M. Thatcher, *Let Our Children Grow Tall*, Centre for Policy Studies, 1977, p.4.
5. S. Lukes, *Essays in Social Theory*, Macmillan, 1977, p.111.
6. I. Bradley, *William Morris and his World*, Thames and Hudson, 1978, p.77.
7. K. Popper, *The Open Society and its Enemies*, Routledge & Kegan Paul, 1966, vol. 1, ch. 10.
8. Isaiah Berlin, 'The Hedgehog and the Fox', in *Russian Thinkers*, edited by H. Hardy and A. Kelly, Hogarth Press, 1978, p.22.
9. A. W. Wright, *G. D. H. Cole and Socialist Democracy*, Clarendon Press, 1979, p.136.
10. G. D. H. Cole, 'What Next? Anarchists or Bureaucrats?', *Fabian Journal*, April 1954.
11. Berlin, op. cit., Introduction, p. xv.
12. Michel Rocard, in *Le Monde*, 21 June 1977.
13. Cole, op. cit.
14. *North–South: A Programme for Survival*, Pan Books, 1980.

2. THE DECENTRALIST TRADITION

1. W. Morris, in *Commonweal*, 25 January 1890.
2. M. Cole, *The Story of Fabian Socialism*, Heinemann, 1961, p.185.
3. G. D. H. Cole, 'Guild Socialism Twenty Years Ago and Now', *New English Weekly*, September 1934.
4. S. Webb, 'A Stratified Democracy', *New Commonwealth*, 28 November 1919.

5. Morris, op. cit.
6. C. A. R. Crosland, *The Future of Socialism*, Jonathan Cape, 1956, p.84.
7. C. A. R. Crosland, *Socialism Now*, Jonathan Cape, 1974, pp.65–6.
8. 'The Miners' Next Step', quoted in H. Pelling, *A History of British Trade Unionism*, Penguin, 1971, p.141.
9. B. Webb, *My Apprenticeship*, Longman, 1926, p.377.
10. S. and B. Webb, *A History of Trade Unionism*, Longman, 1894, p.760.
11. *For Socialism and Peace*, Labour Party, 1934.
12. Quoted in R. Miliband, *Parliamentary Socialism*, Merlin Press, 1973, p.289.
13. R. H. Tawney, *The Radical Tradition*, Allen and Unwin, 1964.
14. *Local Government in England*, Cmnd 4040, HMSO, 1969.
15. *Local Government Finance*, Cmnd 6453, HMSO, 1976.
16. *Industrial Democracy*, Cmnd 6706, HMSO, 1977.
17. A. Crosland, *The Future of Socialism*, pp.521–2.
18. A. Crosland, in *New Fabian Essays*, ed. R. H. S. Crossman, Turnstile Press, 1952, p.42.
19. A. Crosland, *Socialism Now*, p.34.
20. A. Crosland, *The Conservative Enemy*, Jonathan Cape, 1962, p.127.

3. THE GROWTH OF CORPORATISM

1. R. Miliband, *The State in Capitalist Society*, Weidenfeld and Nicolson, 1969.
2. A. J. P. Taylor, *English History 1914–45*, Oxford University Press, 1965, p.1.
3. K. Middlemass, *Politics in Industrial Society*, André Deutsch, 1979, p.20.
4. Taylor, op. cit., p.507.
5. Middlemass, op. cit., p.22.
6. A. H. Halsey, A. F. Heath and J. M. Ridge, *Origins and Destinations*, Oxford University Press, 1980.
7. Miliband, op. cit.
8. C. Welch, 'Crosland Reconsidered', *Encounter*, January 1979, p.91.
9. G. Dalton, *Economic Systems and Society*, Penguin, 1974, p.149.
10. *Report of the Royal Commission on Trade Unions and Employers' Associations*, Cmnd 3623, HMSO, 1968.
11. J. Elliott, *Conflict or Co-operation? The Growth of Industrial Democracy*, Kogan Page, 1978, p.139.
12. R. Undy, 'The Devolution of Bargaining Levels and Responsibilities in the Transport and General Workers' Union, 1965–75', *Industrial Relations*, Autumn 1978, pp.44–56.
13. S. Walkland (ed.), *The House of Commons in the Twentieth Century*, Clarendon Press, 1979, p.277.
14. S. Holland, *The Socialist Challenge*, Quartet Books, 1975.
15. M. Kogan, *The Politics of Education*, Penguin, 1971, pp.44–5.
16. M. Meacher, 'It takes 2,700 to quango', *New Society*, 20 September 1979.

4. THE SOCIAL DEMOCRATIC TRADITION

1. J. Braunthal, *History of the International, World Socialism 1943–68*, Gollancz, 1980.
2. Ibid.
3. Ibid.
4. The Frankfurt Declaration, quoted in Braunthal, op. cit.
5. W. E. Paterson in Paterson and Campbell, *Social Democracy in Post-War Europe*, Macmillan, 1974.
6. Ibid.
7. Ibid.
8. P. M. Williams, *Hugh Gaitskell, A Political Biography*, Jonathan Cape, 1979, p.570.
9. Ibid., p.631.
10. L. Kolakowski, quoted by Denis Healey in the Sarah Barker Memorial Lecture, 8 September 1979.
11. M. Kolinsky and W. E. Paterson, *Social and Political Movements of Western Europe*, Croom Helm, 1976.

5. ECONOMIC POLICY

1. R. Harrod, *Reforming the World's Money*, Macmillan, 1965, p.77.
2. M. Stewart, *The Jeckyll and Hyde Years*, J. M. Dent, 1977, p.247.
3. 'The Global 2000 Report to the President: on entering the twenty-first century', 1979.
4. N. Bosanquet and P. Townsend (eds), *Labour and Equality*, Heinemann, 1980, p.130.
5. Marshall, op. cit., p.78, and *Economic Trends*, no. 316, HMSO, 1980.
6. *New Society*, 27 July 1978, p.174.
7. Hansard, 30 November 1978, col. 298 and 1 May 1980, col. 660. Quoted in H. Parker, *Goodbye Beveridge?*, Outer Circle Policy Unit, 1980, p.28.
8. *Royal Commission on the Distribution of Income and Wealth, Report No. 6*, Cmnd 7175, HMSO, 1978, p.94.
9. Bosanquet and Townsend, op. cit., p.173.
10. F. Hirsh, *Social Limits to Growth*, Routledge & Kegan Paul, 1977, p.9.
11. *Commission of the European Communities Annual Economic Report*, 1979–80, November 1979, table 7.
12. D. Blake and P. Ormerod (eds), *The Economics of Prosperity*, Grant McIntyre, 1980, p.18.
13. Ibid., p.19, and *Cambridge Economic Policy Review*, April 1979, p.38.
14. *Cambridge Economic Policy Review*, March 1976, p.37.
15. Hansard, 23 May 1980, col. 393–4.
16. Bank of England, *Quarterly Bulletin*, June 1980, p.191.
17. P. Forsyth and J. Kay, 'The Economic Implications of North Sea Oil', *Fiscal Studies*, July 1980.
18. *Report of the Committee to Review the Functioning of Financial Institutions*, Cmnd 7937, HMSO, 1980, p.278.

19. *Cambridge Economic Policy Review*, March 1978, p.1.
20. Sir Alan Cottrell, *The Undermining of British Industry*, University of Southampton, Fawley Foundation Lecture, 1979, pp.7–8.
21. *Education, Training and Industrial Performance*, Central Policy Review Staff, HMSO, 1980, p.7.
22. *Outlook on Training: Review of the Employment and Training Act, 1973*, Manpower Services Commission, HMSO, 1980.
23. *Engineering our Future: Report of the Committee of Inquiry into the Engineering Profession*, Cmnd 7794, HMSO, 1980, p.74.
24. Hansard, 6 August 1980, cols 129–30.
25. S. Mukherjee, *The Costs of Unemployment*, Political and Economic Planning Broadsheet, no.561, 1976, quoted in D. Blake and P. Ormerod (eds), *The Economics of Prosperity*, Grant McIntyre, 1980.
26. Report of the Committee to Review the Functioning of Financial Institutions, Cmnd 7933 HMSO 1980, p.261.

6. INCOMES POLICY

1. A. R. Braun, *The Role of Incomes Policy in Industrial Countries Since World War II*, International Monetary Fund Staff Papers, March 1975, p.2.
2. F. T. Blackaby, 'The Reform of the Wage Bargaining System', *National Institute Economic Review*, August 1978, p.51.
3. 'Incomes Policy', *National Institute Economic Review*, February 1976, p.75.
4. *Incomes Data Services International Report*, August 1979, p.1.
5. Braun, op. cit., p.23.
6. *Report of the Royal Commission on Trade Unions and Employers' Associations*, Cmnd 3623, HMSO, 1968, p.28.
7. A. Jones, *The New Inflation*, Deutsch, 1973.
8. A. Dean, 'Incomes Policies and Differentials', *National Institute Economic Review*, August 1978, p.46.
9. R. Elliott and L. Fallick, *Pay Differentials in Perspective: a study of manual and non-manual workers' pay over the period 1951–75*, University of Aberdeen Occasional Paper no. 77–07. Quoted in Dean, op. cit. p.47.
10. Dean, op. cit., p.48.
11. W. Brown, 'Incomes policy and pay differentials: the impact of incomes policy upon workplace wage determination in the engineering industry, 1972–75', *Oxford Bulletin of Economics and Statistics*, February 1976.
12. S. Henry and P. Ormerod, 'Incomes policy and wage inflation: empirical evidence for the United Kingdom 1961–77', *National Institute Economic Review*, August 1978, p.39.
13. Department of Employment, *Prices and earnings, 1951–69: an econometric assessment*, HMSO, 1971.
14. R. Tarling and F. Wilkinson, 'The Social Contract: Post-War Incomes Policies and their Inflationary Impact', *Cambridge Journal of Economics*, 1977.
15. Blackaby, op. cit., p.51.

7. INDUSTRIAL DEMOCRACY

1. Commission of the European Communities, *Employee Participation and Company Structure*, Bulletin of the European Communities, Supplement 8/75.
2. Quoted in J. Elliott, *Conflict or Co-operation? The Growth of Industrial Democracy*, Kogan Page, 1978, p.114.
3. *Report on the Committee of Inquiry on Industrial Democracy*, Cmnd 6706, HMSO, 1977.
4. *Industrial Democracy*, Cmnd 7231, HMSO, 1978.
5. T. Forester, 'Whatever Happened to Industrial Democracy?', *New Society*, 17 July 1980.
6. *In Place of Strife*, Cmnd 3888, HMSO, 1969.
7. *Industrial Democracy*, op. cit., p.9.

8. PARLIAMENTARY GOVERNMENT

1. J. Mackintosh, *Specialist Committees in the House of Commons: have they failed?*, The Waverley Papers, Edinburgh University, 1969.
2. G. K. Fry, *The Growth of Government*, Cass, 1979, pp.2–3.
3. R. H. S. Crossman, *Diaries of a Cabinet Minister*, 3 vols, Jonathan Cape, 1975–7.
4. E. Burke, *Speech to the Electors of Bristol*, 3 November 1774.
5. *Report of the Committee on Financial Aid to Political Parties*, Cmnd 6601, HMSO, 1976, p.56.
6. S. A. de Smith, *Constitutional and Administrative Law*, Penguin, 1971.
7. Crossman, op. cit., vol. 1, *Minister of Housing, 1964–66*, p.21.
8. N. C. Crowther-Hunt and P. Kellner, *The Civil Servants: an Inquiry into Britain's Ruling Class*, Macdonald and Jane's, 1980.
9. *Report of the Committee on Representational Services Overseas*, Cmnd 2276, HMSO, 1964.
10. G. Moorhouse, *The Diplomats: The Foreign Office Today*, Jonathan Cape, 1977, p.121.
11. D. Owen, *The Politics of Defence*, Jonathan Cape, 1972.
12. T. Barnes, *Open Up!*, Fabian Tract 467, Fabian Society, 1980.
13. S. Dresner, *Open Government: Lessons from America*, Outer Circle Policy Unit, 1980, p.132.
14. *Report of the Committee on Data Protection*, Cmnd 7341, HMSO, 1978.
15. H. Fairlie, 'The Lives of Politicians', *Encounter*, vol. XXIX, no. 2, August 1967.

9. CONSTITUTIONAL REFORM

1. *House of Lords Reform*, Cmnd 3799, HMSO, 1968.
2. R. Crossman, *The Diaries of a Cabinet Minister*, vol. 3 *Secretary of State for Social Services 1963–70*, Jonathan Cape, 1977, p.355.

3. *Royal Commission on the Constitution 1969–73,* Vol. 1, *Report,* Cmnd 5460, HMSO, 1973, pp.5–6.
4. Ibid., p.322.
5. Ibid., *Memorandum of Dissent by Lord Crowther-Hunt and Professor A. Peacock,* Cmnd 5460–1, HMSO, 1973, p.viii.
6. V. Bogandor, *Devolution,* Oxford University Press, 1979.

10. LOCAL GOVERNMENT

1. T. Smith quoted in W. Thornhill (ed.), *The Growth and Reform of English Local Government,* Weidenfeld and Nicolson, 1971.
2. F. Gladstone, *Voluntary Action in a Changing World,* National Council of Social Service, 1979, p.3.
3. Cited in Circular 121/77, Department of the Environment.
4. *Policy for the Inner Cities,* Cmnd 6845, HMSO, 1977, p.1.
5. Ibid., p.8.
6. Ibid., p.9.
7. Ibid.
8. T. Burgess and T. Travers, *Ten Billion Pounds,* Grant McIntyre, 1980, pp.23–36.
9. D. Lipsey, 'Councils of Despair', *New Society,* 31 July 1980.
10. Burgess and Travers, op. cit., pp. 14–15.
11. *Local Government in England,* Cmnd 4584, HMSO, 1971.
12. Burgess and Travers, op. cit., p.28.
13. *Report of the Royal Commission on Local Government in England,* Cmnd 4040, HMSO, 1969; *Report of the Royal Commission on Local Government in Scotland,* Cmnd 4150, HMSO, 1969.
14. *Local Government Finance,* Cmnd 6453, HMSO, 1976.
15. Ibid., p.306.
16. Ibid., p.287.
17. Ibid., pp.287–8.
18. N. Barr, S. James and A. Prest, *Self-Assessment for Income Tax,* Heinemann, 1977, p.51.
19. Ibid.
20. Committee of Public Accounts, Minutes of 19 November 1979, para. 1039.
21. *Local Government Finance,* Cmnd 6813, HMSO, 1977, p.18.
22. Committee of Public Accounts, op. cit., para 1055.
23. Ibid., para. 1045.
24. *Local Government Finance,* Cmnd 6813, p.11.
25. *Local Government Finance,* Cmnd 6453, p.248.
26. Ibid., p.250.
27. Ibid.
28. Ibid., p.247.
29. F. Cripps and W. Godley, *Local Government Finance and its Reform,* Cambridge University Department of Applied Economics, 1976, p.11.

30. G. W. Jones, 'Central-Local Government Relations: Grants, Local Responsibility and Minimum Standards', in D. Butler and A. Halsey (eds), *Policy and Politics – Essays in Honour of Norman Chester*, Macmillan, 1978, p.71.
31. Burgess and Travers, op. cit., p.94.
32. Ibid., p.180.
33. R. McAllister, *Local Government: Death or Devolution?*, Outer Circle Policy Unit, 1980.
34. D. Owen, *In Sickness and in Health*, Quartet Books, 1976, p.28.
35. R. Klein, 'Living with its disabilities', *British Medical Journal*, 6 October 1979, p.848.
36. *Report of the Royal Commission on the National Health Service*, Cmnd 7615, HMSO, 1979.
37. Memorandum by the Minister of Health to the Cabinet, 5 October 1945, Public Records Office CAB/129/3.
38. Resources Allocation Working Party, *Allocating Health Resources*, Research Paper, No. 3. Royal Commission on the NHS.
39. *RAWP Deals*, Radical Statistics Health Group, 1979.
40. A. Mitchell, *Resource Allocation Scotland*, Chartered Institute of Public Finance and Accountancy, Conference Papers, 1978.
41. M. Wynn and A. Wynn, 'Administration and Financing of a Health Service: A Note on Swedish elected County Health Authorities and the Swedish County Health Tax', Evidence submitted to the Royal Commission on the NHS.
42. *Report of the Royal Commission on the NHS*, op. cit., p.379.
43. G. N. Marsh, 'Obstetric audit in general practice', *British Medical Journal*, 1977, vol. 2, pp.1004–6.
44. B. Whitaker, *The Police*, Eyre and Spottiswoode, 1964, p.67.

11. NEGOTIATE AND SURVIVE

1. Lord Zuckerman in F. Griffiths and J. C. Polanyi, *The Dangers of Nuclear War*, University of Toronto Press, 1979, p.164.
2. W. McGeorge Bundy, 'The Avoidance of Nuclear War since 1945', in Griffiths and Polanyi, op. cit., p.32.
3. *North-South: A Programme for Survival*, Pan Books, 1980, pp.119–20.
4. Leonard Beaton, *The Reform of Power*, Gollancz, 1968.
5. Ibid.
6. D. Owen, *Human Rights*, Jonathan Cape, 1978, p.133.
7. E. P. Thompson, *Protest and Survive*, Spokesman Pamphlet no. 71, 1980.

12. THE ENABLING STATE

1. *Housing Policy: A Consultative Document*, Cmnd 6851, HMSO, 1977.
2. D. Webster, 'Why Labour Failed on Housing', *New Society*, 17 January 1980.

3. B. Kilroy, 'Housing Finance – Why So Privileged?', *Lloyds Bank Review*, July 1980, p.43.

4. Ibid.

5. M. King and A. Atkinson, 'Housing Policy, Taxation and Reform', *Midland Bank Review*, Spring 1980, p.8.

6. Ibid., p.13.

7. *Local Government Finance*, Cmnd 6453, HMSO, 1976, p.170.

8. King and Atkinson, op. cit., p.13.

9. Ibid.

10. Ibid., p.14.

11. *Supplementary Benefits Commission Annual Report 1979*, Cmnd 8033, HMSO, 1980, p.24.

12. *Can Tenants Run Housing?* Fabian Society, Fabian Research Series 344, April 1980.

13. A. Halsey, A. Heath, and J. Ridge, *Origins and Destinations*, Oxford University Press, 1980.

INDEX